Contents Table

Welcome & What You'll Learn

Welcome to **Flutter Made Easy: A Beginner's Guide to Mobile App Development**. If you're reading this, you're likely curious about the exciting world of mobile app creation, and you've chosen the perfect tool to dive in with: Flutter.

Flutter is Google's UI toolkit designed to create beautiful, natively compiled applications for mobile, web, and desktop from a single codebase. It's a game-changer for developers, offering a streamlined way to build high-quality apps that run seamlessly across different platforms.

Why Flutter? Why This Book?

In this book, we'll guide you through the ins and outs of Flutter, starting from the very basics. You'll learn:

- **The Fundamentals:** We'll demystify what Flutter is and why it's an excellent choice for beginners and experienced developers alike.
- **Your Development Environment:** You'll set up your computer to start building Flutter apps right away. Don't worry, we'll walk you through it step-by-step.
- **The Dart Language:** Flutter uses the Dart programming language. You'll get a crash course on Dart's essentials, making it easy to grasp even if you're new to coding.
- **Widgets:** Widgets are the building blocks of Flutter apps. You'll master how to create, customize, and arrange widgets to build stunning user interfaces.
- **Layouts and Styling:** You'll learn to design app layouts that look great on any screen size and style your apps to make them visually appealing.
- **Interactive Features:** We'll cover how to handle user input, add navigation between screens, work with images, and even fetch data from the internet.
- **Building Real Apps:** The best way to learn is by doing! You'll create several real-world apps, including a to-do list, a news reader, a weather app, and even a personal finance tracker.
- **Advanced Concepts (Optional):** If you're up for a challenge, we'll touch on testing, custom animations, using Firebase for data storage, and the process of publishing your apps.

Who This Book Is For

This book is ideal for:

- **Complete beginners** with no prior programming or app development experience.
- **Developers from other languages** who want to quickly get started with Flutter.
- **Hobbyists** eager to turn their app ideas into reality.
- **Anyone** with a passion for learning and creating!

Your Journey Starts Now

Flutter offers a fantastic opportunity to learn, build, and create. Whether you dream of publishing apps to the app stores or simply want to add a new skill to your repertoire, this book is your guide.

Let's embark on this exciting Flutter adventure together! Turn the page and let's get started.

Section I:
Introduction to Flutter

What is Flutter, and Why Should You Learn It?

Outline

- What is Flutter?
- Why Flutter?
- Benefits of Using Flutter
- Who Uses Flutter?
- Chapter Summary

What is Flutter?

Flutter is Google's open-source UI toolkit designed to craft beautiful, natively compiled applications for mobile (iOS and Android), web, and desktop from a single codebase. Think of it as a powerful set of tools, like a well-stocked toolbox, specifically for creating the visual aspects and interactive elements of your app – the user interface (UI).

Instead of writing separate code for each platform, Flutter allows you to write your app's code once and deploy it across multiple platforms, saving you significant time and effort.

Flutter uses the Dart programming language, also developed by Google. Dart is relatively easy to learn, especially if you have experience with languages like Java, JavaScript, or C#. It's optimized for building user interfaces, making Flutter development smooth and efficient.

To give you a real-world example, the popular Google Ads app is built with Flutter. This showcases Flutter's capability to create high-performance apps that reach millions of users.

Why Flutter?

Cross-Platform Development: Your Code, Everywhere

Traditionally, building apps for different platforms (like iOS and Android) meant writing separate codebases using different languages and tools. This was time-consuming, expensive, and prone to inconsistencies.

Cross-platform development emerged as a solution. The idea is simple yet revolutionary: write your app's code once, and it magically runs on multiple platforms! This not only saves development time and resources but also ensures a more consistent user experience across devices.

Flutter excels at cross-platform development. With a single codebase, you can create apps for:

- **Mobile:** iOS and Android
- **Web:** Runs in modern browsers
- **Desktop:** Windows, macOS, and Linux

This means you can reach a wider audience without the hassle of maintaining multiple codebases.

How Flutter Does It Differently

Unlike some other cross-platform frameworks (like React Native, which relies on bridges to native components), Flutter takes a unique approach. It renders its own UI components directly, using a high-performance rendering engine called Skia. This often results in smoother animations, faster performance, and a more consistent look and feel across platforms.

Let's illustrate this with an analogy:

- **React Native:** Imagine building a house using pre-fabricated rooms from different manufacturers. While convenient, you might encounter compatibility issues and inconsistencies in the overall design.
- **Flutter:** Imagine building a house from scratch using your own custom-designed bricks. You have full control over the design, and the result is a more cohesive and polished structure.

In essence, Flutter gives you the best of both worlds: the efficiency of cross-platform development and the performance and customization of native apps.

Fast Development with Hot Reload: Your Iterative Power Tool

Flutter's **Hot Reload** feature is a game-changer that accelerates your development workflow. Imagine being able to modify your app's code and see the changes reflected on your device or emulator almost instantaneously, without having to manually stop, recompile, and restart the entire app. That's the magic of Hot Reload.

How It Works (The Short Version):

1. You make a change to your Dart code.
2. You save the file.
3. Flutter's tooling injects the updated code into the running Dart Virtual Machine (VM).
4. The Flutter framework rebuilds the necessary parts of the widget tree, applying your changes seamlessly.
5. You see the updated UI in a flash!

Why It Matters:

Hot Reload eliminates the frustrating wait times associated with traditional development cycles. Instead of spending valuable minutes or even hours recompiling and relaunching your app for every little tweak, you can now experiment and iterate in real-time.

This means:

- **Faster Feedback Loop:** You get immediate visual feedback on your changes, allowing you to quickly test different ideas and see what works best.
- **Increased Productivity:** You can focus on building features and fixing bugs instead of waiting for your app to restart.
- **Smoother Debugging:** You can easily pinpoint issues and make corrections on the fly, as you see the impact of your changes right away.

Example: Fine-Tuning Your Design

Imagine you're designing the layout of a screen. With Hot Reload, you can adjust the padding, spacing, colors, or fonts in your code and see the results in the blink of an eye. You can fine-tune the UI until it looks perfect, all without interrupting your creative flow.

Hot Reload vs. Traditional Development: It's like comparing a high-speed train to a horse-drawn carriage. The efficiency gains are immense, allowing you to deliver high-quality apps in record time.

Beautiful and Customizable UIs: Your Design Playground

Flutter empowers you to create stunningly beautiful user interfaces (UIs) that captivate users. It achieves this through its extensive collection of customizable widgets – the building blocks of Flutter apps.

Widgets: Your Creative Arsenal

Flutter widgets are not merely pre-designed elements; they're a versatile set of tools you can tailor to your vision. From buttons and text fields to sliders, dialogs, and complex layouts, Flutter provides a comprehensive toolkit for crafting visually rich and interactive experiences.

What sets Flutter apart is its focus on flexibility and customization. You have complete control over the appearance and behavior of your widgets. You can easily change colors, fonts, sizes, animations, and even create entirely new custom widgets to match your app's unique brand identity.

Inspiring Examples

The Flutter community has produced an array of visually stunning apps showcasing the versatility of Flutter's UI capabilities. Apps like Reflectly (a journaling app) and the Xianyu app by Alibaba demonstrate how Flutter can be used to create unique, eye-catching designs that stand out in the crowded app market.

The Native Advantage: Material Design and Cupertino

Flutter goes a step further by offering two sets of pre-designed widgets that adhere to the design guidelines of the major mobile platforms:

- **Material Design:** Google's design language for Android, known for its clean lines, bold colors, and meaningful motion.
- **Cupertino:** Apple's design language for iOS, characterized by subtle gradients, translucent elements, and smooth animations.

By using Material Design or Cupertino widgets, you can ensure that your app looks and feels right at home on either platform, giving users a seamless experience.

Unleash Your Creativity

Whether you're a seasoned designer or just starting out, Flutter provides you with the tools and flexibility to turn your creative ideas into reality. The only limit is your imagination.

Growing Community and Ecosystem: Never Build Alone

Flutter boasts a vibrant and supportive community of developers, designers, and enthusiasts who are passionate about the framework. This dynamic community is a valuable asset for both newcomers and experienced Flutter users.

Benefits of a Strong Community:

- **Learning Resources:** The community offers a wealth of tutorials, blog posts, video courses, and sample projects to help you learn and master Flutter.
- **Support & Collaboration:** You can connect with fellow developers on forums, social media, and dedicated platforms like Discord to get help, share ideas, and collaborate on projects.
- **Events & Conferences:** Flutter conferences and meetups take place around the world, providing opportunities to network, learn from experts, and stay up-to-date with the latest developments.

Key Resources:

- **Flutter Official Documentation:** A comprehensive guide with detailed explanations, code examples, and tutorials.

- **Flutter Community Forum:** A place to ask questions, get help, and engage with other developers.
- **Flutter Awesome:** A curated list of the best Flutter libraries, tools, tutorials, articles, and more.
- **Online Courses:** Platforms like Udemy, Coursera, and Pluralsight offer structured Flutter courses for learners of all levels.

A Thriving Ecosystem of Packages

Flutter's ecosystem is rapidly expanding, with a vast collection of packages (pre-built libraries of code) that extend Flutter's core capabilities. These packages cover a wide range of functionalities, from handling complex animations and integrating with Firebase to implementing advanced UI elements and accessing device features.

Some popular Flutter packages include:

- **provider:** A state management solution for managing shared data across your app.
- **http:** A powerful library for making network requests and fetching data from APIs.
- **image_picker:** A package for selecting images from the device's gallery or camera.
- **flutter_svg:** For rendering scalable vector graphics (SVGs) in your Flutter apps.
- **flutter_bloc:** A popular state management solution based on the BLoC pattern.

This rich ecosystem means you can leverage the work of other developers, saving time and effort while building complex features into your apps. It's a testament to Flutter's growing popularity and the collaborative spirit of its community.

Benefits of Using Flutter: A Powerful Toolkit

Flutter offers a compelling combination of features and advantages that make it a powerful choice for mobile app development:

- **Rapid Development:** Flutter's Hot Reload feature allows you to see changes instantly, accelerating your development cycle. The ability to write code once and deploy it across multiple platforms (iOS, Android, web, and desktop) further streamlines the process.
- **Expressive and Flexible UI:** Flutter's rich set of customizable widgets gives you the freedom to create beautiful and unique user interfaces. You can achieve pixel-perfect designs, implement complex animations, and tailor the look and feel of your app to match your brand identity. Material Design and Cupertino widgets ensure your app looks native on both Android and iOS platforms.
- **High Performance:** Flutter apps are compiled to native ARM machine code, resulting in smooth animations, fast rendering, and a responsive user experience. Flutter's architecture bypasses the need for JavaScript bridges, often associated with performance bottlenecks in other cross-platform frameworks.
- **Vibrant Community and Rich Ecosystem:** Flutter has a thriving community of developers who contribute to its growth. This means you have access to extensive documentation, tutorials, forums, and a vast ecosystem of packages that extend Flutter's capabilities. You'll never feel alone on your Flutter journey.
- **Open Source and Backed by Google:** Flutter is an open-source project, meaning it's free to use and modify. It's also backed by Google, a tech giant known for its innovation and commitment to open source software. This ensures Flutter's continued development and support.

Who Uses Flutter?: A Growing Roster of Success Stories

Flutter's popularity has surged in recent years, with a growing number of companies and developers recognizing its potential. Here's a glimpse into the diverse range of organizations that have embraced Flutter:

- **Google:** Flutter's own creator, Google, uses it extensively in apps like Google Ads, Google Pay, and Stadia.
- **Alibaba:** The Chinese e-commerce giant built its Xianyu app (a popular second-hand marketplace) with Flutter.
- **BMW:** The luxury car manufacturer developed its My BMW app using Flutter, allowing users to control various car functions remotely.
- **Nubank:** The Brazilian digital bank chose Flutter to create its user-friendly mobile banking app.
- **eBay Motors:** The online marketplace for vehicles built its mobile app with Flutter to provide a seamless buying and selling experience.
- **Reflectly:** This popular journaling app, known for its beautiful UI and smooth animations, is a testament to Flutter's capabilities.

Case Study: How Flutter Transformed a Business

Reflectly: A Journey of Growth and Innovation

Reflectly is a prime example of how Flutter can empower businesses to achieve remarkable success. Launched in 2017, Reflectly started as a simple mood-tracking app but quickly evolved into a comprehensive mental health companion, incorporating features like journaling, personalized insights, and guided meditations.

By choosing Flutter, Reflectly's development team benefited from:

- **Rapid Iterations:** Flutter's Hot Reload enabled them to quickly test and implement new features, speeding up their development cycle.
- **Beautiful UI:** Flutter's customizable widgets allowed them to create a visually appealing and engaging app that resonated with users.
- **Consistent Experience:** They were able to deliver a consistent user experience across both iOS and Android platforms without compromising on performance.

The results were impressive. Reflectly garnered millions of downloads, received widespread acclaim for its design and functionality, and secured significant investment from venture capitalists. Flutter played a pivotal role in their success, allowing them to build a high-quality app quickly and efficiently.

This demonstrates that Flutter isn't just a tool for hobbyists; it's a robust framework capable of driving real-world business results. Whether you're a startup or an established enterprise, Flutter can be a valuable asset in your app development strategy.

Chapter Summary

In this chapter, you learned about the fundamentals of Flutter. We defined Flutter as Google's UI toolkit for building beautiful, natively compiled applications for mobile, web, and desktop from a single codebase. We explored the key reasons why Flutter is gaining popularity, such as its cross-platform capabilities, fast development with Hot Reload, expressive and customizable UI, and a strong community and ecosystem.

You learned about Flutter's unique approach to cross-platform development, which enables you to write code once and deploy it across multiple platforms, saving time and effort. We also highlighted Flutter's Hot Reload feature, which allows you to see changes in your app instantly, significantly speeding up the development process.

Flutter's rich set of customizable widgets and support for Material Design and Cupertino were discussed, demonstrating how Flutter empowers you to create visually appealing and native-looking user interfaces.

Finally, we touched upon Flutter's vibrant community and growing ecosystem of packages, providing you with ample support, resources, and tools to enhance your Flutter development journey. We also showcased examples of well-known companies using Flutter for their apps, demonstrating its real-world applications and success stories.

Setting Up Your Flutter Development Environment

Outline

- System Requirements
- Installing Flutter
- Installing Android Studio
- Installing Xcode (for iOS Development)
- Installing Visual Studio Code (Optional)
- Configuring Editors
- Setting Up Emulators and Simulators
- Verifying Your Installation
- Chapter Summary

System Requirements

Before diving into Flutter development, it's essential to ensure your system meets the minimum requirements. These requirements vary slightly depending on the platforms you intend to target (mobile, web, or desktop).

Minimum Requirements (All Platforms)

- **Operating System:**
  - **Windows:** Windows 10 64-bit or later.
  - **macOS:** macOS 10.14 Mojave or later.
  - **Linux:** Most modern Linux distributions (e.g., Ubuntu, Debian, Fedora).
- **Disk Space:** At least 1.65 GB of free disk space (excluding space for IDE/tools).
- **Tools:**
  - Flutter depends on these command-line tools being available in your environment:
    - **Windows:** PowerShell 5.0 or later (this is pre-installed with Windows 10), Git for Windows (2.x).
    - **macOS:** bash, mkdir, rm, git, curl, unzip, which.
    - **Linux:** bash, mkdir, rm, git, curl, unzip, which.

Additional Requirements for Mobile Development

- **Android Studio:** For Android development, you'll need to install Android Studio and set up an Android emulator or connect a physical Android device.
- **Xcode:** For iOS development, you'll need to install Xcode and set up an iOS simulator or connect a physical iOS device. This requires a Mac running macOS.

Additional Requirements for Web Development

- **Chrome:** Recommended for debugging and testing web applications.
- **Web browser:** Any modern web browser to run and test your Flutter web apps.

Additional Requirements for Desktop Development

- **Windows:** Visual Studio 2022 or later with the "Desktop development with C++" workload installed.
- **macOS:** Xcode is needed to run and build macOS desktop apps.

Recommended Specifications (All Platforms)

While the minimum requirements will get you started, a more powerful machine will generally provide a smoother and more efficient development experience. Here are some recommended specifications:

- **Processor:** Multi-core processor with 64-bit support (Intel Core i5 or equivalent).
- **RAM:** 8 GB or more.
- **Disk Space:** A fast SSD with at least 20 GB of free space.
- **Display:** High-resolution display (1920x1080 or higher).

Mobile vs. Web/Desktop: Key Differences

The main difference in requirements lies in the additional tools needed for mobile development. To build and test apps for iOS and Android, you'll need to install platform-specific IDEs and SDKs (Android Studio and Xcode). These tools are not necessary for web or desktop development.

By understanding the specific requirements for your target platforms, you can ensure a seamless setup and a productive Flutter development experience.

Installing Flutter

To begin your Flutter journey, you'll need to download and install the Flutter Software Development Kit (SDK). Follow these step-by-step instructions for your specific operating system:

1. Download the Flutter SDK

- Go to the official Flutter website: https://docs.flutter.dev/get-started/install
- Select your operating system (Windows, macOS, or Linux).
- Download the latest stable release of the Flutter SDK for your platform. This will be a zip file.

2. Extract the Flutter SDK

- Extract the downloaded zip file to your desired location.
  - For Windows, you can use a tool like 7-Zip or the built-in Windows extractor.
  - For macOS and Linux, you can use the `unzip` command in your terminal:
    ```
    unzip ~/Downloads/flutter_macos_stable.zip
    ```

3. Add Flutter to Your PATH

Adding Flutter to your system's PATH environment variable allows you to run Flutter commands from any terminal or command prompt window.

- **Windows:**
  1. Open the Start menu and search for "env."
  2. Select "Edit the system environment variables."
  3. Click the "Environment Variables…" button.
  4. Under "System variables," find the "Path" variable and click "Edit."
  5. Click "New" and add the path to the `flutter\bin` directory (e.g., `C:\flutter\bin`).
  6. Click "OK" on all open windows.
- **macOS and Linux:**
  1. Open your shell's configuration file (`.bashrc`, `.zshrc`, or similar).
  2. Add the following line (replacing <path_to_flutter> with the actual path to your Flutter SDK):
     ```
     export PATH="$PATH:<path_to_flutter>/bin"
     ```
  3. Save the file and run `source <your_shell_config_file>` in your terminal to apply the changes.

4. Verify Installation

To confirm that Flutter is installed correctly, open a new terminal window and run the following command:

```
flutter doctor
```

This command will check your system for all the necessary dependencies and give you a report. If any issues are found, follow the instructions provided by the `flutter doctor` command to resolve them.

Congratulations! You've successfully installed Flutter and are ready to start building awesome apps!

Installing Android Studio: Your Flutter Workshop

While you can use various code editors for Flutter development, Android Studio is the official Integrated Development Environment (IDE) recommended by Google. It provides a powerful, feature-rich environment specifically tailored for building Android and Flutter applications.

Why Android Studio?

Android Studio offers several advantages that make it the preferred choice for Flutter developers:

- **Seamless Integration:** Android Studio comes with built-in support for Flutter and Dart. This means you get features like code completion, syntax highlighting, debugging tools, and project management out of the box.
- **Visual Layout Editor:** The visual layout editor allows you to drag and drop widgets to design your app's UI, making it easier to visualize and refine your layouts.
- **Emulator and Device Integration:** Android Studio makes it easy to create and manage Android Virtual Devices (AVDs) for testing your app on various Android versions and screen sizes. It also simplifies the process of connecting and deploying to physical Android devices.
- **Robust Debugging Tools:** Android Studio offers a powerful debugger that helps you identify and fix errors in your code. It provides features like breakpoints, variable inspection, and step-through execution.
- **Extensive Plugin Ecosystem:** You can extend Android Studio's capabilities by installing a wide range of plugins from the JetBrains Marketplace. These plugins offer features like code analysis, version control integration, and theme customization.

Installing Android Studio

1. **Download:** Go to the Android Studio website (https://developer.android.com/studio) and download the installer for your operating system.
2. **Run the Installer:** Follow the on-screen instructions to install Android Studio. This may take some time as it downloads additional components.
3. **Launch Android Studio:** After installation, launch Android Studio. You might be prompted to import settings from a previous installation; choose the option that suits you.

Installing the Flutter and Dart Plugins

1. **Open Plugin Settings:** Go to "File" -> "Settings" (or "Android Studio" -> "Preferences" on macOS).
2. **Browse Repositories:** In the Settings dialog, navigate to "Plugins."
3. **Search and Install:** Search for "Flutter" and click "Install." Android Studio will automatically find and suggest the Dart plugin as well. Install it too.
4. **Restart Android Studio:** After installing both plugins, restart Android Studio to apply the changes.

You're now ready to create your first Flutter project in Android Studio and embark on your app development journey!

Installing Xcode (for iOS Development)

If you plan to build and test Flutter apps for iOS devices or use the iOS simulator, you'll need to install Xcode. This powerful integrated development environment (IDE) by Apple is essential for iOS development.

Why Xcode for iOS?

Xcode provides a comprehensive set of tools for creating, testing, and debugging iOS apps. Here's why it's crucial for Flutter iOS development:

- **iOS SDK and Tools:** Xcode includes the iOS Software Development Kit (SDK), which contains the libraries, frameworks, and tools needed to build iOS apps.
- **iOS Simulator:** Xcode comes with a built-in iOS simulator that allows you to test your Flutter app on different iPhone and iPad models without needing physical devices.
- **Debugging and Profiling:** Xcode provides robust tools for debugging and profiling your iOS app, helping you identify and fix issues related to performance, memory usage, and more.
- **Deployment:** When you're ready to publish your Flutter app to the App Store, you'll use Xcode to package and submit your app.

Important Note: Xcode is exclusive to macOS. If you're developing on Windows or Linux, you won't be able to install Xcode or build iOS apps directly. However, you can still use Flutter for Android and web development.

Installing Xcode

1. **App Store:** Open the App Store on your Mac.
2. **Search:** Search for "Xcode" and click the "Get" button to download and install it. Xcode is a large application, so the download might take some time.
3. **Launch Xcode:** After installation, launch Xcode. You might be prompted to agree to the Xcode license agreement; accept it to proceed.
4. **Install Command Line Tools:**
   - Open Xcode preferences (Xcode -> Preferences).
   - Go to the "Locations" tab.
   - In the "Command Line Tools" dropdown, select the Xcode version you just installed.
5. **Additional Configuration (Recommended):** To ensure a smooth Flutter development experience, run the following command in your terminal:

   ```
   sudo xcodebuild
   ```

   This command performs some additional configuration tasks that can help prevent issues later on.

Now you're ready to use Xcode for iOS development with Flutter!

Installing Visual Studio Code (Optional)

While Android Studio is the official IDE for Flutter, Visual Studio Code (VS Code) offers a compelling alternative. VS Code is a free, open-source code editor developed by Microsoft, known for its speed, versatility, and extensive customization options.

Why Choose VS Code for Flutter?

- **Lightweight and Fast:** VS Code is considerably lighter than Android Studio, making it a great choice for less powerful machines or if you prefer a snappier editor.

- **Customizable:** VS Code allows you to personalize your development environment with various themes, extensions, and settings.
- **Wide Range of Extensions:** VS Code's vast library of extensions covers everything from language support to productivity tools, making it adaptable to your specific workflow.
- **Integrated Terminal:** VS Code includes a built-in terminal, which is convenient for running Flutter commands and debugging.
- **Cross-Platform:** VS Code is available for Windows, macOS, and Linux, allowing you to use the same editor across different operating systems.

Installing Visual Studio Code

1. **Download:** Visit the Visual Studio Code website (https://code.visualstudio.com/) and download the installer for your operating system.
2. **Install:** Run the installer and follow the on-screen instructions.
3. **Launch VS Code:** Open Visual Studio Code once the installation is complete.

Installing the Flutter Extension

1. **Open Extensions Marketplace:** Click on the Extensions icon in the sidebar (or press `Ctrl+Shift+X` or `Cmd+Shift+X`).
2. **Search and Install:** Search for "Flutter" and click "Install" on the official Flutter extension. This extension will automatically install the Dart extension as well.
3. **Reload VS Code:** Once both extensions are installed, reload VS Code to activate them.

Key Benefits in Action

With the Flutter extension, VS Code offers a streamlined Flutter development experience:

- **Rich Language Support:** Syntax highlighting, code completion, and error checking for Dart and Flutter code.
- **Debugging:** Integrated debugging tools to help you find and fix errors in your app.
- **Hot Reload:** Support for Flutter's Hot Reload feature for faster development cycles.
- **Project Creation and Management:** Easily create new Flutter projects and manage existing ones.

Choosing Your Editor

Both Android Studio and VS Code are excellent choices for Flutter development. The best one for you depends on your personal preferences and specific requirements.

- **If you prefer a full-featured IDE with extensive built-in tools and visual design capabilities, Android Studio might be the better choice.**
- **If you prefer a lightweight, customizable editor with a focus on code and a vibrant extension ecosystem, VS Code could be a good fit.**

Ultimately, the choice is yours! Experiment with both editors to see which one feels more comfortable and suits your workflow best.

Configuring Editors

Whether you choose Android Studio or Visual Studio Code (VS Code), taking a few moments to configure your code editor can significantly enhance your Flutter development experience. This involves enabling helpful features like code formatting, auto-completion, and customizing the editor to suit your personal preferences.

Why Configure Your Editor?

Configuring your editor helps you:

- **Write Cleaner Code:** Code formatting tools automatically organize your code, making it easier to read and maintain.
- **Code Faster:** Auto-completion suggests code snippets and functions as you type, reducing the need to memorize syntax.
- **Catch Errors Early:** Linters analyze your code for potential errors and style inconsistencies, helping you avoid mistakes.
- **Work Efficiently:** Custom keybindings and themes can streamline your workflow and reduce repetitive tasks.

Configuring Android Studio

1. **Enable Dart Analysis:**
   - Go to File > Settings (or Android Studio > Preferences on macOS).
   - Navigate to Languages & Frameworks > Flutter.
   - Ensure the "Enable Dart support for the project 'your_project_name'" checkbox is selected.
2. **Code Formatting:**
   - Go to File > Settings > Editor > Code Style > Dart (or Flutter).
   - Customize the formatting options (e.g., indentation, line breaks, spacing) to your liking.
   - Use the "Reformat Code" action (Ctrl+Alt+L or Cmd+Option+L) to apply formatting to your code.
3. **Auto-completion:** Android Studio comes with built-in code completion for Dart and Flutter. You can trigger it by pressing Ctrl+Space or Cmd+Space.
4. **Customizing Appearance and Keybindings:**
   - Explore the Settings dialog to customize themes, fonts, and color schemes.
   - Go to File > Settings > Keymap to modify keyboard shortcuts.

Configuring Visual Studio Code

1. **Install Flutter and Dart Extensions:** Ensure you have the official Flutter and Dart extensions installed (see the previous section for instructions).
2. **Code Formatting:**
   - Open the Command Palette (Ctrl+Shift+P or Cmd+Shift+P).
   - Type "Format Document" and press Enter. VS Code will automatically format your Dart code.
   - Customize formatting options in Settings (File > Preferences > Settings) by searching for "dart.format."
3. **Auto-completion:** VS Code's Flutter extension provides code completion for Dart and Flutter. You can trigger it by typing a few characters and then pressing Ctrl+Space or Cmd+Space.
4. **Customizing Appearance and Keybindings:**
   - Use the Extensions Marketplace to install themes and customize the look and feel of VS Code.
   - Go to File > Preferences > Keyboard Shortcuts to modify keybindings.

Additional Tips

- **Use Linters:** Consider installing a linter extension like "Dart Linter" or "Flutter Linter" to get real-time feedback on code quality and style.
- **Explore Extensions:** Both Android Studio and VS Code have extensive plugin/extension ecosystems. Explore and install extensions that can further enhance your productivity and workflow.
- **Experiment:** Don't be afraid to try different settings and configurations to find what works best for you.

By investing a little time in configuring your editor, you can set yourself up for a more efficient, enjoyable, and productive Flutter development journey.

Setting Up Emulators and Simulators

Emulators and simulators are essential tools for Flutter development. They allow you to test your apps on various virtual devices without needing to own a collection of physical phones and tablets. This section will guide you through setting up and optimizing emulators for Android (using Android Virtual Devices in Android Studio) and simulators for iOS (using Xcode).

Android Emulators with Android Virtual Devices (AVDs)

1. **Open AVD Manager:** In Android Studio, go to **Tools** -> **Device Manager** (or click the AVD Manager icon in the toolbar).
2. **Create a New AVD:** Click the "Create Virtual Device" button.
3. **Choose a Device:** Select a hardware profile that resembles the device you want to emulate (e.g., Pixel 5, Nexus 6). You can also create custom hardware profiles.
4. **Select a System Image:** Choose a system image that matches the Android version and API level you want to target. Download it if it's not already installed.
5. **Configure AVD Options:** Customize options like the AVD's name, startup orientation, camera emulation, and more. Click "Finish" to create the AVD.
6. **Launch the AVD:** In the Device Manager, select your newly created AVD and click the "Play" button to launch it.

iOS Simulators with Xcode

1. **Open Xcode:** Launch Xcode.
2. **Open Simulator:** Go to **Xcode** -> **Open Developer Tool** -> **Simulator**.
3. **Choose a Device:** From the menu bar, go to **Hardware** -> **Device** and select the iPhone or iPad model you want to simulate.
4. **Run Your App:** In your Flutter project, select the desired simulator as the target device and run your app.

Optimizing Emulator and Simulator Performance

- **Hardware Acceleration:** Enable hardware acceleration in both Android Studio and Xcode settings for faster emulation and simulation.
- **Allocate More Resources:** Increase the allocated RAM and CPU cores for your emulators and simulators. You can usually adjust these settings in the AVD Manager or Simulator preferences.
- **Cold Boot vs. Quick Boot:** In Android Studio, you can choose between a "cold boot" (full system startup) or a "quick boot" (snapshot-based resume) for your AVD. Quick boot is generally faster, but a cold boot might be necessary for troubleshooting.
- **Use Physical Devices:** For the most accurate testing and performance assessment, consider testing your app on physical Android and iOS devices.

Pro Tip: Create multiple AVDs and simulators to cover a variety of screen sizes, Android versions, and iOS versions. This will help you ensure your app looks and performs well on different devices.

Verifying Your Installation

After following the installation steps, it's time for a quick checkup to ensure everything is set up correctly. Flutter provides a handy command called `flutter doctor` that diagnoses your environment and reports any issues.

Running flutter doctor

1. **Open a Terminal/Command Prompt:** Launch your terminal (macOS/Linux) or command prompt (Windows).
2. **Run the Command:** Type the following and press Enter:

```
flutter doctor
```

3. **Review the Report:** Flutter doctor will run a series of checks, looking for:
   - Flutter SDK version
   - Android Studio (and Flutter/Dart plugins)
   - Connected devices (physical or emulators/simulators)
   - Xcode (for iOS development)

The output will look something like this:

Doctor summary (to see all details, run flutter doctor -v):
[✓] Flutter (Channel stable, 3.10.5, on macOS 13.5 22G74 darwin-arm, locale en-US)
[✓] Android toolchain - develop for Android devices (Android SDK version 33.0.2)
[✓] Xcode - develop for iOS and macOS (Xcode 14.3.1)
[✓] Chrome - develop for the web
[✓] Android Studio (version 2022.2)
[✓] Connected device (3 available)
[✓] HTTP Host Availability

• No issues found!

Troubleshooting Common Issues

If you see any errors or warnings in the `flutter doctor` report, don't panic! Here are some common issues and how to fix them:

- **Android license status unknown:** Run `flutter doctor --android-licenses` to accept the Android SDK licenses.
- **Xcode not installed:** Install Xcode from the App Store and configure it as explained in the previous section.
- **No devices available:** Connect a physical device via USB or create an emulator/simulator.
- **Missing dependencies:** Follow the instructions in the `flutter doctor` output to install any missing tools or SDKs.

Pro Tip: Run `flutter doctor -v` for a more detailed report that includes information about the versions of your tools and dependencies.

You're Ready to Go!

If your `flutter doctor` report shows all green checkmarks (✓), congratulations! Your Flutter development environment is set up and ready to go. You can now move on to the next chapter and start building your first Flutter app.

Chapter Summary

In this chapter, you took the crucial first steps in your Flutter development journey by setting up your development environment. You learned about the minimum system requirements for developing Flutter apps on different platforms and how to download and install the Flutter SDK.

We guided you through the process of installing Android Studio, the recommended IDE for Flutter development, and installing the necessary Flutter and Dart plugins. We also covered the installation of Xcode, essential for iOS development, and introduced Visual Studio Code as an alternative editor for those who prefer a lightweight option.

Additionally, you learned how to configure your chosen editor to optimize your workflow, enabling features like code formatting and auto-completion. We also explained how to set up Android emulators and iOS simulators for testing your Flutter apps on different devices.

Finally, we showed you how to verify your installation using the `flutter doctor` command and provided troubleshooting tips for common issues. Now that your environment is set up, you're ready to dive into the exciting world of Flutter development and start building your first app!

A Tour of Dart: The Language Behind Flutter

Outline

- Why Dart?
- Dart Basics
- Variables and Data Types
- Operators
- Control Flow
- Functions
- Classes and Objects
- Collections
- Error Handling
- Chapter Summary

Why Dart?

Google didn't just randomly select Dart as the language for Flutter. They carefully evaluated its strengths and found it to be the ideal partner for their UI toolkit. Here's why:

- **Hot Reload: Your Productivity Booster**

Imagine being able to change your code and instantly see the results in your app. That's the magic of Dart's Hot Reload feature. It dramatically speeds up development cycles, allowing you to experiment, iterate, and fine-tune your UI in real-time. Say goodbye to tedious rebuilds and restarts!

- **AOT Compilation: Power and Performance**

When it's time to release your app, Dart's ahead-of-time (AOT) compilation takes over. Your code is compiled into native machine code, ensuring fast startup times, smooth animations, and a snappy user experience. Your app will feel like a true native citizen on every platform.

- **JIT Compilation: The Best of Both Worlds**

During development, Dart leverages just-in-time (JIT) compilation. This enables the Hot Reload magic by quickly injecting updated code into the running app. In production, the switch to AOT compilation ensures top-notch performance.

- **Object-Oriented: Familiarity Breeds Productivity**

If you've worked with languages like Java, C#, or JavaScript, you'll feel right at home with Dart. Its object-oriented nature (classes, objects, inheritance) makes it easy to structure and manage your code, promoting reusability and maintainability.

- **Easy to Learn: Your Onboarding Ramp**

Dart's syntax is clean, intuitive, and approachable. It's designed to be easy to read and understand, even if you're new to programming. This gentle learning curve makes it a great starting point for beginners who want to dive into mobile app development.

- **Optimized for UI Development:** Dart includes language features specifically tailored for UI development, such as:
    - **Cascade Notation (. .):** Concisely chain together method calls on the same object.

○ **Spread Operator (...):** Conveniently insert elements from one collection into another.
○ **Null Safety (Sound Null Safety):** Prevent null pointer exceptions at compile time.

Dart and Flutter are like two puzzle pieces that fit together perfectly. Their combined strengths create a harmonious development environment that empowers you to build beautiful, high-performance apps with ease.

Dart Basics

Dart's syntax shares similarities with other popular programming languages, making it relatively easy to pick up. Let's dive into the core elements that form the backbone of your Dart code.

Syntax and Structure

- **Statements:** In Dart, a statement is a single instruction or action. It's the basic unit of computation. Think of it as a single sentence in a paragraph.
- **Semicolons:** Each statement in Dart ends with a semicolon (;). It's like a period at the end of a sentence.
- **Code Blocks:** Statements are often grouped together into blocks using curly braces ({}). Blocks define the scope of variables and control the flow of your code. You'll encounter blocks when working with functions, conditional statements, loops, and more.

The `main()` Function: Your Starting Point

Every Dart program must have a `main()` function. It's the entry point for your code – the place where execution begins. Think of it as the front door to your house. When you run your Dart program, the Dart runtime looks for the `main()` function and starts executing the code inside it.

"Hello, World!" in Dart: Your First Steps

Let's see how all of this comes together with a classic "Hello, World!" example:

```dart
void main() { print('Hello, World!'); }
```

Let's break this down:

1. `void main() {`: This line declares the `main()` function. The `void` keyword indicates that the function doesn't return any value.
2. `print('Hello, World!');`: This line is a statement that calls the `print()` function to display the text "Hello, World!" in the console.
3. `}`: This closing curly brace marks the end of the `main()` function's code block.

To run this code:

1. **Save:** Save this code as a file named `main.dart`.
2. **Execute:** Open a terminal and navigate to the directory where you saved the file. Then run the following command:

   ```
   dart run main.dart
   ```

   You should see "Hello, World!" printed in your terminal.

Congratulations! You've just written and executed your first Dart program. This simple example demonstrates the basic structure of Dart code and how to use the `print()` function for output.

Comments

Comments are like little notes you leave in your code for yourself or other developers. They don't affect how your program runs, but they're invaluable for:

- **Explaining the purpose of code:** Comments help you (or others) understand *why* a particular piece of code exists and what it's trying to achieve.
- **Providing context:** Comments can clarify the logic behind complex algorithms or data structures.
- **Documenting assumptions:** Comments can state any assumptions you're making about the code's input or environment.
- **Temporary disabling code:** You can use comments to temporarily "comment out" sections of code that you don't want to execute while testing or debugging.

Single-Line Comments

Single-line comments start with two forward slashes (//). Everything after the // and until the end of the line is ignored by the Dart compiler:

```
// This is a single-line comment print('Hello, World!'); // This comment
explains the print statement
```

Multi-Line Comments

Multi-line comments start with /* and end with */. Anything between these symbols is considered a comment, even if it spans multiple lines:

```
/* This is a multi-line comment. It can span across multiple lines. */
```

Best Practices for Comments

- **Be clear and concise:** Write comments that are easy to understand and get straight to the point.
- **Keep comments up-to-date:** As you modify your code, make sure to update any relevant comments.
- **Use comments sparingly:** Too many comments can clutter your code and make it harder to read. Focus on explaining the *why*, not the *how*.
- **Avoid obvious comments:** Don't waste time commenting on things that are self-explanatory from the code itself.
- **Use doc comments:** Dart has a special type of comment called a "doc comment" that starts with /// or /**. These are used to generate documentation for your code.

By using comments effectively, you can make your code more readable, maintainable, and easier to collaborate on with others.

Printing Output

The print() function is your primary tool for displaying messages and data to the console (the output area of your code editor or terminal). It's invaluable for debugging, providing feedback during development, and logging information.

Basic Output with print()

To display a message, simply pass it as an argument to the print() function:

```
print('This is a simple message.'); print(42); // You can also print numbers
print(true); // And boolean values (true/false)
```

String Interpolation: Dynamic Output

String interpolation lets you embed variables and expressions directly within string literals. This makes it easier to create dynamic messages and output data in a readable format.

There are two main ways to use string interpolation in Dart:

1. **Using $ for Variables:** Prefix a variable name with $ to insert its value into a string:
   ```
   var name = 'Alice'; print('Hello, $name!'); // Output: Hello, Alice!
   ```
2. **Using ${...} for Expressions:** Enclose an expression within ${...} to evaluate it and insert the result into a string:
   ```
   var x = 10; var y = 20; print('The sum of $x and $y is ${x + y}.'); //
   Output: The sum of 10 and 20 is 30.
   ```
   You can put anything inside the curly braces that returns a value. For instance:
   ```
   print('The area of a circle with radius 5 is ${3.14159 * 5 * 5}');
   ```

Examples of String Interpolation

```
var age = 30; var price = 19.99; var isMember = true; print('Name: $name, Age:
$age'); print('Price: \$$price'); print('Member status: $isMember');
```

Console Output:

Name: Alice, Age: 30
Price: $19.99
Member status: true

By mastering string interpolation, you can create informative and dynamic console output that aids in debugging and understanding your Flutter applications.

Variables and Data Types

Variables are fundamental building blocks in programming. They act as containers for storing data that your program can use and manipulate. In Dart, variables are dynamic, meaning they can hold different types of values throughout their lifetime.

Declaring Variables: The `var` Keyword

Dart provides the `var` keyword for declaring variables. The neat thing is that you don't need to explicitly specify the data type when you use `var`. Dart's type inference figures it out for you based on the initial value assigned to the variable.

```
var name = 'Alice'; // A String var age = 30; // An int var price = 19.99; //
A double var isStudent = true; // A bool
```

Core Data Types: The Variety Pack

Dart offers a variety of built-in data types to represent different kinds of information:

- **Numbers:**
  - `int`: Represents whole numbers (e.g., 42, -10).
  - `double`: Represents floating-point numbers with decimal places (e.g., 3.14, -0.5).
- **Strings:**

- String: Represents a sequence of characters (e.g., "Hello, World!", "Flutter is awesome!").
- **Booleans:**
  - bool: Represents logical values (either true or false).
- **Collections:**
  - List: An ordered collection of items (e.g., [1, 2, 3], ["apple", "banana", "orange"]).
  - Map: A collection of key-value pairs (e.g., {"name": "Alice", "age": 30}).
- **Special Types:**
  - dynamic: Can hold any type of value. Use with caution, as it disables type checking.
  - Null: Represents the absence of a value.

Type Safety: Dart's Guardian Angel

Dart is a type-safe language. This means it checks the types of values you assign to variables and ensures that they match the declared type (or the inferred type when using var). If you try to assign an incompatible value, Dart will raise an error.

```
var age = 30; age = 'thirty'; // Error! Type 'String' is not a subtype of type 'int'
```

Type safety is your friend. It helps you catch potential errors early on, making your code more reliable and less prone to unexpected crashes.

Benefits of Static Typing (Type Safety)

- **Early Error Detection:** Type safety helps you catch potential errors during development, rather than at runtime when they can cause crashes.
- **Improved Code Readability:** Explicit types make your code more self-documenting and easier for others (and your future self) to understand.
- **Better Tooling:** IDEs and code editors can provide better code completion, refactoring, and error highlighting with the help of static types.
- **Performance Optimization:** Dart's AOT compiler can generate more optimized code when it knows the types of values in advance.

When to Use var vs. Explicit Types

- **Use var when:**
  - The type is obvious from the assigned value.
  - You want to take advantage of type inference.
- **Use explicit types when:**
  - The type is not immediately clear from the value.
  - You want to document the intended type of the variable.
  - You need to work with APIs or libraries that require specific types.

In general, using var for local variables and explicit types for class members and function parameters is a good practice.

Operators

Operators are special symbols that perform specific operations on values or variables. Dart offers a variety of operators for arithmetic calculations, assignments, comparisons, and logical operations.

Arithmetic Operators: The Math Toolkit

Operator	Description	Example
+	Addition	2 + 3 (result is 5)
–	Subtraction	5 – 2 (result is 3)
*	Multiplication	4 * 6 (result is 24)
/	Division	10 / 2 (result is 5.0)
~/	Integer Division (truncates)	10 ~/ 3 (result is 3)
%	Modulus (remainder)	10 % 3 (result is 1)

Assignment Operators: Putting Values into Variables

Operator	Description	Example	Equivalent To
=	Assignment	x = 5;	
+=	Add and Assign	x += 3;	x = x + 3;
-=	Subtract and Assign	x -= 2;	x = x - 2;
*=	Multiply and Assign	x *= 4;	x = x * 4;
/=	Divide and Assign	x /= 2;	x = x / 2;
~/=	Integer Divide and Assign	x ~/= 3;	x = x ~/ 3;
%=	Modulus and Assign	x %= 5;	x = x % 5;

Comparison Operators: Checking Relationships

Operator	Description	Example
==	Equal to	5 == 5 (true)
!=	Not equal to	5 != 3 (true)
>	Greater than	7 > 4 (true)
<	Less than	2 < 6 (true)
>=	Greater than or equal to	8 >= 8 (true)
<=	Less than or equal to	3 <= 9 (true)

Logical Operators: Combining Conditions

Operator	Description	Example

&&	Logical AND (both conditions must be true)	`(age > 18) && (isStudent)`
||	Logical OR (at least one condition must be true)	`(hasMoney) || (hasCreditCard)`
!	Logical NOT (inverts the truth value)	`!(isRaining)`

Control Flow

In programming, control flow refers to the order in which statements are executed. Dart provides tools to make decisions, repeat actions, and control the flow of your program based on specific conditions.

Conditional Statements

Conditional statements allow your program to take different paths based on whether a certain condition is true or false. Dart provides several ways to achieve this:

1. The if Statement

The `if` statement checks if a given condition is true. If so, it executes the block of code within its curly braces. If the condition is false, it skips the block.

```
var score = 85; if (score >= 90) { print('Excellent!'); }
```

2. The if-else Statement

The `if-else` statement provides an alternative path to take if the initial `if` condition is false.

```
var score = 75; if (score >= 90) { print('Excellent!'); } else { print('Good job!'); }
```

3. The else-if Ladder

You can use multiple `else if` blocks to check additional conditions.

```
var score = 65; if (score >= 90) { print('Excellent!'); } else if (score >= 80) { print('Very good!'); } else if (score >= 70) { print('Good job!'); } else { print('Keep trying!'); }
```

Conditional Expressions (Ternary Operator):

For simple conditions, you can use a compact syntax called a *conditional expression* (sometimes referred to as the ternary operator).

```
var isAdult = age >= 18 ? true : false;
```

This is equivalent to:

```
var isAdult; if (age >= 18) { isAdult = true; } else { isAdult = false; }
```

Key Points:

- **Boolean Expressions:** The condition inside the parentheses of an if statement must be a boolean expression. This is an expression that evaluates to either true or false.
- **Nesting:** You can nest if statements within other if statements to handle more complex scenarios.
- **Logical Operators:** Use logical operators (&& for AND, || for OR, ! for NOT) to combine multiple conditions.

By understanding and using conditional statements effectively, you can create more flexible and dynamic Flutter apps that respond intelligently to different situations.

Loops

Loops are essential tools for automating repetitive tasks in your code. Dart provides several types of loops, each with its own strengths for specific situations.

1. The for Loop: Counting Your Way Through

The for loop is ideal when you know in advance how many times you want to repeat a block of code. It consists of three parts:

- **Initialization:** A statement executed once at the beginning of the loop. Typically used to initialize a loop counter variable.
- **Condition:** A boolean expression checked before each iteration. The loop continues as long as this condition is true.
- **Update:** A statement executed at the end of each iteration. Often used to modify the loop counter.

```
for (var i = 0; i < 5; i++) { print('Iteration: $i'); }
```

This loop will print "Iteration: 0" through "Iteration: 4".

2. The while Loop: Repeat Until False

The while loop is useful when you want to repeat a block of code as long as a certain condition remains true. The condition is checked before each iteration, and the loop terminates when the condition becomes false.

```
var count = 0; while (count < 5) { print('Count: $count'); count++; }
```

3. The for-in Loop: Iterating Over Collections

The for-in loop simplifies the process of iterating over elements in a collection, such as a List or Set. It automatically handles the iteration process, assigning each element to a variable for you to use within the loop.

```
var numbers = [1, 2, 3, 4, 5]; for (var number in numbers) { print(number); }
```

Controlling Loop Execution: break and continue

- **break;:** Immediately terminates the loop, even if the loop condition is still true.
- **continue;:** Skips the rest of the current iteration and proceeds to the next one.

```
for (var i = 1; i <= 10; i++) { if (i % 2 == 0) { // Skip even numbers
continue; } print(i); // Print only odd numbers if (i == 7) { // Stop at
7 break; } }
```

This loop will print "1", "3", "5", and then "7" before terminating.

Choosing the Right Loop

The best loop type depends on your specific use case:

- `for:` When you know the exact number of iterations in advance.
- `while:` When you want to repeat as long as a condition is true.
- `for-in:` When you want to easily iterate over items in a collection.

Functions

Functions are self-contained chunks of code designed to perform specific tasks. Think of them like little machines within your program, each with a specific job to do. Functions are essential for:

- **Reusability:** You write the code for a function once, and then you can call (use) it as many times as you need, avoiding repetition.
- **Modularity:** Functions break down complex tasks into smaller, more manageable pieces, making your code easier to understand and maintain.
- **Abstraction:** Functions hide implementation details, allowing you to focus on what a piece of code does, rather than how it does it.

Defining Functions: Giving Your Code a Name

Here's the basic structure of a Dart function:

```
returnType functionName(parameters) { // Function body (code to be executed) }
```

- `returnType:` The data type of the value the function returns (e.g., `int`, `String`, `bool`). If the function doesn't return anything, use the `void` keyword.
- `functionName:` A descriptive name for your function. It should indicate what the function does.
- `parameters:` A list of values (inputs) that you can pass to the function when you call it.

Example: A Simple Function

```
int addNumbers(int a, int b) { return a + b; } var result = addNumbers(5, 3);
// Call the function and store the result print(result); // Output: 8
```

Optional Parameters: Flexibility for Function Calls

You can make parameters optional by enclosing them in square brackets ([ ]). Optional parameters must be placed at the end of the parameter list.

```
String greet(String name, [String greeting = 'Hello']) { return '$greeting,
$name!'; } print(greet('Alice')); // Output: Hello, Alice! print(greet('Bob',
'Hi')); // Output: Hi, Bob!
```

Named Parameters: Clarity and Order Independence

Named parameters allow you to specify the name of each argument when calling a function. This improves code readability and eliminates the need to remember the order of arguments.

```
String createEmail(String name, String domain, {bool isStudent = false}) {
return '$name${isStudent ? '.student' : ''}' '@$domain.com'; }
print(createEmail('alice', 'example', isStudent: true)); // Output:
alice.student@example.com print(createEmail('bob', 'example')); // Output:
bob@example.com
```

Default Values: Simplifying Function Calls

You can assign default values to parameters, making them optional for the caller. If the caller doesn't provide a value, the default value is used.

```
String greet(String name, [String greeting = 'Hello']) { return '$greeting,
$name!'; } print(greet('Alice')); // Outputs 'Hello, Alice!' because
'greeting' uses its default value
```

Arrow Functions (=>): Shorthand for Single-Expression Functions

Arrow functions provide a concise way to write functions that have a single expression in their body.

```
int multiply(int a, int b) => a * b; // Equivalent to: int multiply(int a, int
b) { return a * b; }
```

Classes and Objects

Object-oriented programming (OOP) is a powerful paradigm for organizing and structuring your code. It revolves around the concepts of classes and objects, which help you model real-world entities and their interactions.

Core OOP Concepts:

- **Class:** A blueprint or template for creating objects. It defines the properties (data) and methods (actions) that objects of that class will have.
- **Object:** An instance of a class. It represents a specific entity with its own unique state (values for properties) and behavior (ability to perform actions).
- **Properties:** The data associated with an object, representing its characteristics or attributes.
- **Methods:** The actions that an object can perform. They are functions defined within a class.

Defining Classes and Objects in Dart

Here's how you define a class in Dart:

```
class Person { String name; // Property (instance variable) int age; //
Property (instance variable) Person(this.name, this.age); // Constructor void
sayHello() { // Method print('Hello, my name is $name and I am $age years
old.'); } }
```

Let's break this down:

- The class name is Person.
- We have two properties: name and age
- A constructor to initialize those properties

- A method called `sayHello` that prints a message.

To create an object (an instance) of this class, you use the new keyword (though it's optional in newer Dart versions) and the constructor:

```
var person = Person('Alice', 30); person.sayHello(); // Output: Hello, my name
is Alice and I am 30 years old.
```

Inheritance: Building Hierarchies

Inheritance allows you to create new classes (subclasses) that inherit properties and methods from existing classes (superclasses). This promotes code reuse and models hierarchical relationships.

```
class Student extends Person { String major; Student(String name, int age,
this.major) : super(name, age); // calls parent constructor void study() {
print('$name is studying $major.'); } }
```

In this example, the `Student` class inherits from the `Person` class.

Polymorphism: Many Forms

Polymorphism allows objects of different classes to be treated as if they were objects of a common superclass. This provides flexibility and makes your code more adaptable.

```
Person student = Student('Bob', 20, 'Computer Science'); student.sayHello();
// Output: Hello, my name is Bob and I am 20 years old. (student as
Student).study(); // Output: Bob is studying Computer Science.
```

Key OOP Principles:

- **Encapsulation:** Bundling data and methods that operate on that data within a class, hiding internal details.
- **Abstraction:** Simplifying complex systems by modeling them with classes and objects, focusing on essential features.
- **Inheritance:** Creating hierarchies of classes where subclasses inherit properties and behaviors from superclasses.
- **Polymorphism:** The ability of objects of different classes to respond to the same method call in their own way.

By mastering OOP concepts and applying them in your Flutter projects, you can create well-structured, maintainable, and scalable codebases that are easier to understand and extend.

Collections

Collections are like containers that hold multiple pieces of data. Dart offers a variety of collection types, but we'll focus on the two most common ones: Lists and Maps.

Lists: Ordered Sequences

A `List` in Dart is an ordered collection of elements. Think of it as a numbered list where each item has a specific position (index). Lists are incredibly versatile and can store items of the same or different data types.

Creating a List

```
var numbers = [1, 2, 3, 4, 5]; // A list of integers var fruits = ['apple',
'banana', 'orange']; // A list of strings
```

Accessing Elements

```
print(numbers[0]); // Access the first element (1) print(fruits[2]); // Access
the third element ("orange")
```

Modifying Lists

```
numbers.add(6); // Add an element to the end fruits.removeAt(1); // Remove the
element at index 1 ("banana") fruits[0] = 'grape'; // Change the first element
to "grape"
```

Common List Methods

- `length`: Returns the number of elements in the list.
- `add(item)`: Adds an item to the end of the list.
- `insert(index, item)`: Inserts an item at a specific index.
- `remove(item)`: Removes the first occurrence of an item.
- `removeAt(index)`: Removes the item at a specific index.
- `contains(item)`: Checks if the list contains a specific item.
- `indexOf(item)`: Returns the index of the first occurrence of an item.
- `clear()`: Removes all elements from the list.
- `sort()`: Sorts the elements of the list in ascending order.

Maps: Key-Value Pairs

A Map in Dart stores data as key-value pairs. Each key is associated with a unique value. This allows you to look up values based on their keys, like a dictionary.

Creating a Map

```
var person = { 'name': 'Alice', 'age': 30, 'isStudent': true }; // Or using
Map constructor Map<String, dynamic> anotherPerson = Map();
anotherPerson['name'] = 'Bob'; anotherPerson['age'] = 25;
anotherPerson['isStudent'] = false;
```

Accessing Values

```
print(person['name']); // Access the value associated with the key "name"
print(person['age']); // Access the value associated with the key "age"
```

Modifying Maps

```
person['age'] = 31; // Update the value associated with the key "age"
person['city'] = 'New York'; // Add a new key-value pair
```

Common Map Methods

- `length`: Returns the number of key-value pairs in the map.
- `keys`: Returns an iterable containing all the keys.
- `values`: Returns an iterable containing all the values.
- `containsKey(key)`: Checks if the map contains a specific key.
- `containsValue(value)`: Checks if the map contains a specific value.
- `remove(key)`: Removes the key-value pair with the specified key.
- `clear()`: Removes all key-value pairs from the map.

By understanding lists and maps, you'll be equipped to handle and organize various types of data within your Flutter applications.

Error Handling

Errors are inevitable in any software program, and Flutter apps are no exception. When something goes wrong during your app's execution, it can lead to unexpected crashes and frustrated users. That's where error handling comes in.

Exceptions: Your App's Alarm System

In Dart, errors are represented as exceptions. Think of exceptions as alarms that go off when something unexpected happens. They can be triggered by various factors, such as:

- Invalid user input
- Network issues
- File operations gone wrong
- Programming mistakes (e.g., dividing by zero)

When an exception is thrown, the normal flow of your program is interrupted. If not handled properly, this can cause your app to terminate abruptly.

The `try-catch` Block: Catching Exceptions

Dart provides the `try-catch` block to handle exceptions. It works like this:

1. **try:** The code you suspect might throw an exception is placed inside a `try` block.
2. **catch:** If an exception occurs within the `try` block, execution jumps to the corresponding `catch` block. You can have multiple `catch` blocks to handle different types of exceptions.
3. **finally (optional):** The `finally` block is always executed, regardless of whether an exception was thrown or not. It's often used for cleanup tasks like closing files or releasing resources.

```
try { var result = 10 ~/ 0; // Attempt to divide by zero (throws an
IntegerDivisionByZeroException) } catch (e) { print('Error: $e'); //
Catch and print the exception message } finally { print('This will always
be printed.'); // Always executed }
```

`throw`: Triggering Exceptions Manually

Sometimes you'll want to throw an exception intentionally to signal an error condition. You can do this using the `throw` keyword followed by the exception object you want to raise.

```
if (age < 0) { throw ArgumentError('Age cannot be negative.'); }
```

Handling Specific Exception Types

Dart provides various built-in exception types for different error scenarios. Some common ones include:

- `FormatException`: Thrown when a string cannot be parsed as a number.
- `IOException`: Thrown for errors during input/output operations (e.g., file not found).
- `ArgumentError`: Thrown when a function argument is invalid.

You can catch specific exceptions in your `catch` blocks using the on keyword:

```
try { // ... } on FormatException catch (e) { print('Invalid format: $e'); }
on IOException catch (e) { print('I/O error: $e'); }
```

Graceful Error Handling: A User-Friendly Approach

When an exception occurs, don't just let your app crash. Instead, handle the error gracefully by:

- **Logging the error:** Record details about the exception (type, message, stack trace) to help you diagnose the issue later.
- **Displaying a user-friendly message:** Inform the user about the error in a clear and concise way. Avoid technical jargon or overwhelming them with details.
- **Providing recovery options:** If possible, offer ways for the user to recover from the error (e.g., retrying a failed network request, correcting invalid input).

By incorporating robust error handling into your Flutter apps, you can create a more reliable and enjoyable user experience.

Chapter Summary

In this chapter, you embarked on a whirlwind tour of Dart, the language that powers Flutter. You learned why Dart is a perfect fit for Flutter due to its features like hot reload, AOT and JIT compilation, object-oriented nature, and ease of learning.

We covered the essentials of Dart syntax and structure, including statements, semicolons, and code blocks. You also wrote your first "Hello, World!" program to see how these elements combine.

We then explored the concept of variables and data types, emphasizing the importance of type safety in Dart. You learned about the different data types available in Dart, including numbers, strings, booleans, lists, maps, and more.

You also became familiar with Dart's operators for arithmetic, assignment, comparison, and logical operations, allowing you to manipulate and combine values in your code.

We then dived into control flow statements, learning how to use `if`, `else`, and `else if` to make decisions in your code and how to use `for` and `while` loops for repetition. Additionally, we covered the `for-in` loop for iterating over collections like lists and sets.

Finally, you explored the concept of functions as reusable blocks of code, learning how to define functions, pass parameters, and return values. We also touched upon advanced function features like optional parameters, named parameters, default values, and arrow functions.

With this foundational understanding of Dart, you're well-equipped to tackle the next chapters and start building interactive and dynamic Flutter applications.

Section II:
Core Building Blocks: Widgets

Understanding Widgets: The Heart of Flutter UI

Outline

- What is a Widget?
- The Widget Tree
- Basic Widget Types
- Widget Composition and Nesting
- Building a Simple UI with Widgets
- Chapter Summary

What is a Widget?

In the Flutter universe, widgets are the stars of the show. They are the fundamental building blocks that you use to construct the user interface (UI) of your app. **Everything you see and interact with in a Flutter app is a widget**, or a combination of widgets working together.

Think of widgets like Lego bricks. You have a wide variety of bricks in different shapes, sizes, and colors. You combine these bricks in various ways to build anything you can imagine – a simple house, a towering skyscraper, or even a spaceship! Similarly, Flutter offers a rich assortment of pre-built widgets for text, buttons, images, layouts, and much more. By assembling these widgets in different configurations, you can create any UI you desire.

The Declarative Approach: Describe, Don't Dictate

Flutter embraces a declarative approach to UI development. This means that instead of giving step-by-step instructions on *how* to build the UI (imperative style), you simply *describe* what you want the UI to look like at a particular moment in time.

For example, if you want to display a text message in your app, you don't tell Flutter to "create a text object, set its font size, position it here, and then display it." Instead, you simply declare: "I want a text widget with this content, this style, and this position."

Flutter's framework then takes care of the rest. It determines the most efficient way to build and render that widget, taking into account factors like screen size, device orientation, and user interactions. This declarative approach frees you from low-level details and allows you to focus on the high-level design of your UI.

Key Points About Widgets:

- **Immutable:** Widgets are immutable, meaning their properties cannot be changed once they are created. To update the UI, you rebuild the widget with the desired changes.
- **Composable:** Widgets can be combined and nested to create complex layouts and structures.
- **Reusable:** You can easily reuse widgets throughout your app to maintain consistency and reduce code duplication.

In essence, widgets are the DNA of your Flutter app, carrying the instructions for how it should look and behave. By mastering the art of widget composition, you'll unlock the full potential of Flutter's expressive and flexible UI framework.

The Widget Tree

In Flutter, widgets don't exist in isolation; they form a family tree called the **widget tree**. This tree-like structure is the backbone of your app's UI, defining how widgets are organized, nested, and ultimately rendered on the screen.

Understanding the Hierarchy

- **Parent and Child Widgets:** Every widget in your app can act as a parent to other widgets, which are called its children. A parent widget can have zero, one, or many child widgets.
- **Branching Out:** Child widgets can, in turn, have their own children, creating a branching structure that resembles a tree.
- **Root Widget:** At the very top of the widget tree, you have a single root widget. This is usually a special type of widget (like `MaterialApp` or `CupertinoApp`) that defines the overall structure and theme of your app.

Visualizing the Widget Tree

Let's consider a simple example:

```
Column( children: [ Text('Hello, Flutter!'),
Image.asset('assets/flutter_logo.png'), ElevatedButton( onPressed: () { /*
button action */ }, child: Text('Click Me'), ), ], );
```

In this code, the `Column` widget is the parent. It has three children: a `Text` widget, an `Image` widget, and an `ElevatedButton` widget. The `ElevatedButton` widget, in turn, has a `Text` widget as its child.

We can visualize this as a tree:

```
Column
├── Text('Hello, Flutter!')
├── Image.asset('assets/flutter_logo.png')
└── ElevatedButton
    └── Text('Click Me')
```

How the Widget Tree Shapes Your UI

The structure of your widget tree directly determines how your app's UI is laid out and rendered. Here's how it works:

1. **Root Widget:** The root widget sets the overall theme and structure for your app.
2. **Layout Widgets:** Widgets like Row, `Column`, and `Stack` are used to organize and position child widgets within the screen.
3. **Content Widgets:** Widgets like `Text`, `Image`, and `ElevatedButton` provide the actual content (text, images, buttons) that users see and interact with.

When Flutter builds your app's UI, it starts from the root widget and traverses down the widget tree. Each widget is responsible for building its own UI and passing layout constraints down to its children. The final result is a visual representation of your widget tree on the screen.

The Power of Composition

The ability to nest and compose widgets in this hierarchical way is what makes Flutter's UI system so flexible and powerful. You can build complex and intricate UIs by combining simple widgets into larger, more sophisticated ones. This modular approach also promotes code reusability and maintainability.

By understanding the widget tree concept, you'll gain a deeper appreciation for how Flutter constructs UIs and be well on your way to creating beautiful, interactive user interfaces for your apps.

Basic Widget Types

Flutter provides two fundamental categories of widgets, each designed for different purposes:

Stateless Widgets: Simple and Unchanging

A stateless widget is a widget that does not have any internal state to keep track of. This means its appearance and behavior are determined solely by the configuration information passed to it when it's created. Once a stateless widget is built, it remains static and does not change unless it's explicitly rebuilt with different parameters.

Common Stateless Widgets:

- **Text:** Displays a piece of text on the screen.
- **Icon:** Renders an icon from Flutter's built-in icon library or a custom icon font.
- **Image:** Displays an image from various sources (assets, network, file).
- **RaisedButton, TextButton, IconButton, etc.:** Different types of buttons that trigger actions when pressed.
- **Container:** A versatile widget for applying padding, margins, borders, and other styles to its child.

Example: A Text Widget

```
Text( 'Hello, Flutter!', style: TextStyle(fontSize: 24.0, color: Colors.blue),
);
```

Stateful Widgets: Dynamic and Interactive

A stateful widget, on the other hand, maintains internal state that can change over time. This state can be updated due to user interactions, network responses, timer events, or any other triggers. When the state of a stateful widget changes, it automatically rebuilds its UI to reflect the new state.

Common Stateful Widgets:

- **Checkbox:** A checkbox that can be toggled on or off.
- **Slider:** A slider for selecting a value from a range.
- **TextField:** A text field for user input.
- **Switch:** A switch that can be toggled on or off.
- **AnimatedContainer:** A container that can smoothly animate its properties (size, color, etc.).

Example: A Checkbox Widget

```
Checkbox( value: isChecked, // The current state (checked or unchecked)
onChanged: (bool? newValue) { setState(() { isChecked = newValue!; // Update
the state when the checkbox is toggled }); }, );
```

Choosing the Right Widget Type

The decision to use a stateless or stateful widget depends on whether your widget needs to manage changing data:

- **Use a stateless widget if:** The widget's appearance and behavior are determined solely by its initial configuration and do not change over time.
- **Use a stateful widget if:** The widget needs to keep track of internal data that can change and dynamically update its UI in response to those changes.

By understanding the distinction between stateless and stateful widgets, you can choose the appropriate widget type for each element in your app's UI, ensuring efficient rendering and a smooth user experience.

Widget Composition and Nesting

Flutter's power lies in its ability to combine and nest widgets effortlessly. This allows you to create complex and sophisticated user interfaces by assembling smaller, simpler widgets like building blocks.

Nesting Widgets: Creating Hierarchy

Nesting widgets involves placing one widget (the child) inside another widget (the parent). The parent widget acts as a container or layout manager, dictating the position, size, and other properties of its child.

Example: A Column of Widgets

```
Column( children: [ Text('Title'), Image.asset('assets/image.png'),
ElevatedButton( onPressed: () { /* button action */ }, child: Text('Click
Me'), ), ], );
```

In this code, the `Column` widget arranges its three children (a `Text`, an `Image`, and an `ElevatedButton`) vertically in a single column.

Example: A Row of Widgets

```
Row( children: [ Icon(Icons.favorite), Text('Like'), SizedBox(width: 10), //
Add some spacing Icon(Icons.share), Text('Share'), ], );
```

Here, the Row widget arranges its children horizontally in a single row.

Common Layout Widgets: Your UI Toolbox

Flutter provides a set of versatile layout widgets to help you organize and arrange your widgets effectively:

- **Row:** Arranges its children horizontally in a row.
- **Column:** Arranges its children vertically in a column.
- **Stack:** Overlays its children on top of each other, allowing for complex layering and positioning.
- **Container:** A versatile widget for adding padding, margins, borders, background colors, and other styles to its child.

Advanced Layouts:

For more complex layouts, you can explore other layout widgets like:

- **Expanded:** Allows a child of Row, Column, or Flex to fill the available space.

- **Wrap:** Displays its children in multiple rows or columns, automatically wrapping them when they overflow.
- **GridView:** Arranges its children in a grid layout.
- **ListView:** Displays its children in a scrollable list.

The Flexibility of Composition

By combining these layout widgets and nesting them within each other, you can build virtually any kind of UI layout you can imagine.

- A login screen might consist of a Column to arrange a logo, text fields, and a button.
- A product listing could use a GridView to display items in a visually appealing grid.
- A chat app might employ a ListView to present a scrolling list of messages.

The possibilities are endless, and the ability to compose and nest widgets is a key factor in Flutter's strength as a UI framework.

By mastering widget composition, you'll be well on your way to creating beautiful, responsive, and engaging user interfaces for your Flutter applications.

Building a Simple UI with Widgets

Let's bring all this widget knowledge to life by creating a basic Flutter app that displays a simple yet visually appealing UI. We'll combine text, images, and layout widgets to create a visually engaging composition.

Setting the Stage with MaterialApp

```
import 'package:flutter/material.dart'; void main() => runApp(MyApp()); class
MyApp extends StatelessWidget { @override Widget build(BuildContext context) {
return MaterialApp( // Your UI code goes here ); } }
```

- **MaterialApp:** This is our root widget. It sets up the foundation for Material Design (Google's design language for Android) and provides essential features like navigation and theming.

Building the Scaffold: The App's Structure

```
// ...inside MaterialApp home: Scaffold( appBar: AppBar( title: Text('Welcome
to Flutter'), ), body: // ... ),
```

- **Scaffold:** This widget provides a basic structure for your app, including an app bar and a body area where you'll place the main content.
- **AppBar:** A widget that displays a bar at the top of the screen with a title and optional actions.

Crafting the Body: Layout and Content

```
// ...inside Scaffold body: Center( // Centers the content child: Column( //
Arranges children vertically mainAxisAlignment: MainAxisAlignment.center, //
Centers the column vertically children: [
Image.asset('assets/flutter_bird.png', height: 200, width: 200),
SizedBox(height: 20), // Add spacing Text( 'Hello, Flutter!', style:
```

```
TextStyle(fontSize: 24, fontWeight: FontWeight.bold), ), Text( 'Building
Beautiful UIs', style: TextStyle(fontSize: 18), ), ], ), ),
```

- **Center:** This widget centers its child widget within itself.
- **Column:** This widget arranges its children (an image and two text widgets) vertically in a column.
- **Image.asset:** This widget displays an image from your app's assets folder. We've set the height and width to control its size.
- **SizedBox:** This widget adds empty space between widgets.
- **Text:** This widget displays text. We've customized the style to make it larger and bold for the first text widget.

Experiment and Explore!

This is just a simple example. You can customize it by:

- **Adding more widgets:** Experiment with other widget types like buttons, icons, and input fields.
- **Using different layouts:** Try arranging widgets with Row or Stack instead of Column.
- **Changing styles:** Play with different colors, fonts, and sizes to personalize the look and feel of your app.

As you gain experience, you'll discover the vast array of widgets and layout options available in Flutter, allowing you to create truly unique and stunning user interfaces.

Key Points

- **Widget Composition:** Combine and nest widgets to build complex UIs.
- **Start Simple:** Begin with basic widgets and layouts to grasp the fundamentals.
- **Experiment:** Play around with different widget combinations to unleash your creativity.
- **Read the Docs:** Refer to Flutter's documentation for a comprehensive list of widgets and their properties.

Chapter Summary

In this chapter, you delved into the heart of Flutter's UI magic – widgets. You learned that widgets are the fundamental building blocks of Flutter apps, and everything you see on the screen is a widget or a combination of widgets. We explored the declarative nature of Flutter's UI development, where you describe what you want, and Flutter takes care of the how.

You discovered the concept of the widget tree, a hierarchical structure that organizes widgets and defines the layout of your app's UI. We also introduced the two main types of widgets: stateless widgets, which are simple and unchanging, and stateful widgets, which can dynamically update their appearance based on data changes.

Furthermore, we explored the power of widget composition and nesting, demonstrating how you can combine simple widgets to create complex UI structures. We introduced common layout widgets like Row, Column, Stack, and Container, giving you the tools to arrange widgets in various configurations.

Finally, you embarked on your first hands-on Flutter project, building a simple UI using a combination of text, images, and layout widgets. This exercise allowed you to put theory into practice and gain a deeper understanding of how widgets work together to create a visually appealing interface.

Armed with this foundational knowledge of widgets, you're well-prepared to move on to the next chapters, where we'll explore different widget types in more detail and learn how to create even more sophisticated and interactive user interfaces.

Stateless Widgets: Simple and Efficient UI Elements

Outline

- The Power of Stateless Widgets
- Anatomy of a Stateless Widget
- Essential Stateless Widgets
- Creating Your Own Stateless Widgets
- Best Practices for Stateless Widgets
- Chapter Summary

The Power of Stateless Widgets

Stateless widgets are the unsung heroes of Flutter UI development. While their name might imply simplicity, they are the workhorses behind many of the visual elements you see in Flutter apps. They're designed to handle UI components that don't require dynamic updates or interactions.

Why Stateless? The Efficiency Advantage

Stateless widgets are inherently efficient because they are **immutable**. Once you build a stateless widget, its appearance and behavior are fixed. It won't change unless you explicitly rebuild it with different parameters.

This immutability means that Flutter doesn't need to waste time re-rendering stateless widgets when other parts of your app change. This leads to a significant performance boost, especially in larger and more complex UIs where unnecessary rebuilds can quickly become a bottleneck.

When to Use Stateless Widgets: The Right Tool for the Job

Stateless widgets are perfect for scenarios where you need to display static content that doesn't change in response to user interactions or data updates. Some common use cases include:

- **Text:** Displaying labels, headings, paragraphs, or other static text elements.
- **Images:** Rendering images from assets, network sources, or local files.
- **Icons:** Showing icons from Flutter's built-in icon library or custom icon fonts.
- **Basic Layouts:** Arranging widgets in simple configurations using Row, `Column`, or `Container`.
- **Decorative Elements:** Adding visual embellishments like dividers, spacers, or progress indicators.

Stateless Widgets: Your Efficiency Powerhouse

By utilizing stateless widgets for appropriate UI elements, you can:

- **Optimize Performance:** Reduce unnecessary widget rebuilds and improve your app's overall responsiveness.
- **Simplify Development:** Stateless widgets are easier to reason about and maintain since they don't have internal state to manage.
- **Improve Code Readability:** Your UI code becomes more concise and focused, making it easier to understand.
- **Promote Reusability:** Stateless widgets are often highly reusable, saving you time and effort.

In the next sections, we'll delve deeper into how stateless widgets work and explore some of the most commonly used ones in Flutter. By mastering stateless widgets, you'll lay a strong foundation for building efficient and performant Flutter UIs.

Anatomy of a Stateless Widget

Let's dissect a stateless widget to understand its inner workings. We'll create a simple example and break down the key components that make it tick.

Code Example: A Hello Widget

```
import 'package:flutter/material.dart'; class HelloWidget extends
StatelessWidget { final String message; const HelloWidget({super.key, required
this.message}); // Constructor @override Widget build(BuildContext context) {
return Container( padding: const EdgeInsets.all(16.0), // Add padding child:
Text( message, style: const TextStyle(fontSize: 20), ), ); } }
```

Breaking Down the Code

1. **Class Definition (HelloWidget):**
   - We define a new class called HelloWidget.
   - It extends the StatelessWidget class, indicating that it's a stateless widget.
2. **Constructor (HelloWidget({...})):**
   - The constructor initializes the widget's properties.
   - In this case, we have a message property that stores the text to be displayed.
   - We make the message required, meaning it must be provided when creating an instance of this widget.
   - The super.key call is used for managing widget keys (more on that later).
3. **build() Method:**
   - This is the heart of a stateless widget. It describes how to build the widget's visual representation.
   - The build() method takes a BuildContext as a parameter and returns a Widget object.
   - In our example, it returns a Container widget that has padding and contains a Text widget to display the message.
4. **BuildContext Parameter:**
   - The BuildContext provides information about the widget's location within the widget tree.
   - It's used to access theme data, obtain information about the widget's parent, and interact with other parts of the widget tree.

How It Works in Practice

When you create an instance of HelloWidget and include it in your widget tree, Flutter calls its build() method. This method creates and returns a Container widget that contains the specified message text. Flutter then renders this widget tree on the screen.

Important Considerations

- The build() method is called whenever the widget's configuration changes (e.g., when you pass a different message to the constructor).

- Stateless widgets are immutable, so you can't directly modify their properties after they're created. Instead, you rebuild the widget with the updated configuration.

By understanding the anatomy of a stateless widget, you'll be able to create your own custom widgets and build complex, modular UIs with ease.

Essential Stateless Widgets

Flutter offers a rich collection of pre-built stateless widgets that serve as the backbone of your app's UI. Let's explore some of the most commonly used ones, along with examples of how to incorporate them into your code:

Text: The Wordsmith

The Text widget is your go-to tool for displaying text in your Flutter app. You can customize the font style, size, color, alignment, and many other properties to achieve the desired look.

```
Text( 'This is a text widget', style: TextStyle(fontSize: 18, fontWeight:
FontWeight.bold), );
```

Icon: The Visual Cue

Icons are a powerful way to convey meaning and add visual interest to your UI. Flutter provides a vast library of Material Design and Cupertino icons that you can easily use.

```
Icon(Icons.favorite, color: Colors.red);
```

Image: Painting with Pixels

The Image widget lets you display images from various sources:

- **Asset Images:** Images bundled with your app (e.g., logos, backgrounds).
- **Network Images:** Images loaded from a URL.
- **File Images:** Images loaded from a file on the device's storage.

```
Image.asset('assets/logo.png');
Image.network('https://www.example.com/image.jpg');
//Image.file(File('path/to/image.jpg'));
```

Container: The Chameleon

The Container widget is a versatile workhorse. It's essentially a blank canvas that you can style and customize to your heart's content. You can use it to add padding, margins, borders, background colors, shadows, and more to its child widget.

```
Container( padding: EdgeInsets.all(16.0), margin:
EdgeInsets.symmetric(vertical: 8.0), decoration: BoxDecoration( color:
Colors.lightBlue, borderRadius: BorderRadius.circular(10.0), ), child:
Text('This is inside a container'), );
```

SizedBox: The Spacer

The SizedBox widget creates an empty box with a specific size. It's handy for adding spacing between widgets or creating fixed-size gaps in your layout.

```
SizedBox(width: 20, height: 10); // A box with width 20 and height 10
```

Divider: The Separator

The Divider widget creates a thin horizontal or vertical line that acts as a visual separator between elements.

```
Divider(color: Colors.grey); // A horizontal divider
```

(To create a vertical divider, use it inside a Row with crossAxisAlignment: CrossAxisAlignment.stretch.)

By combining these essential stateless widgets and exploring their various properties, you can construct a wide range of UI elements, from simple text displays to complex layouts.

Creating Your Own Stateless Widgets

While Flutter provides a rich set of built-in widgets, you'll often want to create your own custom widgets to encapsulate specific UI elements or to reuse common patterns throughout your app. Let's walk through the process step-by-step.

1. Define a New Class

Start by creating a new Dart class that extends the StatelessWidget class. Give your widget a descriptive name that reflects its purpose.

```
import 'package:flutter/material.dart'; class CustomCard extends
StatelessWidget { // ... (Add properties and constructor here) @override
Widget build(BuildContext context) { // ... (Build your widget's UI here) } }
```

2. Add Properties and Constructor

Declare the properties that your widget needs to receive from its parent. These properties will determine the appearance and behavior of your widget. Create a constructor to initialize these properties.

```
// ... inside CustomCard class final String title; final String subtitle;
const CustomCard({Key? key, required this.title, required this.subtitle}) :
super(key: key);
```

In this example, our CustomCard widget will have two properties: title and subtitle. We use the required keyword to ensure that the parent widget provides values for these properties when creating an instance of CustomCard.

3. Implement the build() Method

The build() method is where you assemble the UI of your custom widget. Use Flutter's built-in widgets and any other custom widgets you've created to construct the desired visual representation.

```
// ... inside CustomCard class @override Widget build(BuildContext context) {
return Card( child: ListTile( leading: Icon(Icons.check_circle, color:
```

```
Colors.green), // Add an icon title: Text(title, style: TextStyle(fontWeight:
FontWeight.bold)), // Use the title property subtitle: Text(subtitle), // Use
the subtitle property ), ); }
```

In this example, the build() method returns a Card widget containing a ListTile that displays the title and subtitle text, along with a leading icon.

4. Using Your Custom Widget

Now you can use your CustomCard widget in your main app:

```
class MyApp extends StatelessWidget { @override Widget build(BuildContext
context) { return MaterialApp( home: Scaffold( appBar: AppBar(title:
Text('Custom Widget Demo')), body: Center( child: CustomCard( title: 'My First
Custom Widget', subtitle: 'This is a simple card widget.', ), ), ), ); } }
```

Key Takeaways:

- **Modularity:** Custom widgets make your code more modular and easier to maintain.
- **Reusability:** You can use your custom widget multiple times throughout your app, saving you from writing repetitive code.
- **Flexibility:** You have full control over the appearance and behavior of your custom widget.
- **Experimentation:** Don't be afraid to create different types of custom widgets to encapsulate various UI patterns.

This example demonstrates how to create a basic custom widget. With practice and creativity, you can build complex, reusable UI components that elevate the look and feel of your Flutter applications.

Best Practices for Stateless Widgets

While stateless widgets are inherently simpler than their stateful counterparts, following some best practices will ensure that your Flutter UIs are not only visually appealing but also efficient, maintainable, and scalable.

Keep It Simple and Lightweight

Remember, stateless widgets are meant for static UI elements. Avoid adding unnecessary logic or complex operations within them. Instead, focus on their core responsibility: rendering the UI based on the configuration they receive. This keeps your widgets small, focused, and easier to understand.

Embrace Widget Composition

Don't be afraid to break down complex UI elements into smaller, more manageable stateless widgets. This approach, known as *widget composition*, allows you to:

- **Reuse Widgets:** Create reusable components that you can easily incorporate throughout your app, reducing code duplication and promoting consistency.
- **Improve Readability:** By breaking down complex structures into smaller units, you make your code more organized and easier to read.
- **Simplify Testing:** Smaller, focused widgets are easier to test independently, leading to more robust code.

Think of it like building with LEGOs: you combine smaller pieces to create larger structures. In Flutter, you compose simple widgets to construct elaborate UIs.

Use `const` Constructors

When creating stateless widgets that have no internal state, use the `const` keyword in their constructors. This tells Flutter that the widget's configuration is constant and can be optimized during compilation. This can lead to improved performance, especially when you're dealing with a large number of widgets.

```
class MyWidget extends StatelessWidget { final String title; const
MyWidget({Key? key, required this.title}) : super(key: key); // Const
constructor @override Widget build(BuildContext context) { // ... } }
```

Choose Stateless Widgets Wisely

Stateless widgets are not suitable for every scenario. Use them judiciously for UI elements that:

- **Display static content:** Text, images, icons, and other elements that don't need to update dynamically.
- **Have simple layouts:** Arrangements of widgets using Row, `Column`, or `Stack`, where the structure doesn't change frequently.
- **Don't need to handle user interactions:** Widgets that don't require responding to taps, gestures, or other input events.

For dynamic UI elements that need to respond to user actions or data changes, you'll typically need to use stateful widgets (covered in the next chapter). However, by strategically using stateless widgets, you can optimize your Flutter apps for performance and maintainability.

Chapter Summary

In this chapter, you've gained a solid understanding of stateless widgets, the essential building blocks for creating efficient and maintainable Flutter user interfaces. You learned how these widgets excel at displaying static content and how their immutability leads to performance gains.

We explored the anatomy of a stateless widget, breaking down its structure and highlighting the role of the `build` method and the `BuildContext` parameter. You also discovered some of the most commonly used stateless widgets in Flutter, such as `Text`, `Icon`, `Image`, `Container`, `SizedBox`, and `Divider`, along with code examples demonstrating their basic usage.

We then walked through the process of creating your own custom stateless widgets, empowering you to encapsulate reusable UI components and tailor them to your specific needs.

Finally, we discussed best practices for working with stateless widgets, emphasizing the importance of simplicity, widget composition, and the use of `const` constructors. By following these guidelines, you can ensure that your Flutter apps are not only visually appealing but also performant and easy to maintain.

Armed with this knowledge, you're now equipped to create a wide variety of UI elements using stateless widgets. In the next chapter, we'll dive into the world of stateful widgets, exploring how to build interactive and dynamic components that respond to user input and data changes.

Stateful Widgets: Interactive and Dynamic Components

Outline

- Embracing Change with Stateful Widgets
- The State Management Lifecycle
- The setState( ) Method
- Common Stateful Widgets
- Creating Your Own Stateful Widgets
- When to Use Stateful Widgets
- Best Practices for State Management
- Chapter Summary

Embracing Change with Stateful Widgets

While stateless widgets are great for static elements, the real magic of Flutter's interactivity lies in stateful widgets. These dynamic components are essential for building user interfaces that respond to user input, fetch data from the network, or adapt to changing conditions.

What is State?

In the Flutter world, **state** refers to the data or variables associated with a widget that can change over time. This could be anything from a simple counter value to a complex data structure representing the contents of a shopping cart.

Think of state as the memory of a widget. It remembers information that influences how the widget looks or behaves. For example, a checkbox widget might have a isChecked boolean variable that determines whether the checkbox is checked or unchecked.

Why Stateful Widgets?

Stateful widgets are the key to building responsive and interactive UIs because they allow you to:

- **React to User Input:** When a user interacts with a widget (e.g., tapping a button, entering text in a field), you can update the widget's state to reflect that interaction and trigger a rebuild of its UI.
- **Handle Asynchronous Operations:** If your widget needs to fetch data from a network or perform other time-consuming tasks, you can use stateful widgets to manage the loading process and update the UI when the data arrives.
- **Create Dynamic UIs:** You can use stateful widgets to build UIs that change their appearance or behavior based on various factors, such as user preferences, device orientation, or the current time.

Common Use Cases for Stateful Widgets

Here are some examples of UI elements that often rely on stateful widgets:

- **Counters:** A widget that displays a number that can be incremented or decremented by the user.
- **Forms:** Input fields, checkboxes, radio buttons, and other form elements need to track their values as the user interacts with them.

- **Progress Indicators:** Widgets that show the progress of a task (e.g., loading data, downloading a file) need to update their display as the task progresses.
- **Animated Widgets:** Widgets that perform animations need to manage their state to control the animation's progress and appearance.
- **Any UI that Changes:** Essentially, any part of your UI that needs to change in response to events or data should likely be implemented as a stateful widget.

By understanding the role of state and leveraging stateful widgets effectively, you can create Flutter apps that are not just visually appealing but also engaging and responsive to user interactions.

The State Management Lifecycle

Understanding the lifecycle of a stateful widget is crucial for managing its state effectively and building responsive UIs. This lifecycle consists of several methods that are called at different stages of the widget's existence.

The State Object: Your Widget's Memory

A stateful widget doesn't hold its state directly. Instead, it delegates state management to a separate object called a `State` object. This separation ensures that the state persists even if the widget itself is rebuilt due to configuration changes.

The Lifecycle Methods:

1. `createState()`:
   - This is the first method called when a stateful widget is inserted into the widget tree.
   - It's responsible for creating and returning the initial `State` object associated with the widget.
   - You override this method in your `StatefulWidget` class to provide your custom `State` implementation.
2. `initState()`:
   - This method is called only once, immediately after the `State` object is created.
   - It's the perfect place to initialize variables, fetch initial data, or start listening to streams or other events.
   - Avoid calling `setState()` in `initState()` as it can lead to unexpected behavior.
3. `build()`:
   - The core method of any widget, responsible for constructing the UI based on the current state.
   - Called whenever the widget's state changes or the widget needs to be rebuilt for other reasons.
   - It returns a `Widget` object that represents the UI of the stateful widget.
4. `didUpdateWidget(covariant oldWidget)`:
   - Called whenever the parent widget rebuilds and provides this widget with new configuration.
   - It gives you the opportunity to compare the new configuration (`widget`) with the old configuration (`oldWidget`) and update the state accordingly.
   - Use `setState()` to trigger a UI rebuild if necessary.
5. `deactivate()`:
   - Called when the widget is removed from the widget tree.
   - This could happen due to navigation, a change in the parent widget's configuration, or other factors.
   - Use this method to cancel timers, subscriptions, or other ongoing operations that are no longer needed.
6. `dispose()`:

○ Called when the State object is permanently removed from the tree and will not be rebuilt.
○ This is the final opportunity to clean up resources like subscriptions, animations, or any objects that might cause memory leaks.

Visualizing the Lifecycle

The following illustrates the typical flow of a stateful widget's lifecycle:

createState() --> initState() --> build() --> didUpdateWidget() --> deactivate() --> dispose()

By understanding the sequence of these lifecycle methods, you can manage the state of your widgets effectively and create dynamic UIs that respond to changes and user interactions.

The setState() Method

The setState() method is your trusty companion when working with stateful widgets. It's the bridge that connects your widget's internal state with its visual representation on the screen.

How setState() Works: The Refresh Button

Think of setState() as a button that tells Flutter: "Hey, something in my state has changed! Please rebuild my UI to reflect the latest data."

Here's a simplified breakdown of what happens when you call setState():

1. **State Change:** You modify one or more variables within your stateful widget's State object.
2. **Notification:** Calling setState() notifies Flutter that the state has been updated.
3. **Rebuild:** Flutter re-executes the build() method of your stateful widget.
4. **Re-render:** Flutter uses the updated state values to rebuild the widget's UI, updating the display to match the new state.

Use setState() Wisely: Performance Matters

While setState() is incredibly useful, it's important to use it judiciously. Each call to setState() triggers a rebuild of the widget's subtree, which can be computationally expensive. If you overuse setState() for state changes that don't actually affect the UI, you could inadvertently degrade your app's performance.

Rule of Thumb: Only call setState() when a state change directly impacts how your widget should be displayed.

setState() in Action: Code Examples

Let's see how to use setState() in a simple counter app:

```
class MyCounterApp extends StatefulWidget { @override _MyCounterAppState
createState() => _MyCounterAppState(); } class _MyCounterAppState extends
State<MyCounterApp> { int _counter = 0; void _incrementCounter() { setState(()
{ _counter++; }); } @override Widget build(BuildContext context) { return
Center( child: Column( mainAxisAlignment: MainAxisAlignment.center, children:
<Widget>[ Text('You have pushed the button this many times:'), Text(
```

```
'$_counter', style: Theme.of(context).textTheme.headlineMedium, ),
ElevatedButton( onPressed: _incrementCounter, child: Text('Increment'), ), ],
), ); } }
```

In this code, when the button is pressed, the _incrementCounter() method is called, which in turn calls setState(). The setState() call updates the _counter variable and triggers a rebuild of the UI. The Text widget displaying the counter value is then updated to reflect the new state.

Common Stateful Widgets

Flutter provides a variety of built-in stateful widgets that are essential for creating interactive and dynamic user interfaces. Let's explore some of the most commonly used ones:

Checkbox: Toggling Options

The Checkbox widget allows users to select or deselect an option. Its state represents whether it's checked or unchecked.

```
bool isChecked = false; // Initial state Checkbox( value: isChecked,
onChanged: (bool? newValue) { setState(() { isChecked = newValue!; }); }, );
```

Explanation

1. isChecked variable holds the current checked state.
2. The onChanged callback is triggered when the user toggles the checkbox.
3. Inside onChanged, we use setState to update the isChecked variable and trigger a rebuild to reflect the new state.

TextField: Capturing User Input

The TextField widget allows users to enter text. Its state is the text that has been entered.

```
String inputText = ''; // Initial state TextField( onChanged: (String
newValue) { setState(() { inputText = newValue; }); }, );
```

Explanation

1. inputText variable stores the current input text.
2. The onChanged callback is triggered whenever the text changes.
3. Inside onChanged, we use setState to update inputText and refresh the UI.

Radio: Exclusive Selection

The Radio widget allows users to select one option from a group. It's state represents which option is currently selected.

```
int selectedValue = 0; // Initial state Row( children: [ Radio( value: 0,
groupValue: selectedValue, onChanged: (int? newValue) { setState(() {
selectedValue = newValue!; }); }, ), Text('Option 1'), Radio( value: 1,
groupValue: selectedValue, onChanged: (int? newValue) { setState(() {
selectedValue = newValue!; }); }, ), Text('Option 2'), ], );
```

Explanation

1. `selectedValue` holds the index of currently selected option.
2. Each `Radio` has its own value. The `groupValue` determines if the radio should be selected (when it matches the `selectedValue`).
3. `onChanged` updates `selectedValue` to the value of the selected radio using `setState`.

`Slider`: Continuous Values

The `Slider` widget lets users select a value within a range by dragging a thumb. Its state is the current selected value.

```
double currentValue = 0.5; // Initial state Slider( value: currentValue,
onChanged: (double newValue) { setState(() { currentValue = newValue; }); },
);
```

`DropdownButton`: Selecting from a List

The `DropdownButton` widget presents a list of options in a dropdown menu. Its state is the currently selected item.

```
String selectedItem = 'Option 1'; // Initial state DropdownButton<String>(
value: selectedItem, items: <String>['Option 1', 'Option 2', 'Option 3']
.map<DropdownMenuItem<String>>((String value) { return
DropdownMenuItem<String>( value: value, child: Text(value), ); }).toList(),
onChanged: (String? newValue) { setState(() { selectedItem = newValue!; }); },
);
```

By utilizing these and other stateful widgets, you'll be able to create rich, interactive, and dynamic user experiences in your Flutter apps.

Creating Your Own Stateful Widgets

Custom stateful widgets are essential for creating interactive and dynamic UI elements that respond to changes in your app. Let's break down the process of crafting your own stateful widgets:

1. The `StatefulWidget` Class: Configuration Blueprint

Begin by defining a class that extends `StatefulWidget`. This class will act as a blueprint for your widget, storing any configuration parameters you want to pass to it.

```
class FavoriteButton extends StatefulWidget { final bool isFavorite; //
Initial favorite state final Function onToggle; // Callback for toggle action
const FavoriteButton({ super.key, required this.isFavorite, required
this.onToggle, }); @override _FavoriteButtonState createState() =>
_FavoriteButtonState(); }
```

In this example, FavoriteButton has two properties:

- `isFavorite`: Indicates whether the button is currently in a favorite state.

- onToggle: A callback function to be executed when the button is tapped (used to update the state in the parent widget).

The createState() method returns an instance of a _FavoriteButtonState class (defined in the next step), which will manage the widget's state.

2. The State Class: State Management and UI Building

Next, create a separate class that extends State<YourWidget>. This is where you'll define the widget's state variables, handle user interactions, and build the actual UI.

```
class _FavoriteButtonState extends State<FavoriteButton> { bool _isFavorite =
false; // Internal state variable (starts with '_') @override void initState()
{ super.initState(); _isFavorite = widget.isFavorite; // Initialize from
configuration } @override Widget build(BuildContext context) { return
IconButton( icon: Icon(_isFavorite ? Icons.favorite : Icons.favorite_border),
onPressed: () { setState(() { _isFavorite = !_isFavorite; // Toggle the state
}); widget.onToggle(); // Notify the parent about the state change }, ); } }
```

Let's break this down:

1. _isFavorite: This variable holds the internal state of whether the button is favorited.
2. initState(): We initialize _isFavorite using the initial value from the widget's configuration.
3. build(): This method creates the UI. It uses _isFavorite to decide which icon to display and updates _isFavorite and calls the onToggle callback when the button is pressed.

Separation of Concerns

Notice how the StatefulWidget class focuses on configuration (what the widget should look like initially), while the State class handles the actual state management and UI building. This separation makes your code more organized, reusable, and testable.

Using Your Custom Stateful Widget

Now you can use your FavoriteButton widget in other parts of your app:

```
// ... in your main app's build method FavoriteButton( isFavorite:
isFavorited, onToggle: () { setState(() { isFavorited = !isFavorited; }); }, )
```

Key Takeaways:

- **Stateful widgets are essential for building interactive UIs.**
- **setState() is the key to updating the UI when the state changes.**
- **Separate configuration from state management for clean code.**
- **Use custom stateful widgets to encapsulate complex UI interactions.**

When to Use Stateful Widgets

Stateful widgets are your go-to solution for building UI elements that evolve and react to changes. They shine in scenarios where your UI needs to be dynamic, interactive, or responsive to data updates.

Here are some key scenarios where stateful widgets are the right choice:

1. Interactive UI Elements

If a widget needs to change its appearance or behavior based on user interactions, it's a prime candidate for a stateful widget. Examples include:

- **Buttons:** When a button is pressed, you might want to change its color, disable it, or trigger other actions.
- **Sliders and Switches:** These widgets need to track their current value as the user adjusts them.
- **Form Fields:** Text fields, checkboxes, radio buttons, and dropdowns need to store the data that the user enters or selects.
- **Tappable Elements:** Widgets that respond to taps or other gestures might need to update their appearance to indicate selection or highlight.

2. Asynchronous Data Loading

When your widget needs to fetch and display data that takes time to load (e.g., from a network request), a stateful widget is essential. It allows you to manage the loading state (e.g., showing a loading indicator) and update the UI when the data is available.

- **News Feeds:** Widgets that display articles fetched from a news API.
- **Weather Apps:** Widgets that show weather forecasts retrieved from a weather service.
- **Social Media Feeds:** Widgets that display posts or messages fetched from a social network.

3. Animated or Transitional UIs

If you want to create smooth animations or transitions between different states, stateful widgets are your best friend. They can store the animation's progress and update the UI accordingly.

- **Progress Bars:** Widgets that animate to show the completion percentage of a task.
- **Expanding/Collapsing Panels:** Widgets that smoothly reveal or hide content.
- **Animated Icons:** Icons that transform from one state to another (e.g., a heart icon that fills in when liked).

When NOT to Use Stateful Widgets

Remember, stateless widgets are more efficient than stateful widgets because they don't require rebuilding as often. So, if your UI element is purely static and doesn't need to change based on data or user input, a stateless widget is a better choice.

Key Takeaway: Stateful widgets empower you to create responsive, interactive, and dynamic user interfaces that keep your users engaged and delighted.

Best Practices for State Management

Effectively managing state is crucial for building scalable and maintainable Flutter applications. As your app grows in complexity, choosing the right state management approach and adhering to best practices becomes increasingly important.

State Management Approaches: A Glimpse

Flutter offers several options for managing state:

- **setState():** The simplest approach, suitable for small to medium-sized apps. We've already covered this in detail.
- **Provider:** A popular state management package that provides an easy way to access and manage state in a widget tree.

- **BLoC (Business Logic Component):** A pattern that separates business logic from UI components, making your code more testable and reusable.
- **Riverpod:** A newer state management solution designed to be simpler and more flexible than Provider.

We'll dive deeper into these state management approaches in Chapter 13, where you'll learn how to choose the right one for your specific project.

Lifting State Up: Sharing is Caring

In Flutter, it's often necessary to share state between widgets that are not directly related in the widget tree. This is where the concept of "lifting state up" comes into play.

The idea is to move the shared state to a common ancestor widget higher up in the widget tree. This ancestor widget then passes the state down to its child widgets as needed. This way, multiple widgets can access and modify the same state, ensuring consistency and avoiding duplication.

Tips for Efficient State Management:

- **Minimize Rebuilds:** Avoid unnecessary rebuilds by using `const` widgets where possible. These widgets are optimized by Flutter and won't rebuild unless their configuration changes.
- **Use `setState()` Sparingly:** Only call `setState()` when a state change actually requires the UI to be updated. Excessive use of `setState()` can lead to performance issues.
- **Choose the Right Approach:** For simple apps, `setState()` might be sufficient. For larger, more complex apps with intricate state interactions, consider using Provider, BLoC, or Riverpod for better organization and maintainability.
- **Think Reactively:** Embrace reactive programming principles (e.g., using streams or reactive frameworks like RxDart) to manage asynchronous data and events more effectively.

By adopting these best practices, you'll be able to create Flutter apps that are not only visually appealing but also performant, maintainable, and scalable as they grow.

Chapter Summary

In this chapter, you delved into the dynamic world of stateful widgets, exploring how they bring interactivity and responsiveness to your Flutter UIs. You learned that stateful widgets are essential for managing data that changes over time and for updating the UI in response to user interactions, network events, or other triggers.

We covered the lifecycle of a stateful widget, starting from the creation of its associated `State` object through `createState()` and progressing through various methods like `initState()`, `build()`, `didUpdateWidget()`, `deactivate()`, and `dispose()`. Each of these methods plays a specific role in managing the widget's state and rendering its UI.

The `setState()` method was introduced as the key mechanism for triggering UI updates when the state changes. We emphasized the importance of using it judiciously to avoid unnecessary rebuilds and performance bottlenecks.

You also explored some commonly used stateful widgets in Flutter, such as `Checkbox`, `TextField`, `Radio`, `Slider`, and `DropdownButton`. You saw code examples demonstrating how to manage their state and update their UIs accordingly.

We then walked you through creating your own custom stateful widgets, highlighting the separation of concerns between the `StatefulWidget` and `State` classes. You learned how to create these classes, override the necessary methods, and use `setState()` to trigger UI updates.

Finally, we discussed the scenarios where stateful widgets are the right tool for the job, focusing on interactive UI elements, asynchronous data loading, and animated transitions. We also touched upon best practices for state management, emphasizing the importance of minimizing rebuilds, using `setState()` carefully, and choosing the right state management approach for your app's complexity.

With this knowledge, you're now equipped to create engaging, interactive, and dynamic user interfaces in Flutter that respond to user input and data changes. In the next chapter, we'll shift our focus to layout widgets, exploring how to arrange and position widgets to create visually appealing and well-structured UIs.

Layouts in Flutter: Designing Your App's Structure

Outline

- The Importance of Layouts
- Fundamental Layout Widgets
- Advanced Layout Widgets
- Common Layout Patterns
- Responsive Design for Different Screens
- Practical Tips for Layout Design
- Chapter Summary

The Importance of Layouts

Imagine a house without walls, a book without paragraphs, or a painting without composition. Chaos, right? Similarly, in the world of mobile app development, layouts provide the essential structure that transforms a collection of UI elements into a cohesive and visually pleasing experience.

Why Layouts Matter:

1. **Visual Organization:**
   - Layouts create order out of potential chaos. They define how different UI elements (widgets) are arranged on the screen.
   - Without a well-defined layout, widgets could overlap, clutter the screen, or simply not fit properly, leading to a confusing and frustrating user experience.
   - A good layout strategically positions elements, giving each item a designated space and ensuring that the content is easy to scan and digest.
2. **User Guidance:**
   - Layouts guide the user's eye through your app's content. By using visual hierarchy and placement, you can direct the user's attention to the most important elements first.
   - Consider a news app: headlines might be larger and bolder, followed by summaries and then images. This layout guides the user to the most relevant information quickly.
   - Effective layouts also use whitespace and visual cues to create a natural flow, making it effortless for users to navigate and interact with your app.
3. **Consistency and Branding:**
   - Consistent layouts create a sense of familiarity and professionalism. When users navigate through different screens or sections of your app, a consistent layout helps them feel at ease and understand how to use your app.
   - Layouts are also an opportunity to reinforce your brand identity. By using consistent colors, fonts, and spacing, you create a recognizable visual style that users will associate with your app.
4. **Adaptability (Responsiveness):**
   - In the mobile world, screen sizes and orientations vary widely. A well-designed layout should adapt seamlessly to these different contexts.
   - Responsive layouts ensure that your app looks great and functions correctly on everything from a small phone to a large tablet, whether in portrait or landscape mode.
   - Flutter provides a range of tools and widgets to help you achieve responsiveness, but the foundation lies in thoughtful layout design.

Think of layouts as the architecture of your app. A well-designed layout is like a sturdy, well-organized building. It provides a solid framework for the content, makes navigation intuitive, and leaves a lasting impression on the user.

Fundamental Layout Widgets

Flutter provides a set of core layout widgets that you'll use extensively to structure your app's UI. These widgets are your building blocks for organizing and arranging other widgets (like text, images, and buttons) into visually appealing and functional layouts.

Row: Arranging Widgets Horizontally

The Row widget aligns its children in a horizontal row. You can control the spacing, alignment, and size of the row using various properties.

```
Row( children: [ Icon(Icons.star), // An icon SizedBox(width: 8.0), // Some
spacing Text('Favorite'), // Text widget ], );
```

Key properties:

- mainAxisAlignment: Controls how the children are aligned along the main axis (horizontally in this case).
- crossAxisAlignment: Controls how the children are aligned along the cross axis (vertically in this case).
- mainAxisSize: Determines whether the row should take up the minimum or maximum available space.

Column: Arranging Widgets Vertically

The Column widget arranges its children in a vertical column. It's similar to Row, but the children are stacked on top of each other.

```
Column( children: [ Text('User Profile'), Icon(Icons.person), Text('John
Doe'), ], );
```

Stack: Layering Widgets

The Stack widget allows you to overlap widgets on top of each other. The first widget in the children list is at the bottom of the stack, and the last one is on top.

```
Stack( children: [ Image.asset('assets/background.jpg'), // Background image
Positioned( // Position a child widget top: 16.0, left: 16.0, child:
Text('Overlay Text'), // Text on top of the image ], ], );
```

Container: The Swiss Army Knife

The Container widget is extremely versatile. It allows you to apply padding, margins, borders, background colors, and many other styles to its child widget.

```
Container( padding: EdgeInsets.all(16.0), margin: EdgeInsets.only(bottom:
8.0), decoration: BoxDecoration( color: Colors.lightBlue, borderRadius:
BorderRadius.circular(10.0), ), child: Text('This is inside a container'), );
```

Center: Keeping It Simple

The Center widget does exactly what its name suggests: it centers its single child widget within the available space.

```
Center( child: Text('This text is centered'), );
```

By understanding and mastering these fundamental layout widgets, you'll be equipped to create virtually any kind of layout you need for your Flutter apps. Remember, you can combine and nest these widgets to build more complex structures and achieve your desired UI design.

Advanced Layout Widgets

While the fundamental layout widgets provide a solid foundation for building UIs, Flutter offers a range of more sophisticated layout widgets that unlock additional flexibility and control over your designs. These widgets empower you to create complex and dynamic layouts that adapt to different screen sizes and content variations.

Expanded: Filling the Space

The Expanded widget is your go-to tool for making a child widget fill the available space within a Row, Column, or Flex. It automatically distributes the remaining space among its children based on their flex factor (a numerical value indicating how much space each child should occupy).

```
Row( children: [ Icon(Icons.search), Expanded( // Takes all available space
child: TextField(), ), ], );
```

In this example, the TextField will expand to fill the remaining horizontal space in the row after the icon.

Wrap: Flowing with Content

The Wrap widget is ideal for situations where you have a variable number of widgets and want them to wrap onto new lines or columns when they run out of space. It's perfect for creating dynamic layouts like tag clouds or galleries.

```
Wrap( spacing: 8.0, // Gap between adjacent chips runSpacing: 4.0, // Gap
between lines children: <Widget>[ Chip(label: Text('Flutter')), Chip(label:
Text('Dart')), Chip(label: Text('Widgets')), Chip(label: Text('Layouts')), ],
);
```

GridView: Grids Galore

The GridView widget allows you to arrange widgets in a scrollable grid layout. You can customize the number of columns, the spacing between items, and the scroll direction.

```
GridView.count( crossAxisCount: 2, // Two columns children: List.generate(8,
(index) { return Center( child: Text('Item $index'), ); }), );
```

ListView: Scrolling Lists

The ListView widget is a staple for displaying a scrolling list of items. It's incredibly versatile and can be used to display various types of content, from simple text lists to complex custom-designed items.

```
ListView.builder( itemCount: 20, itemBuilder: (context, index) { return
ListTile( title: Text('Item $index'), ); }, );
```

SingleChildScrollView: Scrolling Individual Widgets

The SingleChildScrollView widget allows you to make a single widget scrollable, even if it wouldn't normally overflow its container. It's helpful for cases where you have a large amount of content that needs to be displayed within a limited space.

```
SingleChildScrollView( child: Column( children: [ // Your content here ], ),
);
```

By combining these advanced layout widgets with the fundamental ones (and even your own custom widgets), you can unlock limitless possibilities for designing sophisticated and adaptable UIs in Flutter.

Common Layout Patterns:

Flutter makes it easy to implement common UI layout patterns that you'll find in countless mobile apps. These patterns provide familiar structures for organizing your content and enhancing user navigation.

AppBar and Body: A Classic Combo

The AppBar and Body layout is a fundamental structure in mobile app design. The AppBar typically contains the app title, actions (e.g., search, settings), and navigation controls. The body area holds the main content of the screen.

```
Scaffold( appBar: AppBar( title: Text('My App'), ), body: Center( child:
Text('Main Content'), ), );
```

Side Drawer Navigation: The Hidden Menu

A side drawer (or navigation drawer) is a panel that slides out from the side of the screen, typically containing navigation links or additional controls.

```
Scaffold( appBar: AppBar(title: Text('My App')), drawer: Drawer( // Add a
drawer child: ListView( children: [ ListTile(title: Text('Home'), onTap: ()
{}), ListTile(title: Text('Settings'), onTap: () {}), ], ), ), body:
Center(child: Text('Main Content')), );
```

Tabbed Interface: Switching Views Seamlessly

A tabbed interface allows users to switch between different views (or sections) of your app using tabs. Flutter provides the TabBar and TabBarView widgets to implement this pattern.

```
DefaultTabController( length: 3, // Number of tabs child: Scaffold( appBar:
AppBar( bottom: TabBar( tabs: [ Tab(icon: Icon(Icons.directions_car)),
Tab(bike)}, ], ), title: Text('Tabs Demo'), ), body: TabBarView( children: [
Center(child: Text("Car Tab")}, Center(child: Text("Transit Tab")},
Center(child: Text("Bike Tab")}, ], ), ), );
```

Master-Detail Layout: Optimized for Tablets

The Master-Detail layout is a two-pane layout often used on tablets. The master pane typically displays a list of items, and the detail pane shows the details of the currently selected item.

```
// This requires a bit more code, but the core is using two widgets // (e.g.,
`ListView` and another widget) side-by-side in a `Row`. You'll // need logic
to manage which item is selected in the master list // and update the details
shown in the detail widget.
```

Let me know if you'd like a more detailed code example for the master-detail layout.

Key Considerations

- **Navigation:** Choose the navigation pattern that best suits your app's structure and content.
- **Screen Size:** Consider how your layout will adapt to different screen sizes, especially when using complex patterns like master-detail.
- **Flexibility:** Use layout widgets like Expanded and Flexible to make your layouts adaptable to varying content sizes.
- **Performance:** Be mindful of potential performance impacts when using complex layouts with many widgets.
- **User Experience:** Ensure that your layout choices prioritize a clear and intuitive user experience.

Responsive Design for Different Screens

Mobile devices come in a vast array of sizes and shapes, from compact smartphones to expansive tablets. Creating a responsive design ensures your app looks and functions beautifully on all these devices, regardless of screen dimensions or orientation.

Why Responsive Design Matters

Responsive design isn't just about aesthetics; it's about user experience. If your app looks awkward or cramped on a small screen, users will likely abandon it. Conversely, a responsive app that adapts to different sizes feels polished and professional.

Here's why it's crucial:

- **Reach a Wider Audience:** Cater to users with various devices, maximizing your app's reach and potential user base.
- **Improved User Experience:** Provide a comfortable and intuitive experience, regardless of the device being used.
- **Adaptability:** Ensure your app functions correctly in both portrait and landscape modes.
- **Future-Proofing:** Prepare your app for new screen sizes and devices that might emerge in the future.

The MediaQuery Class: Your Screen Detective

Flutter's MediaQuery class is your secret weapon for building responsive UIs. It provides valuable information about the current screen, including:

- size: The width and height of the screen.
- orientation: Whether the device is in portrait or landscape mode.
- devicePixelRatio: The pixel density of the screen.
- textScaleFactor: A multiplier for system font sizes.

You can access this information within your `build` method using `MediaQuery.of(context)`.

Layout Widgets for Flexibility

Flutter offers several layout widgets that help you create responsive UIs:

- **Expanded:** Automatically distributes available space among its children, making your layout flexible and adaptable.
- `Wrap:`** Dynamically wraps its children onto new lines or columns when they exceed the available space.
- **LayoutBuilder:** A powerful widget that gives you more control over layout decisions based on the available space.

Example: Responsive Column

```
LayoutBuilder( builder: (context, constraints) { return SingleChildScrollView(
child: ConstrainedBox( constraints: BoxConstraints( minHeight:
constraints.maxHeight, ), child: IntrinsicHeight( child: Column( children: [
Container( height: constraints.maxHeight * 0.3, // 30% of screen height color:
Colors.blue, ), Expanded( // Takes remaining space child: Container( color:
Colors.green, ),on ), ], ), ), ), ); }, );
```

In this example, `LayoutBuilder` and `ConstrainedBox` are used to create a responsive `Column` layout where the first item takes 30% of the screen height, and the second item takes the remaining space.

By leveraging `MediaQuery` and these layout widgets, you can create beautiful and functional Flutter apps that adapt gracefully to different screen sizes and orientations, providing an optimal experience for all your users.

Practical Tips for Layout Design

Designing effective and visually appealing layouts is an art that combines creativity with technical understanding. Here are some practical tips to help you master the art of layout design in Flutter:

1. **Plan Before You Code:**
- **Sketch Your Vision:** Start by sketching out your UI on paper or a whiteboard. This helps you visualize the overall structure, the placement of elements, and the flow of the user experience.
- **Wireframes and Mockups:** Consider creating more detailed wireframes or mockups using design tools like Figma, Adobe XD, or Sketch. This allows you to refine your design, experiment with different layouts, and get feedback before you start coding.
- **Component-Based Thinking:** Break down your UI into smaller, reusable components (widgets). This modular approach makes your code more organized, easier to maintain, and promotes consistency.
2. **Choose the Right Layout Widgets:**
- **Understand Your Options:** Familiarize yourself with the full range of Flutter's layout widgets. Choose the ones that best suit your specific layout requirements.
- **Nest Widgets Strategically:** Don't be afraid to nest layout widgets within each other to create complex arrangements.
- **Leverage Flexibility:** Use Expanded, `Flexible`, and `Wrap` to create layouts that adapt to different screen sizes and content variations.
3. **Optimize Performance:**

- **const is Key:** Use the `const` keyword whenever possible to create constant widgets. This tells Flutter that the widget's configuration won't change, allowing it to optimize performance.
- **Minimize Rebuilds:** Avoid unnecessary widget rebuilds by using state management techniques like `Provider` or BLoC to isolate state changes to specific parts of your UI.
- **Lazy Loading:** For long lists or grids, use `ListView.builder` or `GridView.builder` to load items only when they're visible on the screen.
- **Profiling:** Use Flutter's performance profiling tools to identify potential bottlenecks in your layout and optimize them.
4. **Iterate and Experiment:**
- **Don't be Afraid to Try:** Layout design is often an iterative process. Experiment with different layouts, widget combinations, and styling options until you find what works best for your app.
- **Get Feedback:** Share your designs with others and gather feedback to refine your UI.
- **Stay Updated:** Flutter is constantly evolving, so stay up-to-date with the latest layout widgets and best practices.

By applying these practical tips, you'll be well on your way to crafting beautiful, user-friendly, and performant layouts for your Flutter apps. Remember, layout design is both a science and an art, and mastering it takes practice, experimentation, and a willingness to learn and iterate.

Chapter Summary

In this chapter, you gained a deeper understanding of the importance of layouts in crafting exceptional Flutter apps. Layouts are not just about aesthetics; they're about organizing content, guiding users, ensuring consistency, and adapting to various screen sizes.

You explored the fundamental building blocks of Flutter layouts, including the `Row`, `Column`, `Stack`, `Container`, and `Center` widgets. You learned how to use their properties and combine them to create simple yet effective layouts.

We then ventured into the realm of advanced layout widgets like `Expanded`, `Wrap`, `GridView`, `ListView`, and `SingleChildScrollView`, which offer more flexibility and power for handling complex UI arrangements.

You discovered common layout patterns found in mobile apps, such as the classic AppBar and Body structure, side drawer navigation, tabbed interfaces, and the master-detail layout, along with how to implement them in Flutter.

We also emphasized the significance of responsive design, showing you how to use Flutter's `MediaQuery` class and layout widgets to create UIs that adapt beautifully to different screen sizes and orientations.

Finally, we provided practical tips for approaching layout design in Flutter, from planning and sketching to optimizing performance and iterating on your designs. By incorporating these best practices, you'll be well-equipped to craft user interfaces that not only look great but also provide a seamless and enjoyable user experience.

Styling Widgets: Colors, Themes, and Typography

Outline

- The Power of Styling in Flutter
- Working with Colors
- Text Styling with Typography
- Themeing Your App
- Styling Best Practices
- Chapter Summary

The Power of Styling in Flutter

Think of your Flutter widgets as the raw ingredients of a dish. They provide the functionality, but it's the styling that transforms them into a delectable culinary masterpiece. In the same way, styling takes your basic Flutter widgets and elevates them into a visually appealing and cohesive user interface (UI).

Styling: More Than Just Looks

Styling isn't merely about making your app look pretty (though that's certainly important!). It plays a crucial role in several aspects of your app's success:

1. **Branding:**
   - A well-styled app reinforces your brand identity. Carefully chosen colors, fonts, and visual elements create a consistent look and feel that users associate with your brand.
   - This helps build trust, recognition, and a sense of professionalism.
2. **User Experience (UX):**
   - Good styling enhances the usability of your app. Clear visual cues, appropriate font sizes, and well-organized layouts guide users intuitively through your app.
   - Consistent styling throughout your app creates a sense of familiarity, making it easier for users to learn and navigate.
3. **Accessibility:**
   - Styling considerations are critical for making your app accessible to users with disabilities.
   - For example, using sufficient color contrast between text and background ensures that users with visual impairments can easily read the content.
   - Properly sized text and touch targets accommodate users with motor skill difficulties.

Flutter's Styling Toolbox: Your Creative Arsenal

Flutter provides a variety of ways to style your widgets:

1. **Inline Styles:**
   - This is the simplest way to apply styles directly within a widget's `build` method. It's suitable for quick tweaks and simple styling needs.
   - Example: `Text('Hello', style: TextStyle(fontSize: 24.0, color: Colors.blue),)`
2. **Widget-Specific Styling:**
   - Many widgets have properties dedicated to styling specific aspects of their appearance (e.g., `Container`'s `padding`, `margin`, `decoration`).
   - This approach is more organized and helps keep styling code closer to the relevant widget.
3. **Themes:**

- Themes are a powerful way to define a consistent visual style for your entire app. They allow you to centralize styling decisions and easily apply them across your widget tree.
- Example: Using ThemeData in MaterialApp to define default colors, fonts, and styles for your app.

In the following sections, we'll dive deeper into each of these styling mechanisms, exploring how to use colors, typography, and themes to create beautiful, user-friendly, and accessible Flutter apps.

Working with Colors

Colors are the lifeblood of any visual design. In Flutter, you have an artist's palette at your disposal, allowing you to create vibrant and engaging user interfaces.

The Colors Class: Your Color Palette

Flutter's Colors class is your gateway to a wide spectrum of colors. It provides a rich collection of pre-defined colors, from classic shades like Colors.red and Colors.blue to more nuanced options like Colors.teal and Colors.amber.

```
Container( color: Colors.blue, child: Text('Blue Container'), );
```

Creating Custom Colors: Mixing and Matching

Sometimes, you'll need a color that's not available in the pre-defined set. Flutter makes it easy to create custom colors using various color models:

- **RGB (Red, Green, Blue):** The most common way to define colors. You specify the intensity of red, green, and blue components (0-255 each) to create a specific color.
- **ARGB (Alpha, Red, Green, Blue):** Similar to RGB, but with an additional alpha component (0-255) that controls the color's transparency.
- **HSL (Hue, Saturation, Lightness):** An alternative way to define colors based on their hue (color), saturation (intensity), and lightness (brightness).

Creating Custom Colors in Code

You can create custom colors using the Color.fromRGBO(), Color.fromARGB(), or Color.fromHSL() constructors:

```
Color myCustomColor = Color.fromRGBO(255, 128, 0, 1.0); // Orange (fully
opaque) Color myTransparentColor = Color.fromARGB(128, 0, 0, 255); //
Semi-transparent blue
```

Applying Colors: The color and foregroundColor Properties

To apply colors to your widgets, you'll typically use two properties:

- **color:** Sets the background color of a widget.
- **foregroundColor:** Sets the color of the text or icon within a widget (e.g., in a Text or Icon widget).

```
Container( color: Colors.amber, // Yellow background child: Text(
'Hello', style: TextStyle(foregroundColor: Colors.black), // Black text
), );
```

Controlling Transparency with `Opacity`

The `Opacity` widget allows you to adjust the transparency of any widget. You can specify an opacity value between 0.0 (completely transparent) and 1.0 (fully opaque).

```
Opacity( opacity: 0.5, // 50% opacity child: Container(color: Colors.red), //
Semi-transparent red container );
```

By mastering these color techniques, you'll have the tools to craft visually striking and expressive Flutter UIs that leave a lasting impression on your users.

Text Styling with Typography

Typography is the art and technique of arranging type to make written language legible, readable, and appealing when displayed. In Flutter, the `TextStyle` class is your key to unlocking the full potential of typography, allowing you to craft text that is both visually pleasing and informative.

The `TextStyle` Class: Your Text Stylist

The `TextStyle` class is a powerful tool that enables you to customize virtually every aspect of your text's appearance. Here are some of the most commonly used properties:

- **fontSize:** Controls the size of the text (in logical pixels).
- **fontWeight:** Determines the thickness of the characters (e.g., `FontWeight.normal`, `FontWeight.bold`).
- **fontStyle:** Specifies whether the text should be italicized (`FontStyle.italic`) or normal (`FontStyle.normal`).
- **fontFamily:** The name of the font family to use (e.g., "Roboto", "Open Sans").
- **color:** Sets the color of the text. You can use predefined colors from the `Colors` class or create custom colors.
- **letterSpacing:** Adjusts the space between letters.
- **wordSpacing:** Adjusts the space between words.
- **height:** Sets the height of the line (as a multiplier of the font size).

Applying `TextStyle`

To apply a `TextStyle` to a Text widget, simply pass the `TextStyle` object as the value for the `style` property:

```
Text( 'This is styled text', style: TextStyle( fontSize: 20, fontWeight:
FontWeight.bold, fontFamily: 'Roboto', ), );
```

You can also apply `TextStyle` to other widgets that display text, such as:

- `AppBar` (for the title):

  ```
  AppBar( title: Text('My App', style: TextStyle(fontSize: 22)), );
  ```

- `TextButton`:

```
TextButton( onPressed: () {}, child: Text('Click Me', style:
TextStyle(color: Colors.white)), );
```

Choosing the Right Typography: Readability and Aesthetics

When choosing fonts and styles for your app, consider both readability and aesthetics:

- **Readability:** Ensure your text is easy to read, especially on smaller screens. Choose font sizes that are large enough and avoid overly decorative or complex fonts.
- **Aesthetics:** Select fonts that complement your app's overall design and brand identity. Experiment with different font combinations to find a style that's both visually appealing and effective.
- **Consistency:** Maintain a consistent typographic hierarchy throughout your app. Use different font sizes, weights, and styles to differentiate headings, body text, and other elements.
- **Accessibility:** Ensure sufficient contrast between text and background colors to accommodate users with visual impairments.

By paying attention to typography, you can transform plain text into a powerful tool for communication and engagement in your Flutter apps.

Themeing Your App

Imagine if you had to manually style every single widget in your Flutter app. That would be tedious and error-prone, right? Thankfully, Flutter offers a powerful theming system that allows you to define a consistent visual style for your entire app and apply it globally.

Themes: Your App's Wardrobe

Think of a theme as a wardrobe for your app. It contains a collection of colors, fonts, and styles that define how various elements of your app should look. By using themes, you can ensure that your app's UI elements (buttons, text fields, app bars, etc.) share a cohesive and harmonious design.

ThemeData: The Style Guide

The ThemeData class is the heart of Flutter's theming system. It's a comprehensive class that encapsulates all the styling parameters for your app's theme. With ThemeData, you can customize the following aspects:

- **Colors:** Primary, secondary, background, error, and other colors.
- **Typography:** Font families, sizes, and styles for different text elements (headings, body text, etc.).
- **Icon Themes:** Define default styles for icons.
- **Component Themes:** Customize the appearance of specific components like buttons, text fields, and sliders.

Creating and Applying a Custom Theme

Here's how you can create a custom theme and apply it to your Flutter app:

```
import 'package:flutter/material.dart'; void main() => runApp(MyApp()); class
MyApp extends StatelessWidget { @override Widget build(BuildContext context) {
return MaterialApp( title: 'Custom Theme Demo', theme: ThemeData(
primarySwatch: Colors.purple, // Use a purple color scheme fontFamily:
'Roboto', // Set the default font family textTheme: const TextTheme( //
Customize text styles bodyMedium: TextStyle(fontSize: 16), titleMedium:
```

```
TextStyle(fontSize: 20, fontWeight: FontWeight.bold), ), ), home: Scaffold(
appBar: AppBar( title: Text('Custom Theme'), ), body: Center( child:
Text('This text uses the custom theme'), ), ), ); } }
```

In this example, we create a custom theme with a purple primary color, the Roboto font, and specific text styles for the body and title. We then apply this theme to the entire app using the `theme` property of the `MaterialApp` widget.

The Benefits of Themes

- **Consistency:** Ensure a uniform look and feel across your app's UI elements.
- **Customization:** Easily change your app's appearance by modifying the theme.
- **Maintainability:** Centralize your styling in one place, making it easier to update and manage.
- **Light/Dark Mode:** Easily switch between light and dark themes to accommodate user preferences or environmental conditions.

By embracing Flutter's theming system, you can streamline your styling workflow, create visually cohesive apps, and deliver a more polished and professional user experience.

Styling Best Practices

Styling isn't just about making your app look good; it's about creating a consistent and user-friendly experience. Here are some best practices to help you master the art of styling in Flutter:

1. **Consistent Color Palette:**
   - Define a limited color palette for your app. This ensures visual harmony and reinforces your brand identity.
   - Use a color tool like Coolors - https://coolors.co/ to create harmonious palettes.
   - Consider using shades and tints of your primary colors to create variations for different UI elements.
   - Ensure sufficient contrast between text and background colors for accessibility.
   - Leverage semantic color names (e.g., `Colors.primary`, `Colors.accent`) to make your code more readable and maintainable.
2. **Thoughtful Typography:**
   - Choose a few fonts (ideally no more than two or three) that complement your app's design.
   - Define a typographic scale that specifies font sizes and styles for different elements (headings, body text, buttons).
   - Ensure your font sizes are large enough for readability on various screen sizes.
   - Use font weights and styles to create visual hierarchy and emphasis.
3. **Design Systems and Style Guides:**
   - If you're working on a larger project, consider creating a design system or style guide. This is a collection of reusable components, styles, and guidelines that ensure consistency across your app.
   - Design systems streamline the design process, promote collaboration between designers and developers, and make your app easier to maintain and update.
4. **Centralize Styling with ThemeData:**
   - Use the `ThemeData` class in `MaterialApp` to define default colors, fonts, and styles for your entire app.
   - This centralizes your styling decisions, making it easier to change the overall look and feel of your app by simply updating the theme.
   - `ThemeData` also allows you to easily switch between light and dark modes.
5. **Debugging with Flutter Inspector:**

- ○ Flutter Inspector is a powerful tool that helps you visualize the widget tree, inspect widget properties, and diagnose styling issues.
- ○ Use it to see how your widgets are rendered, check their sizes and positions, and identify any layout problems.
- ○ You can access Flutter Inspector in Android Studio or VS Code.

Additional Tips:

- • **Don't Overdo It:** Avoid excessive use of colors and styles. Keep your UI clean and uncluttered for a better user experience.
- • **Test on Different Devices:** Make sure your styles look good on various devices and screen sizes.
- • **Learn from Others:** Explore open-source Flutter apps and libraries to get inspiration for styling and layout.
- • **Embrace Feedback:** Get feedback from designers and users to refine your app's visual design.

By following these styling best practices, you'll be well on your way to creating Flutter apps that are not only visually stunning but also intuitive, accessible, and a joy to use.

Chapter Summary

In this chapter, you delved into the art of styling Flutter widgets, transforming them from basic building blocks into visually appealing and cohesive UI elements. We explored how styling plays a crucial role in branding, user experience, and accessibility, making it an essential aspect of Flutter app development.

You learned how to work with colors in Flutter, accessing predefined colors and creating custom colors using RGB, ARGB, or HSL values. We discussed how to apply these colors to widgets using the `color` and `foregroundColor` properties, and how to adjust transparency with the `Opacity` widget.

We also explored text styling with typography, introducing the `TextStyle` class and its various properties for customizing font size, weight, style, family, color, and spacing. You learned how to apply `TextStyle` to `Text` widgets and other widgets that display text, and how to make informed choices for optimal readability and aesthetics.

Furthermore, we introduced the concept of themes in Flutter, explaining how to create a custom theme using `ThemeData` and apply it globally to your app using `MaterialApp`. We discussed the benefits of themes, including consistency, customization, maintainability, and the ability to switch between light and dark modes.

Finally, we provided a set of best practices for styling Flutter apps, emphasizing the use of consistent color palettes and typography, leveraging design systems or style guides, centralizing styling with `ThemeData`, and using the Flutter Inspector for debugging.

By applying these techniques and principles, you're now equipped to create visually stunning and user-friendly Flutter apps that truly stand out. In the next chapter, we'll shift our focus to handling user input, allowing your apps to become interactive and responsive.

Handling User Input: Buttons, Text Fields, and Gestures

Outline

- The Importance of User Input
- Button Widgets
- Text Input with Text Fields
- Gesture Detection
- Combining Input Methods
- Practical Tips for Handling User Input
- Chapter Summary

The Importance of User Input

Imagine an app that only displays information without allowing any interaction. It would be like a one-sided conversation, wouldn't it? Handling user input is the key to transforming your Flutter app from a passive display into an engaging, interactive experience.

Why User Input Matters:

1. **Control and Interaction:**
- User input is the primary way users communicate with your app and guide its behavior.
- Whether it's tapping a button, entering text in a search bar, or swiping through a gallery, user input empowers them to control what happens next.
- A well-designed app anticipates user needs and provides intuitive ways for them to express those needs through input mechanisms.
2. **Data Collection:**
- Many apps require users to provide data, such as login credentials, personal information, or preferences.
- User input is how you collect this essential data to personalize the experience, offer relevant features, or complete transactions.
- Forms, text fields, and selection controls (like checkboxes and radio buttons) are common ways to gather user data.
3. **Navigation and Exploration:**
- User input facilitates navigation within your app.
- Buttons and links allow users to move between screens, explore different sections, and access various features.
- Even simple gestures like swiping or tapping can trigger navigation actions.

The Impact on User Experience:

The quality of your app's input mechanisms directly impacts the overall user experience.

- **Positive Experience:**
   - Well-designed input methods are intuitive, responsive, and easy to use.
   - They provide clear feedback to the user, confirming their actions and guiding them through the app.
   - This results in a positive experience, where users feel in control and can achieve their goals effortlessly.
- **Negative Experience:**

○ Poorly designed input can lead to frustration and confusion.
○ If buttons are unresponsive, text fields are difficult to use, or gestures are misinterpreted, users are likely to become annoyed and abandon your app.

In essence, user input is the lifeblood of your app. It's how users express their intentions, provide information, and navigate through your creation. By mastering the art of handling user input, you can build Flutter apps that are not only functional but also enjoyable and intuitive to use.

Button Widgets

Buttons are the quintessential elements of user interaction. They provide a clear way for users to initiate actions, make choices, and navigate within your Flutter app. Flutter offers a variety of button widgets, each with its own distinct style and purpose.

Button Types: A Button for Every Occasion

- **ElevatedButton:**
  ○ A button with a raised appearance, ideal for highlighting important actions or calls to action.
  ○ Provides visual prominence to make it stand out.

  ```
  ElevatedButton( onPressed: () { // Code to execute when the button
  is pressed print('ElevatedButton pressed'); }, child: const
  Text('Elevated Button'), );
  ```

- **TextButton:**
  ○ A flat button with a text label.
  ○ Used for less prominent actions or within a group of buttons.

  ```
  TextButton( onPressed: () { // Code to execute when the button is
  pressed print('TextButton pressed'); }, child: const Text('Text
  Button'), );
  ```

- **OutlinedButton:**
  ○ A button with a visible border but no background fill.
  ○ Often used for secondary actions or to visually group related buttons.

  ```
  OutlinedButton( onPressed: () { // Code to execute when the button
  is pressed print('OutlinedButton pressed'); }, child: const
  Text('Outlined Button'), );
  ```

- **IconButton:**
  ○ A button that displays an icon instead of text.
  ○ Perfect for actions that are easily recognized by a visual symbol.

  ```
  IconButton( icon: const Icon(Icons.favorite), onPressed: () { //
  Code to execute when the button is pressed print('IconButton
  pressed'); }, );
  ```

- **FloatingActionButton:**
  ○ A circular button that floats above the UI, typically used for the primary action on a screen.
  ○ Provides a prominent and visually appealing way to trigger an action.

```
FloatingActionButton( onPressed: () { // Code to execute when the
button is pressed print('FloatingActionButton pressed'); }, child:
const Icon(Icons.add), );
```

Handling Button Taps with `onPressed`

All button widgets have an onPressed callback function that you define to specify what should happen when the user taps the button. Inside this callback, you can write code to perform actions like:

- Navigate to a different screen
- Update data or variables in your app
- Show a dialog or snackbar
- Send data to a server
- Trigger animations or transitions
- …and much more!

Styling Buttons:

Customize the appearance of buttons using the `style` property. You can change the background color, text color, font size, border style, elevation (for `ElevatedButton`), and more.

```
ElevatedButton( style: ElevatedButton.styleFrom( backgroundColor:
Colors.green, textStyle: const TextStyle(fontSize: 20), }, // ... (Rest of the
button code) );
```

Experiment and Explore!

Feel free to try out different button types and styling options. Mix and match buttons with icons, text, and other widgets to create user interfaces that are both functional and visually engaging.

Text Input with Text Fields

Text fields are the backbone of user input in many apps. They allow users to enter information like names, emails, messages, search queries, and more. In Flutter, the `TextField` widget is your go-to tool for creating text input fields.

Understanding the `TextField` Widget

The `TextField` widget provides a user-friendly interface for text input. Here's how it works:

1. **User Types:** When a user taps on a text field, the keyboard appears, and they can start typing.
2. **Text Updates:** As the user types, the text field's content is updated in real-time.
3. **Input Handling:** You can access the entered text and react to changes using various callbacks and properties.

Key `TextField` Properties

- `controller:`
  - A `TextEditingController` object that allows you to programmatically read, write, and manipulate the text field's content.
  - Use this to set the initial value, clear the field, or get the current text.
- `onChanged:`

- A callback function that is triggered whenever the text in the field changes.
- This is useful for validating input, updating other parts of the UI, or performing actions based on the input.
- **decoration:**
  - This property allows you to customize the appearance of the text field.
  - You can add a label, hint text, helper text, error messages, icons, and customize the border style.

Code Example: Basic Text Field

```
String _enteredText = ''; // Store the input text final TextEditingController
_controller = TextEditingController(); TextField( controller: _controller, //
Attach the controller onChanged: (text) { setState(() { _enteredText = text;
}); }, decoration: InputDecoration( labelText: 'Enter your name', ), ); //
Display the entered text Text(_enteredText),
```

Handling Different Input Types

- **Password Input:** Set obscureText: true to hide the entered characters as dots.
- **Multiline Input:** Set maxLines: null to allow the text field to expand as needed.
- **Number Input:** Use TextInputType.number for numeric keyboards.
- **Email Input:** Use TextInputType.emailAddress for email-specific keyboards.

Input Validation

Use the onChanged callback to validate user input as they type:

```
onChanged: (text) { if (text.isEmpty) { // Show an error message } else { //
Clear any previous error messages } },
```

By understanding the capabilities of TextField and its properties, you'll be able to create intuitive and user-friendly input forms in your Flutter apps.

Gesture Detection

Taps, swipes, drags, long presses—these gestures are the building blocks of touch interactions in mobile apps. Flutter makes it easy to detect and respond to a wide array of gestures, enhancing the user experience and making your apps more intuitive.

Gestures: The Language of Touch

Gestures are the way users communicate with your app through touch. They go beyond simple taps and encompass a rich vocabulary of interactions:

- **Tap:** A single quick touch of the screen.
- **Double Tap:** Two quick taps in succession.
- **Long Press:** A sustained touch on the screen.
- **Drag:** Moving a finger across the screen.
- **Swipe:** A quick, directional flick of the finger.
- **Scale:** Zooming in or out by pinching two fingers together or spreading them apart.

The GestureDetector Widget: Your Gesture Interpreter

The `GestureDetector` widget is Flutter's Swiss Army knife for gesture detection. You can wrap any widget with a `GestureDetector` to make it sensitive to touch events.

The `GestureDetector` provides a rich set of callbacks that you can use to respond to specific gestures:

- **onTap:** Triggered when the user taps the widget.
- **onDoubleTap:** Triggered when the user double-taps the widget.
- **onLongPress:** Triggered when the user long-presses the widget.
- **onPanStart, onPanUpdate, onPanEnd:** Triggered when the user drags a finger across the widget.
- **onScaleStart, onScaleUpdate, onScaleEnd:** Triggered when the user performs a scaling gesture (pinch-to-zoom).

Code Example: Detecting a Tap

```
GestureDetector( onTap: () { // Code to execute when the wrapped widget is
tapped print('Tapped!'); }, child: Container( // ... your widget content here
}, );
```

Examples of Gesture-Driven Interactions

- **Swipeable Cards:** Use onHorizontalDragEnd or onVerticalDragEnd to detect swipes and dismiss cards.
- **Draggable Items:** Use onPanStart, onPanUpdate, and onPanEnd to track finger movements and move items around.
- **Zoomable Images:** Use onScaleStart, onScaleUpdate, and onScaleEnd to implement pinch-to-zoom functionality.

Beyond the Basics: Custom Gestures

While the built-in gesture detectors cover most common use cases, you can also create custom gesture detectors for more specialized interactions. Flutter's gesture system is highly customizable, allowing you to define your own gesture recognizers tailored to your specific needs.

By mastering gesture detection in Flutter, you can transform your apps into truly interactive experiences that delight your users.

Combining Input Methods

In real-world Flutter apps, you'll rarely use input methods in isolation. You'll often need to combine buttons, text fields, and gesture detection to create more complex and intuitive user interactions.

Example: A Form with Keyboard Dismissal

Let's create a simple login form with two text fields (for username and password) and a submit button. We'll also add gesture detection to dismiss the keyboard when the user taps outside the text fields.

```
import 'package:flutter/material.dart'; class LoginForm extends StatefulWidget
{ @override _LoginFormState createState() => _LoginFormState(); } class
_LoginFormState extends State<LoginForm> { final _formKey =
GlobalKey<FormState>(); // For form validation @override Widget
build(BuildContext context) { return GestureDetector( onTap: () {
```

```
FocusScope.of(context).unfocus(); // Dismiss keyboard on tap outside }, child:
Form( key: _formKey, child: Column( children: [ TextFormField( decoration:
InputDecoration(labelText: 'Username'), validator: (value) { if (value == null
|| value.isEmpty) { return 'Please enter a username'; } return null; // Return
null if valid }, ), TextFormField( decoration: InputDecoration(labelText:
'Password'), obscureText: true, validator: (value) { if (value == null ||
value.isEmpty) { return 'Please enter a password'; } return null; }, ),
ElevatedButton( onPressed: () { if (_formKey.currentState!.validate()) { //
Form is valid, process the data print('Form submitted'); } }, child:
Text('Submit'), }, ], ), ), ); } }
```

In this example:

1. We wrap the entire form with a `GestureDetector`.
2. The onTap callback of the `GestureDetector` calls `FocusScope.of(context).unfocus()` to dismiss the keyboard when the user taps outside the text fields.
3. We use `TextFormField` widgets for input, along with `validator` functions for basic input validation.
4. The `ElevatedButton` submits the form if all fields are valid.

Encapsulating Input Methods in Custom Widgets

For better code organization and reusability, you can create custom widgets that encapsulate multiple input methods. For example, you could create a `CustomSearchWidget` that combines a text field for search queries with an icon button for triggering the search. This allows you to easily reuse the search functionality across different screens in your app.

Key Takeaways

- Combining input methods allows you to create more complex and intuitive interactions.
- Dismissing the keyboard on tap outside text fields is a common UX pattern.
- Encapsulating multiple input methods in custom widgets improves code reusability and maintainability.

By mastering these techniques, you'll be able to create rich, user-friendly input experiences that seamlessly integrate buttons, text fields, and gestures.

Practical Tips for Handling User Input

Creating a smooth and intuitive user input experience is crucial for the success of your Flutter app. Here are some practical tips to help you achieve that goal:

1. **Prioritize User-Friendliness:**
- **Clear and Concise Labels/Hints:** Use descriptive labels and hint text within text fields to guide users on what information is expected.
- **Intuitive Input Types:** Choose the appropriate keyboard type (`TextInputType`) for the data you're collecting (e.g., email, number, password).
- **Responsive Feedback:** Provide visual cues (e.g., button animations, progress indicators) or auditory feedback (e.g., sound effects) to acknowledge user actions promptly.
- **Error Handling:** Display clear and helpful error messages when the user enters invalid input. Guide them on how to correct their mistakes.

- **Visual Hierarchy:** Use visual elements like spacing, dividers, and grouping to organize input fields logically and make forms easier to navigate.
2. **Provide Clear Feedback:**
- **Visual Cues:** Use animations, colors, or icons to indicate that a button has been pressed or a text field is selected.
- **Progress Indicators:** When performing asynchronous tasks (e.g., network requests), display a progress indicator to reassure the user that something is happening.
- **Validation Feedback:** Highlight invalid fields with visual cues (e.g., red borders, error messages) to help users identify and correct errors.
3. **Handle Edge Cases and Unexpected Input:**
- **Input Validation:** Validate user input to ensure it conforms to the expected format and data type.
- **Error Handling:** Implement robust error handling mechanisms to catch exceptions and gracefully handle unexpected input.
- **Defensive Programming:** Assume that users might enter incorrect or unexpected data, and write code that can handle those situations gracefully.
4. **Form Validation:**
- **Real-time Validation:** Validate input as the user types, providing immediate feedback on errors.
- **Submit-time Validation:** Validate the entire form when the user submits it, ensuring all fields are valid before proceeding.
- **Custom Validation:** Create custom validation rules to enforce specific requirements for your app's data.
5. **Thorough Testing:**
- **Test on Different Devices:** Test your input mechanisms on various Android and iOS devices to ensure they work correctly on different screen sizes, resolutions, and input methods.
- **Emulators and Simulators:** Utilize emulators and simulators to test your app on a wider range of devices without needing physical hardware.
- **User Testing:** Involve real users in testing your app to get valuable feedback on the usability and effectiveness of your input mechanisms.

Remember: A positive user experience often hinges on how well your app handles user input. By following these best practices, you can create intuitive and user-friendly input mechanisms that make your Flutter app a joy to use.

Chapter Summary

In this chapter, you dove into the essential world of handling user input in Flutter. We began by emphasizing the importance of user input for creating interactive and engaging apps. You learned how user input enables users to control app behavior, provide data, and navigate through different screens, all contributing to a positive user experience.

We explored various button widgets like `ElevatedButton`, `TextButton`, `OutlinedButton`, `IconButton`, and `FloatingActionButton`, showcasing how to handle button taps using the `onPressed` callback and customize their appearance.

Next, you learned how to capture and manage text input using the versatile `TextField` widget. We discussed its key properties like `controller`, `onChanged`, and `decoration`, and showed you how to validate input and handle different input types.

We then explored the realm of gesture detection with the `GestureDetector` widget, allowing you to respond to a wide range of touch interactions like taps, double taps, long presses, drags, and scales. You saw how to implement gesture-based features like swipeable cards, draggable items, and zoomable images.

To enhance the interactivity of your apps, we demonstrated how to combine buttons, text fields, and gestures, providing examples of form submission with keyboard dismissal and the creation of custom widgets that encapsulate multiple input methods.

Finally, we provided practical tips for handling user input, focusing on creating user-friendly interfaces, providing clear feedback, handling edge cases gracefully, and ensuring data integrity through form validation.

With these tools and techniques, you're now equipped to create Flutter apps that actively engage users and respond intuitively to their interactions. In the next chapter, we'll delve into the essential concept of navigation, enabling users to seamlessly move between different screens in your app.

Section III:
Essential Flutter Concepts

Navigating Between Screens

Outline

- The Importance of Navigation in Mobile Apps
- Basic Navigation with `Navigator`
- Routes and the `MaterialPageRoute` Class
- Named Routes
- Passing Data Between Screens
- Navigating with Bottom Navigation Bars
- Navigating with Tabs
- Chapter Summary

The Importance of Navigation in Mobile Apps

Navigation is the backbone of user experience (UX) in mobile apps. It's the roadmap that guides users through your app's content, features, and functionality. Think of it as a GPS system that helps users find their way and discover what your app has to offer.

Seamless Movement: The User's Expectation

Users have come to expect smooth and intuitive navigation in modern apps. They want to effortlessly move between screens to access different sections, complete tasks, and find information. When navigation is well-designed, it feels natural and almost invisible, allowing users to focus on their goals rather than struggling to find their way around.

Why Intuitive Navigation Matters:

- **Engagement:** Easy navigation encourages users to explore your app more deeply, discover hidden features, and spend more time engaging with your content.
- **Task Completion:** Intuitive navigation helps users complete their tasks efficiently, whether it's making a purchase, finding a recipe, or sending a message.
- **Reduced Friction:** When navigation is clear and predictable, it reduces frustration and prevents users from getting lost or feeling overwhelmed.
- **Positive Perception:** Smooth navigation contributes to a positive overall impression of your app, making users more likely to return and recommend it to others.

Avoiding Frustration: The Cost of Poor Navigation

Conversely, poor navigation can be a major source of user frustration. If users find it difficult to move around your app, locate essential features, or understand the overall structure, they're more likely to:

- **Abandon Your App:** Frustrated users will quickly give up and look for alternatives.

- **Leave Negative Reviews:** They might vent their frustration by leaving negative reviews, damaging your app's reputation.
- **Spread Negative Word-of-Mouth:** Dissatisfied users are less likely to recommend your app to others, hindering your growth potential.

Consistency is Key:

One of the cornerstones of good navigation is consistency. Users should be able to predict how to navigate your app based on their previous experiences. This means using familiar navigation patterns (like the back button, tab bars, and menus) and ensuring that these patterns behave consistently throughout your app.

By prioritizing intuitive and consistent navigation, you can create Flutter apps that users love to use.

Basic Navigation with `Navigator`

The `Navigator` class is Flutter's trusty guide for managing screen transitions. It provides methods to move between screens, pass data between them, and maintain a history of where the user has been in your app.

The Navigation Stack: Layers of Screens

Imagine a stack of papers. You can add a new paper on top (push) or remove the top paper (pop). Flutter's navigation system works similarly. Each screen in your app is represented as a `Route` object, and these routes are stacked on top of each other in a navigation stack.

The `Navigator` widget manages this stack, keeping track of the current screen (the one on top of the stack) and providing methods to manipulate it.

`Navigator.push()`: Moving Forward

The `Navigator.push()` method is used to navigate to a new screen. It takes a `Route` object as an argument, which defines the destination screen and the transition animation.

```
Navigator.push( context, MaterialPageRoute(builder: (context) =>
SecondScreen()), );
```

In this example:

1. We use the `context` to tell `Navigator` where we are navigating from.
2. The `MaterialPageRoute` creates a route with a standard slide-in animation.
3. The `builder` function creates an instance of the `SecondScreen` widget, which will be displayed on the new screen.

`Navigator.pop()`: Going Back

The `Navigator.pop()` method is used to return to the previous screen. It removes the current route from the top of the stack, revealing the screen beneath it.

```
Navigator.pop(context);
```

Anonymous Routes: Quick and Easy Navigation

For simple navigation scenarios, you can use anonymous routes. These are routes that are created on the fly without being explicitly named.

```
ElevatedButton( onPressed: () { Navigator.push(context, MaterialPageRoute(
builder: (context) => const SecondScreen(), )); }, child: const Text('Go to
Second Screen'), );
```

In this example, the button's onPressed callback pushes an anonymous route onto the stack, navigating to the SecondScreen.

By using the Navigator and its basic methods, you can easily implement fundamental navigation within your Flutter app. However, for more organized and complex navigation scenarios, you'll want to explore named routes and other advanced navigation techniques, which we'll cover in the upcoming sections.

Routes and the MaterialPageRoute Class

While basic navigation with Navigator.push() and Navigator.pop() is functional, it doesn't give you much control over how your screens transition. That's where routes come in.

Routes: Your App's Map

Think of **routes** as the roads connecting different cities (screens) in your app. Each route defines a specific path that you can take to navigate between screens. Flutter uses the Route class to represent these pathways.

MaterialPageRoute: **The Scenic Route (with Transitions)**

The MaterialPageRoute class is a pre-built route that adheres to the Material Design guidelines. It provides a standard and visually appealing way to transition between screens. By default, it creates a slide-in-from-the-right animation for new screens and a slide-out-to-the-right animation when you go back.

Using MaterialPageRoute

To use MaterialPageRoute, pass it as an argument to Navigator.push(). The MaterialPageRoute constructor has a builder property, which is a function that returns the widget for the destination screen.

```
ElevatedButton( onPressed: () { Navigator.push( context,
MaterialPageRoute(builder: (context) => const SecondScreen()), ); }, child:
const Text('Go to Second Screen'), );
```

In this example:

1. The button's onPressed callback calls Navigator.push().
2. A MaterialPageRoute is created with a builder that constructs the SecondScreen widget.
3. Navigator pushes the SecondScreen onto the navigation stack with a slide-in animation.

The builder Property: On-Demand Widget Creation

The builder function is a crucial part of the MaterialPageRoute. It allows you to create the destination screen's widget on demand, just before it's needed. This is useful when the destination screen requires data from the previous screen or needs to perform some initialization before being displayed.

```
Navigator.push( context, MaterialPageRoute( builder: (context) =>
DetailScreen(item: selectedItem), ), );
```

In this example, we pass `selectedItem` data to the `DetailScreen` widget, which can use it to display the details of the selected item.

Customization Options

`MaterialPageRoute` offers some customization options, such as:

- `fullscreenDialog`: A boolean flag that indicates whether the new route is a full-screen modal dialog.
- `maintainState`: A boolean flag that determines whether the state of the route's widget is preserved when it's not visible (default is `true`).

By understanding `MaterialPageRoute` and its `builder` property, you can create more visually appealing and dynamic navigation experiences in your Flutter apps.

Named Routes

While anonymous routes are quick and easy to use, they can become cumbersome in larger apps with complex navigation structures. Named routes offer a more organized and maintainable approach, making your code easier to read and understand.

The Advantages of Named Routes

- **Improved Code Readability:** Named routes give your screens meaningful identifiers (e.g., `/home`, `/settings`, `/product_details`) instead of generic `MaterialPageRoute` instances. This makes your code more self-explanatory.
- **Reduced Code Duplication:** You can define a named route once in your `MaterialApp` widget and reuse it throughout your app. This eliminates the need to repeat the route creation code in multiple places.
- **Centralized Navigation Management:** The `routes` table in `MaterialApp` acts as a centralized repository for all your named routes, making it easy to manage and update your app's navigation structure.
- **Data Passing Made Easy:** Named routes seamlessly integrate with the `arguments` parameter to pass data to the destination screen.

Defining Named Routes

You define named routes within the `routes` property of your `MaterialApp` widget:

```
MaterialApp( // ... other properties initialRoute: '/', // Optional: Define
the initial route routes: { '/': (context) => HomeScreen(), '/settings':
(context) => SettingsScreen(), '/product/:id': (context) =>
ProductDetailScreen(), // Dynamic route }, );
```

In this example, we define three named routes:

- `/`: The root route, which displays the `HomeScreen`.
- `/settings`: A route for the `SettingsScreen`.
- `/product/:id`: A dynamic route that can display the details of a product based on its ID.

Navigating with `Navigator.pushNamed()`

To navigate to a named route, use the `Navigator.pushNamed()` method:

```
Navigator.pushNamed(context, '/settings'); // Navigate to the settings screen
```

For dynamic routes, you can pass arguments along with the route name:

```
Navigator.pushNamed(context, '/product/123'); // Navigate to the product
detail screen for product ID 123
```

The `arguments` Parameter: Data Delivery Service

The `arguments` parameter of `Navigator.pushNamed()` allows you to pass data as an object to the destination screen. The destination screen can then access this data using `ModalRoute.of(context).settings.arguments`.

```
// In the source screen Navigator.pushNamed( context, '/product/123',
arguments: ProductArguments(id: 123, name: 'Awesome Product'), );

// In the destination screen's build method final args =
ModalRoute.of(context)!.settings.arguments as ProductArguments; // Now you can
use `args.id` and `args.name` to display the product details.
```

By utilizing named routes and the `arguments` parameter, you can create a more organized, flexible, and data-driven navigation system for your Flutter apps.

Passing Data Between Screens

In mobile apps, it's often necessary to share data between different screens. You might want to pass information like user selections, product details, or search queries from one screen to another. Flutter provides several ways to accomplish this, with the choice depending on the complexity of your data and your overall app architecture.

Passing Data with Route Arguments: The Simple Way

For simple data, you can pass it as arguments directly to the named route using the `arguments` parameter of `Navigator.pushNamed()`. This method is convenient and works well for small pieces of data.

Example:

```
// In the source screen Navigator.pushNamed( context, '/product_details',
arguments: {'productId': 12345, 'productName': 'Flutter Book'}, );

// In the destination screen (ProductDetailsScreen) @override Widget
build(BuildContext context) { final args =
ModalRoute.of(context)!.settings.arguments as Map; final productId =
args['productId']; final productName = args['productName']; return Scaffold(
appBar: AppBar(title: Text(productName)), body: Center(child: Text('Product
ID: $productId')), ); }
```

Retrieving Data in the Destination Screen

In the destination screen, you can retrieve the passed data using
`ModalRoute.of(context)!.settings.arguments`. This gives you access to the arguments object
that you passed during navigation.

State Management Solutions: The Scalable Way

For more complex data sharing scenarios or situations where data needs to be accessed by multiple parts
of your app, consider using a state management solution like Provider, Riverpod, or BLoC.

These solutions provide a centralized way to store and manage your app's state, making it accessible
from any widget in the widget tree. This allows for efficient data sharing and eliminates the need to pass
data through multiple layers of widgets.

Example: Using Provider

```
// Create a provider for your data final productProvider =
ChangeNotifierProvider((ref) => Product(id: 12345, name: 'Flutter Book')); //
In the source screen ProviderScope( child: MaterialApp( // ... your app ), );
// In any widget final product = ref.watch(productProvider); // Access the
product data
```

Choosing the Right Approach

- **Route Arguments:** Simple and straightforward for passing small amounts of data directly between
  screens.
- **State Management Solutions:** More scalable and flexible for complex data sharing and when data
  needs to be accessed by multiple parts of your app.

By understanding the different methods for passing data between screens, you can choose the most
appropriate approach for your specific needs and build well-structured Flutter apps that handle data flow
seamlessly.

Navigating with Bottom Navigation Bars

The `BottomNavigationBar` widget in Flutter is a common UI element used to provide navigation
among different pages or views within a mobile app. It's typically used in the bottom of the screen and
allows users to switch between different sections of the app by tapping on the tabs.

Using `BottomNavigationBar` with `Navigator` for Tab-Like Navigation

To implement tab-like navigation using `BottomNavigationBar` in Flutter, you can combine it with the
`Navigator` widget. This approach allows each tab to maintain its own navigation stack, which means
users can navigate within each tab independently.

Code Example

Here is a simple example of a Flutter app with a bottom navigation bar and multiple screens:

```
import 'package:flutter/material.dart'; void main() { runApp(MyApp()); } class
MyApp extends StatelessWidget { @override Widget build(BuildContext context) {
return MaterialApp( title: 'Bottom Navigation Bar Example', home:
```

```
HomeScreen(), ); } } class HomeScreen extends StatefulWidget { @override
_HomeScreenState createState() => _HomeScreenState(); } class _HomeScreenState
extends State<HomeScreen> { int _selectedIndex = 0; static List<Widget>
_widgetOptions = <Widget>[ ScreenA(), ScreenB(), ScreenC(), ]; void
_onItemTapped(int index) { setState(() { _selectedIndex = index; }); }
@override Widget build(BuildContext context) { return Scaffold( appBar:
AppBar( title: Text('Bottom Navigation Bar Example'), ), body:
_widgetOptions.elementAt(_selectedIndex), bottomNavigationBar:
BottomNavigationBar( items: const <BottomNavigationBarItem>[
BottomNavigationBarItem( icon: Icon(Icons.home), label: 'Home', ),
BottomNavigationBarItem( icon: Icon(Icons.business), label: 'Business', ),
BottomNavigationBarItem( icon: Icon(Icons.school), label: 'School', ), ],
currentIndex: _selectedIndex, selectedItemColor: Colors.amber[800], onTap:
_onItemTapped, ), ); } } class ScreenA extends StatelessWidget { @override
Widget build(BuildContext context) { return Center( child: Text( 'Home
Screen', style: TextStyle(fontSize: 24), ), ); } } class ScreenB extends
StatelessWidget { @override Widget build(BuildContext context) { return
Center( child: Text( 'Business Screen', style: TextStyle(fontSize: 24), ), );
} } class ScreenC extends StatelessWidget { @override Widget
build(BuildContext context) { return Center( child: Text( 'School Screen',
style: TextStyle(fontSize: 24), ), ); } }
```

Customizing the `BottomNavigationBar`

You can customize the appearance and behavior of the `BottomNavigationBar` in various ways, such as changing colors, icons, and text. Here are a few common customizations:

1. **Changing the Background Color:**
   ```
   bottomNavigationBar: BottomNavigationBar( backgroundColor: Colors.blue,
   // other properties ),
   ```
2. **Changing the Selected and Unselected Item Colors:**
   ```
   bottomNavigationBar: BottomNavigationBar( selectedItemColor:
   Colors.amber[800], unselectedItemColor: Colors.grey, // other properties
   ),
   ```
3. **Adding or Removing Labels:**
   ```
   bottomNavigationBar: BottomNavigationBar( showSelectedLabels: true,
   showUnselectedLabels: false, // other properties ),
   ```
4. **Customizing the Icon Size:**
   ```
   bottomNavigationBar: BottomNavigationBar( iconSize: 30.0, // other
   properties ),
   ```
5. **Adding a Badge to an Icon (requires additional packages like badges):**
   ```
   import 'package:badges/badges.dart'; BottomNavigationBarItem( icon:
   Badge( badgeContent: Text('3'), child: Icon(Icons.home), ), label:
   'Home', ),
   ```

By using these properties, you can tailor the `BottomNavigationBar` to match your app's design and provide a better user experience.

Navigating with Tabs

Tabbed interfaces are a popular way to organize content within mobile apps. They allow users to quickly switch between different views or sections of your app by tapping on tabs, typically located at the top or bottom of the screen. Flutter provides two primary ways to implement tabbed navigation: TabBar and BottomNavigationBar.

TabBar vs. BottomNavigationBar: Choosing the Right Tool

- **BottomNavigationBar:**
  - Generally used for navigation between the primary sections or views of your app.
  - Usually contains a small number of tabs (3-5).
  - Ideal when you want the tabs to persist across different screens.
  - Provides a familiar user experience consistent with many popular apps.
- **TabBar:**
  - Typically used for switching between different content types within a single screen.
  - Can contain a larger number of tabs.
  - Often positioned at the top of the screen, below the AppBar.
  - Offers more flexibility for customization and can be combined with other layout widgets.

Creating a Tabbed Interface with TabBar and TabBarView

To create a tabbed interface using TabBar, follow these steps:

1. **Use DefaultTabController:**
   - Wrap your Scaffold widget with a DefaultTabController. This controller manages the tab selection state.
   - Specify the length property to indicate the number of tabs you'll have.
2. **Add TabBar to AppBar:**
   - Place a TabBar widget within the AppBar's bottom property. This will display the tabs at the bottom of the app bar.
   - Provide a list of Tab widgets, each representing a single tab with an icon and/or text label.
3. **Link TabBarView to TabBar:**
   - Below the AppBar, add a TabBarView widget. This widget displays the content associated with the currently selected tab.
   - The number of children in TabBarView should match the length property of DefaultTabController.

```
DefaultTabController( length: 3, child: Scaffold( appBar: AppBar(
title: const Text('Tabbed App'), bottom: const TabBar( tabs: [
Tab(icon: Icon(Icons.home)), Tab(icon: Icon(Icons.search)),
Tab(icon: Icon(Icons.settings)), ], ), ), body: const TabBarView(
children: [ Center(child: Text("Home Page")), Center(child:
Text("Search Page")), Center(child: Text("Settings Page")), ], ), ),
);
```

Customizing Tabs and Tab Bars

You can customize the appearance of tabs and tab bars using various properties and styles:

- **Tab properties:**
  - `icon`: The icon to display on the tab.
  - `text`: The text label for the tab.
- **TabBar properties:**
  - `labelColor`, `unselectedLabelColor`: Colors for selected and unselected tab labels.
  - `indicatorColor`: The color of the tab indicator.
  - `labelStyle`, `unselectedLabelStyle`: Styles for tab labels.
  - `indicator`: Customize the appearance of the tab indicator (e.g., size, shape).
  - `isScrollable`: Whether the tabs should scroll horizontally if they don't fit.

By experimenting with these customization options, you can create a tabbed interface that perfectly matches your app's design and provides a seamless navigation experience for your users.

Chapter Summary

In this chapter, you embarked on a journey through the world of navigation in Flutter. You learned that navigation is the backbone of user experience in mobile apps, allowing users to seamlessly move between screens and access various features. We emphasized the importance of intuitive and consistent navigation patterns to avoid frustrating users.

You were introduced to the `Navigator` class, the core tool for managing screen transitions in Flutter. You explored the concept of the navigation stack and learned how to use `Navigator.push()` and `Navigator.pop()` to move between screens using anonymous routes.

We then delved deeper into routes, understanding how they define navigation paths within your app. You were introduced to the `MaterialPageRoute` class, a standard route for Material Design apps that provides visually appealing transitions. You learned how to use the `builder` property of `MaterialPageRoute` to create the destination screen's widget on demand.

Named routes were introduced as a more organized and maintainable approach to navigation. You learned how to define them in the `MaterialApp` widget's `routes` table and navigate to them using `Navigator.pushNamed()`. We also discussed how to pass data between screens using route arguments.

Finally, we explored two common navigation patterns: bottom navigation bars (`BottomNavigationBar`) and tabs (`TabBar` and `TabBarView`). You learned the difference between them and how to implement each pattern to create intuitive and user-friendly navigation experiences in your Flutter apps.

With this knowledge, you're well-equipped to create apps with seamless navigation that guides users through your content and features, enhancing the overall user experience.

Working with Images and Assets

Outline

- The Importance of Images and Assets
- Loading and Displaying Images
- Handling Different Image Formats
- Optimizing Image Loading for Performance
- Using the Image Widget
- Placeholder and Error Handling
- Working with Other Assets
- Managing Assets in Your Project
- Chapter Summary

The Importance of Images and Assets

In the world of mobile apps, a picture truly is worth a thousand words. Images and other visual assets play a crucial role in elevating the user experience, conveying information effectively, and establishing a strong brand identity.

Enhancing Visual Appeal

Imagine an app without images – a sea of text and buttons. It would be rather dull and uninspiring, wouldn't it? Images inject life and personality into your app, making it more visually appealing and engaging.

- **Aesthetics:** Beautiful photos, illustrations, and icons can captivate users and create a positive first impression.
- **Emotional Connection:** Images can evoke emotions and create a deeper connection with users.
- **Visual Hierarchy:** Images can be used to guide the user's eye, highlighting important elements and creating a clear visual hierarchy.

Communicating Information

Images aren't just about decoration; they can also be powerful tools for communication.

- **Visual Representation:** An image can often convey complex information more quickly and effectively than text alone. Think of a weather app using icons to represent sunny, cloudy, or rainy conditions.
- **Product Showcase:** In e-commerce apps, high-quality product images are essential for showcasing items and enticing users to make purchases.
- **Instructions and Tutorials:** Visual guides and diagrams can make instructions easier to understand and follow.

Building Brand Identity

Images and assets play a vital role in establishing and reinforcing your app's brand.

- **Logos and Icons:** Your app's logo and icons are often the first visual elements users encounter, making them crucial for brand recognition.
- **Color Schemes and Styles:** Consistent use of colors and styles in your images and assets helps create a cohesive brand identity that users will recognize and remember.

- **Custom Illustrations:** Unique illustrations or graphics can make your app stand out and create a memorable brand experience.

Quality and Optimization: A Balancing Act

While high-quality images are essential for visual appeal, they can also be large in file size, leading to slower app loading times and increased storage usage. It's crucial to strike a balance between quality and performance by optimizing your images.

- **Compression:** Use image compression techniques to reduce file size without sacrificing too much quality.
- **Resolution:** Provide images in multiple resolutions to cater to different screen densities. Flutter can automatically select the appropriate image based on the device's pixel density.
- **File Format:** Choose the right image format (e.g., PNG, JPEG, WebP) for each asset, considering factors like quality, transparency, and file size.

By thoughtfully incorporating images and assets into your Flutter app, you can create a visually stunning, informative, and engaging user experience that leaves a lasting impression.

Loading and Displaying Images

The Image widget is the cornerstone of displaying images in your Flutter apps. It's a versatile tool that can load and render images from various sources, allowing you to seamlessly integrate visuals into your user interfaces.

The Image Widget: Your Visual Storyteller

At its core, the Image widget is responsible for decoding and displaying image data on the screen. It offers a range of customization options, letting you control the image's size, fit, alignment, and more. We'll delve into these details later in the chapter.

Image Providers: Where Images Come From

Flutter loads images using something called an *ImageProvider*. This is an abstract class that defines how to obtain the raw image data. Flutter provides several concrete implementations of ImageProvider to handle different image sources:

1. Asset Images: Images in Your Pocket

Asset images are bundled with your app's code and are typically stored in the assets folder of your project. This is a great option for images that are essential to your app's functionality or design and don't change frequently.

```
Image.asset('assets/logo.png');
```

- In your pubspec.yaml file, declare the assets:

```
flutter: assets: - assets/logo.png
```

2. Network Images: Images from the Web

Network images are loaded from a URL over the internet. This is useful for displaying images that are hosted remotely or that might change dynamically.

```
Image.network('https://www.example.com/image.jpg');
```

3. File Images: Images from Local Storage

File images are loaded from a file stored on the user's device. This can be useful for images that are captured by the camera, downloaded from the internet, or created within your app.

```
final imageFile = File('/path/to/image.jpg'); Image.file(imageFile);
```

Choosing the Right Image Provider:

- **Asset Images:** Ideal for images that are part of your app's core design and don't need to be updated frequently.
- **Network Images:** Best for images that are hosted remotely or change dynamically (e.g., user avatars).
- **File Images:** Useful for images that are generated or downloaded within your app.

No matter where your image data comes from, the Image widget and its associated image providers empower you to incorporate rich visuals into your Flutter apps with ease.

Handling Different Image Formats

When working with images in Flutter, you'll encounter various image formats. Each format has its own strengths and weaknesses, making them suitable for different use cases. Understanding these formats will help you make informed decisions when choosing images for your app.

Common Image Formats in Flutter

- **PNG (Portable Network Graphics):**
    - **Lossless compression:** Preserves image quality even after compression.
    - **Supports transparency:** Ideal for logos, icons, and images with transparent backgrounds.
    - **Larger file sizes:** Can result in larger file sizes compared to JPEG for complex images.
    - **Best for:** Images with sharp edges, graphics, logos, icons, and images where transparency is needed.
- **JPEG (Joint Photographic Experts Group):**
    - **Lossy compression:** Reduces file size by discarding some image data, which can slightly degrade quality.
    - **Does not support transparency:** Not suitable for images requiring transparent backgrounds.
    - **Smaller file sizes:** Generally results in smaller file sizes than PNG, especially for photographs.
    - **Best for:** Photographs and images where file size is a priority over absolute image quality.
- **SVG (Scalable Vector Graphics):**
    - **Vector format:** Images are defined by mathematical equations, not pixels. This means they can be scaled to any size without losing quality.
    - **Smaller file sizes:** SVG files are often smaller than raster formats like PNG or JPEG, especially for simple graphics and icons.
    - **Limited color support:** Not ideal for complex photographs or images with gradients.
    - **Best for:** Logos, icons, simple illustrations, and any image that needs to be scaled to different sizes without losing quality.
- **WebP:**
    - **Newer format:** Developed by Google, offering both lossy and lossless compression.
    - **Smaller file sizes:** Often smaller than PNG and JPEG while maintaining comparable quality.
    - **Growing support:** Increasingly supported by web browsers and image editors.
    - **Best for:** Photos and images where you want to reduce file size without sacrificing much quality.

Choosing the Right Format: A Decision Tree

Requirement	Best Format
Lossless compression	PNG
Transparency	PNG, SVG
Smallest file size	WebP, SVG (for simple graphics)
Photographs	JPEG, WebP
Scalable graphics/icons	SVG

Additional Tips:

- **Optimize Images:** Compress images to reduce file size while maintaining acceptable quality.
- **Consider Image Dimensions:** Avoid using overly large images as they can slow down your app's loading time.
- **Use the Right Tool:** Consider using image editing software like Adobe Photoshop or GIMP to optimize and convert images to the appropriate format.

By understanding the different image formats and their characteristics, you can make informed choices that will enhance your Flutter app's visual appeal while maintaining optimal performance.

Optimizing Image Loading for Performance

Images can be a double-edged sword in mobile app development. While they enhance the visual appeal, large or unoptimized images can significantly slow down your app and create a frustrating user experience. That's why image optimization is a crucial step in creating performant Flutter apps.

Why Optimize Image Loading?

- **Performance:** Large images take longer to load, leading to delays and sluggishness in your app. Optimizing image loading ensures faster startup times and smoother scrolling.
- **Data Usage:** Loading high-resolution images over cellular networks can consume a lot of data, potentially incurring costs for your users. Optimization helps reduce data usage and conserve bandwidth.
- **User Experience:** Slow-loading images can frustrate users and create a negative impression of your app. Optimized images lead to a snappier and more enjoyable experience.

Image Optimization Techniques

1. Image Compression: Slimmer Images, Same Quality

Image compression involves reducing the file size of an image without significantly compromising its visual quality. There are two main types of compression:

- **Lossless Compression:** Retains all the original image data, but the compression ratio is limited. PNG is a lossless format.
- **Lossy Compression:** Discards some image data to achieve higher compression ratios, but it might result in a slight loss of quality. JPEG is a lossy format.

Use image editing tools or online compression services to optimize your images.

2. Caching: Storing for Speed

Caching involves storing downloaded images locally on the device. This way, when an image needs to be displayed again, it can be loaded from the cache instead of re-downloading it, saving time and bandwidth.

Flutter doesn't have built-in caching for network images, but you can use packages like `cached_network_image` to easily add this functionality.

3. Lazy Loading: Load as You Go

Lazy loading is a technique where images are loaded only when they become visible on the screen. This is especially useful for long lists or grids, as it prevents the app from loading all images at once, improving initial load time and memory usage.

`cached_network_image` Package: Your Optimization Partner

The `cached_network_image` package simplifies image caching and lazy loading in Flutter. It automatically caches network images, handles placeholders and error widgets, and provides a seamless way to integrate optimized image loading into your app.

```
CachedNetworkImage( imageUrl: 'https://www.example.com/image.jpg',
placeholder: (context, url) => CircularProgressIndicator(), errorWidget:
(context, url, error) => Icon(Icons.error), );
```

In this example, `cached_network_image` will display a circular progress indicator while the image is loading and an error icon if the image fails to load.

By employing these optimization techniques, you can significantly enhance your Flutter app's performance, reduce data consumption, and deliver a smoother, more responsive user experience.

Using the `Image` Widget: In-depth

The `Image` widget is incredibly versatile, offering a range of properties to fine-tune how your images are displayed. Let's delve into the key properties and how you can leverage them to create stunning visuals.

Essential `Image` Widget Properties

- **width and height:** Control the dimensions of the displayed image. You can set these to specific pixel values or use relative values like `double.infinity` to fill the available space.
- **fit:** Determines how the image should be resized to fit within its allocated space. Use the `BoxFit` enum to choose from various fitting options (see below).
- **alignment:** Specifies how the image should be positioned within its container when it doesn't fill the entire space. Use the `Alignment` enum to choose from options like `Alignment.center`, `Alignment.topLeft`, etc.
- **color and colorBlendMode:** Apply a color filter or blending mode to the image. This can be used to create tinted images or special effects.
- **repeat:** Controls how the image repeats if it's smaller than its container. Use the `ImageRepeat` enum to choose from options like `repeat`, `repeatX`, `repeatY`, and `noRepeat`.

Mastering `BoxFit`: How Your Image Fits

The `BoxFit` enum gives you precise control over how the image is scaled or cropped to fit within its container.

- BoxFit.contain: The image is scaled to fit within the container while maintaining its aspect ratio.
- BoxFit.cover: The image is scaled to fill the container while maintaining its aspect ratio. Parts of the image may be cropped.
- BoxFit.fill: The image is stretched to fill the container, ignoring its aspect ratio.
- BoxFit.fitWidth: The image is scaled to fit the container's width, maintaining its aspect ratio.
- BoxFit.fitHeight: The image is scaled to fit the container's height, maintaining its aspect ratio.
- BoxFit.none: The image is not scaled or cropped. It may overflow or underflow the container.
- BoxFit.scaleDown: The image is scaled down (if necessary) to fit within the container, maintaining its aspect ratio.

```
Image.asset( 'assets/landscape.jpg', width: 200, height: 100, fit:
BoxFit.cover, // The image fills the container, potentially cropping );
```

Controlling Image Position with `Alignment`

The `Alignment` enum determines where the image is placed within its container when it doesn't fill the entire space. Here are a few common options:

- Alignment.center: Centers the image both horizontally and vertically.
- Alignment.topLeft: Aligns the image to the top-left corner.
- Alignment.bottomRight: Aligns the image to the bottom-right corner.
- Alignment(0.5, -0.5): A custom alignment, shifting the image slightly right and up.

```
Image.asset( 'assets/logo.png', width: 200, height: 200, fit:
BoxFit.contain, alignment: Alignment.topLeft, // Align to top-left );
```

By understanding and utilizing these `Image` widget properties, you can fully customize how images are displayed in your Flutter apps, achieving the perfect balance of visual appeal and performance.

Placeholder and Error Handling

Using placeholder widgets is crucial in mobile apps to enhance user experience. When images are being fetched from the network, there can be a noticeable delay due to various factors such as network speed or server response time. During this delay, showing a placeholder gives users a visual cue that content is being loaded, which helps in maintaining the perceived performance of the app.

Displaying a Placeholder Image Using `loadingBuilder`

The `loadingBuilder` property of the `Image` widget allows you to display a placeholder while an image is loading. This can be a spinner, a static image, or any other widget. Here's how to use it:

```
import 'package:flutter/material.dart'; void main() { runApp(MyApp()); } class
MyApp extends StatelessWidget { @override Widget build(BuildContext context) {
return MaterialApp( home: Scaffold( appBar: AppBar( title: Text('Image Loading
Example'), ), body: Center( child: Image.network(
'https://example.com/your-image.jpg', loadingBuilder: (BuildContext context,
Widget child, ImageChunkEvent? loadingProgress) { if (loadingProgress == null)
{ return child; } else { return Center( child: CircularProgressIndicator(
value: loadingProgress.expectedTotalBytes != null ?
```

```
loadingProgress.cumulativeBytesLoaded / (loadingProgress.expectedTotalBytes ??
1) : null, ), ); } }, ), ), ), ); } }
```

In this example, the `CircularProgressIndicator` is shown while the image is loading. Once the image is fully loaded, the `CircularProgressIndicator` is replaced by the image.

Handling Errors During Image Loading Using `errorBuilder`

The `errorBuilder` property is used to handle errors that occur during image loading, such as network issues or invalid URLs. Here's how to implement it:

```
import 'package:flutter/material.dart'; void main() { runApp(MyApp()); } class
MyApp extends StatelessWidget { @override Widget build(BuildContext context) {
return MaterialApp( home: Scaffold( appBar: AppBar( title: Text('Image Error
Handling Example'), ), body: Center( child: Image.network(
'https://example.com/invalid-image.jpg', loadingBuilder: (BuildContext
context, Widget child, ImageChunkEvent? loadingProgress) { if (loadingProgress
== null) { return child; } else { return Center( child:
CircularProgressIndicator( value: loadingProgress.expectedTotalBytes != null ?
loadingProgress.cumulativeBytesLoaded / (loadingProgress.expectedTotalBytes ??
1) : null, ), ); } }, errorBuilder: (BuildContext context, Object error,
StackTrace? stackTrace) { return Center( child: Column( mainAxisSize:
MainAxisSize.min, children: [ Icon(Icons.error, color: Colors.red, size:
64.0), Text( 'Failed to load image', style: TextStyle(fontSize: 18.0, color:
Colors.red), ), ], ), ); }, ), ), ), ); } }
```

In this example, if the image fails to load, an error icon and a message are displayed instead of the image.

Full Example with Both `loadingBuilder` and `errorBuilder`

Here is the complete example combining both `loadingBuilder` and `errorBuilder`:

```
import 'package:flutter/material.dart'; void main() { runApp(MyApp()); } class
MyApp extends StatelessWidget { @override Widget build(BuildContext context) {
return MaterialApp( home: Scaffold( appBar: AppBar( title: Text('Image Loading
and Error Handling Example'), ), body: Center( child: Image.network(
'https://example.com/invalid-image.jpg', loadingBuilder: (BuildContext
context, Widget child, ImageChunkEvent? loadingProgress) { if (loadingProgress
== null) { return child; } else { return Center( child:
CircularProgressIndicator( value: loadingProgress.expectedTotalBytes != null ?
loadingProgress.cumulativeBytesLoaded / (loadingProgress.expectedTotalBytes ??
1) : null, ), ); } }, errorBuilder: (BuildContext context, Object error,
StackTrace? stackTrace) { return Center( child: Column( mainAxisSize:
MainAxisSize.min, children: [ Icon(Icons.error, color: Colors.red, size:
64.0), Text( 'Failed to load image', style: TextStyle(fontSize: 18.0, color:
Colors.red), ), ], ), ); }, ), ), ), ); } }
```

Explanation

1. **loadingBuilder**:
   - This property allows you to specify a widget to display while the image is loading. In the provided code, a `CircularProgressIndicator` is displayed as the image is being fetched. The progress indicator's value is based on the loading progress if available.
2. **errorBuilder**:
   - This property handles errors that occur during image loading. If the image fails to load, a custom widget is displayed. In the example, an error icon and a text message are shown to indicate the failure.

Breakdown of the Code

- **Image.network**:
  - Loads an image from the given URL. If the URL is invalid or the network request fails, the `errorBuilder` will handle it.
- **loadingBuilder**:
  - Checks if `loadingProgress` is null, which indicates that the image has finished loading. If not, it shows a `CircularProgressIndicator` with a progress value based on the loading progress.
- **errorBuilder**:
  - If an error occurs, this builder displays an error icon and a text message indicating the failure.

This approach ensures that users are given feedback while images are loading and are properly informed if an error occurs, improving the overall user experience.

Working with Other Assets

While images are a crucial part of many apps, Flutter's asset system is much more versatile. You can include a wide variety of resources in your app, from fonts and icons to configuration files, raw data, and even audio and video files.

What are Assets?

Think of assets as the non-code resources that your app needs to function or enhance its user experience. They can be any type of file that you want to bundle and distribute with your app.

Organizing Assets

To keep your project tidy and maintainable, it's recommended to organize your assets in a structured way. Create a top-level `assets` folder in your project's root directory and use subfolders to categorize different types of assets:

```
your_project/
├── assets/
│   ├── fonts/
│   ├── images/
│   ├── icons/
│   ├── data/
│   ├── config.json
│   └── ...
```

Declaring Assets in `pubspec.yaml`

Flutter uses the pubspec.yaml file (located in your project's root directory) to track your project's dependencies and assets. To include assets in your app, you need to declare them under the flutter section:

```
flutter: assets: - assets/fonts/Roboto-Regular.ttf # A font file -
assets/images/logo.png # An image - assets/data/ # Include all files in the
data folder
```

Loading and Using Assets

Flutter provides different mechanisms for loading and using various types of assets:

- **Fonts:**
  - Load fonts using FontManifest.loadFontFromAsset().
  - Use the TextStyle widget to apply the loaded font to your text.

    ```
    // Assuming the font is already loaded Text( 'This is text in a
    custom font', style: TextStyle(fontFamily: 'Roboto'), // Use the
    font family name );
    ```

- **JSON files:**
  - Load JSON data using the rootBundle.loadString() method.
  - Parse the loaded string using jsonDecode from the dart:convert library.

    ```
    import 'dart:convert'; String configString = await
    rootBundle.loadString('assets/config.json'); Map<String, dynamic>
    config = jsonDecode(configString);
    ```

- **Other File Types:**
  - Load raw file data using rootBundle.load().

Remember that you might need to use additional packages or platform-specific code for handling certain types of assets like audio or video files.

By effectively organizing and managing your assets, you can streamline your development workflow, improve code maintainability, and create Flutter apps that deliver a rich and immersive experience.

Managing Assets in Your Project

As your Flutter project grows, so does the number of assets you'll be dealing with. Effective asset management is key to maintaining a clean and organized codebase, ensuring smooth development workflows, and optimizing your app's performance.

Tips for Effective Asset Management:

1. **Structured Organization:**
- Use subfolders within your assets directory to categorize different types of assets (e.g., images, fonts, icons).
- Name your assets consistently and descriptively, using lowercase letters, underscores (_), and avoiding spaces.
- Consider using a naming convention that includes asset dimensions or other relevant details (e.g., logo_200x200.png).

2. **Clear Declaration in `pubspec.yaml`:**
- Accurately list all your assets in the `flutter: assets:` section of your `pubspec.yaml` file.
- Use wildcards (`*`) to include entire folders, but be mindful of potentially including unwanted files.
- Regularly update the `pubspec.yaml` file as you add or remove assets.
3. **Asset Optimization:**
- **Image Compression:** Use tools like TinyPNG or ImageOptim to compress your images without significantly sacrificing quality. This reduces file size and improves app loading times.
- **Vector Graphics (SVG):** For icons and simple graphics, use SVG format whenever possible. SVGs are scalable and can be resized without losing quality.
- **Image Resolution:** Provide images in multiple resolutions to cater to different screen densities. Flutter will automatically select the appropriate image based on the device's screen.
- **Lazy Loading:** Consider using lazy loading techniques to load images only when they are about to become visible on the screen. This can significantly improve initial app load times, especially if you have a large number of images.
4. **Asset Generation and Management Tools:**
- **FlutterGen:** A useful tool that automatically generates Dart code for accessing your assets, eliminating the need for hardcoding asset paths.
- **Flame:** A game engine for Flutter that includes tools for managing and optimizing game assets.

Scaling Your Asset Management

As your app grows, you might find it beneficial to adopt more advanced asset management strategies:

- **Asset Bundling:** Consider using tools like `flutter_assets` to bundle multiple assets into a single file, reducing the number of network requests.
- **Version Control:** Use a version control system like Git to track changes to your assets and revert to previous versions if needed.
- **Cloud Storage:** For large apps with a vast number of assets, consider storing them in the cloud and loading them on demand.

By implementing these asset management best practices, you'll ensure that your Flutter project remains organized, efficient, and scalable as it evolves.

Chapter Summary

In this chapter, you delved into the world of images and assets in Flutter, discovering how they enrich the visual appeal and overall user experience of your apps. You learned that images and assets are not limited to just pictures but encompass a wide range of resources, including fonts, configuration files, and more.

We explored the powerful Image widget, the core tool for displaying images in Flutter, and examined the different ways to load images from assets, networks, and local files. You gained insights into common image formats like PNG, JPEG, SVG, and WebP, understanding their strengths, weaknesses, and ideal use cases.

To ensure your app's performance doesn't suffer from image-related bottlenecks, we discussed essential optimization techniques like image compression, caching, and lazy loading. We also introduced the `cached_network_image` package as a convenient way to implement these optimizations for network images.

Delving deeper into the Image widget, you learned how to harness its properties to control the image's dimensions, fit, alignment, color, and repetition. You mastered the art of fitting images into containers using `BoxFit` and precisely positioning them using `Alignment`.

We touched upon the importance of placeholder widgets and error handling to provide a smooth user experience even when images are loading or encounter issues.

Finally, we explored the broader world of assets beyond images, covering how to organize, declare, and load various asset types in your Flutter project. We also shared tips for efficient asset management, including strategies for organization, optimization, and using specialized tools like FlutterGen.

With this comprehensive knowledge of images and assets, you're now ready to elevate the visual aesthetics and overall experience of your Flutter apps.

Making Network Requests and Fetching Data

Outline

- The Power of Network Communication
- The http Package
- Making GET Requests
- Parsing JSON Data
- Handling Errors and Loading States
- Asynchronous Operations with Futures
- Advanced Networking Techniques
- Best Practices for Networking in Flutter
- Chapter Summary

The Power of Network Communication

Think of your Flutter app as an island. While it might be beautifully designed and full of potential, it's isolated and limited without a way to connect to the outside world. Network communication is the bridge that connects your app to the vast resources and information available on the internet.

Why Network Communication is Essential:

1. **Dynamic Content:**
- **Fresh Data:** Most modern apps don't just rely on static content bundled with the app itself. They fetch up-to-date information from remote servers, ensuring that users always see the latest news, weather forecasts, social media posts, product listings, and more.
- **Personalized Experiences:** Network requests allow you to tailor the app's content to individual users based on their preferences, location, or usage patterns.
- **Real-time Updates:** Apps can receive real-time notifications, messages, or data updates from servers, keeping users informed and engaged.
2. **Cloud Services and APIs:**
- **Cloud Storage:** Many apps store user data, images, and other assets in the cloud, making them accessible from any device.
- **Third-Party APIs:** Apps can leverage the power of third-party APIs (Application Programming Interfaces) to access a wide range of services, such as maps, payment processing, social media integration, and more.
3. **Communication and Collaboration:**
- **Social Interactions:** Social media apps rely heavily on network communication to enable users to share posts, photos, and messages with their friends and followers.
- **Multiplayer Games:** Network requests are used to synchronize game state, send messages, and facilitate interactions between players in real-time.
- **Messaging and Chat:** Instant messaging apps utilize network communication to deliver messages instantly between users.

Real-World Examples:

- **News Apps:** Fetch the latest articles and headlines from news sources around the world.
- **Social Media Apps:** Enable users to share posts, photos, and videos, and interact with their friends.
- **Weather Apps:** Retrieve real-time weather forecasts and display them in an easily digestible format.

- **E-commerce Apps:** Display product catalogs, process orders, and manage customer accounts.
- **Music Streaming Apps:** Stream music and podcasts from online libraries.

The Role of APIs: Your App's Connection Point

APIs act as the intermediaries between your app and external services. They define a set of rules and protocols for how your app can request and receive data from these services. Learning how to interact with APIs is a fundamental skill for any Flutter developer who wants to build modern, connected apps.

In the next sections, we'll dive into the tools and techniques for making network requests in Flutter and handling the data you receive from APIs. By mastering network communication, you'll unlock the full potential of your Flutter apps, enabling them to interact with the world and deliver dynamic, personalized experiences to your users.

The `http` Package

When your Flutter app needs to fetch data from the internet or communicate with a server, the `http` package is your go-to tool. This versatile package provides a simple and effective way to make HTTP requests, the foundation of most web communication.

What is the `http` Package?

The `http` package is a Dart library that simplifies the process of making network requests. It handles the low-level details of sending and receiving data over the internet, allowing you to focus on the logic of your app.

Adding the `http` Package to Your Project

1. **Open pubspec.yaml:** Locate the `pubspec.yaml` file in your project's root directory.
2. **Add the Dependency:** Under the `dependencies` section, add the following line:

```
dependencies: http: ^0.13.5 # Or the latest version available
```

3. **Save and Fetch:** Save the `pubspec.yaml` file. Flutter will automatically fetch and install the `http` package for you.

Using the `http` Package

To use the `http` package in your Dart code:

1. **Import:** Import the package at the top of your file:

```
import 'package:http/http.dart' as http;
```

2. **Make Requests:** Use the package's core functions to make different types of HTTP requests:
- `http.get(Uri.parse(url))`: Retrieves data from the specified URL.
- `http.post(Uri.parse(url), body: data)`: Sends data to the URL and receives a response.
- `http.put(Uri.parse(url), body: data)`: Similar to `post`, but used to update existing data.
- `http.delete(Uri.parse(url))`: Deletes the resource at the specified URL.

Example: A Simple GET Request

```
import 'package:http/http.dart' as http; Future<void> fetchData() async {
final response = await http.get(Uri.parse('https://api.example.com/data')); if
(response.statusCode == 200) { // Request successful String data =
response.body; // Process the fetched data } else { // Handle errors
print('Request failed with status: ${response.statusCode}.'); } }
```

In this example:

- We define an async function called fetchData() to work with asynchronous operations.
- A GET request is sent to the provided URL using http.get.
- We await for the response to be returned.
- Then we check the response.statusCode to see if it was a successful request (200 means success).
- If successful, we extract the data from the response as response.body.
- Otherwise, we can print the error code.

In the following sections, we'll dive deeper into how to parse and utilize the data you receive from network requests.

Making GET Requests

GET requests are the most common type of HTTP request used to retrieve data from a server. Think of it like asking a question and receiving an answer. In the context of APIs, you send a GET request to a specific URL (endpoint), and the server responds with the requested data, usually in a structured format like JSON.

The Anatomy of a GET Request

A GET request typically consists of:

- **URL:** The address of the resource you want to retrieve.
- **Query Parameters (Optional):** Additional parameters appended to the URL to filter or customize the requested data.
- **Headers (Optional):** Metadata about the request, such as authentication tokens or content types.

Making GET Requests with http.get()

The http package makes sending GET requests a breeze. Here's how to do it:

1. **Create a Uri object:** This represents the URL of the endpoint you want to request data from. You can include query parameters in the Uri.

   ```
   final uri = Uri.parse('https://api.example.com/users?limit=10');
   ```

2. **Send the Request:** Use http.get() to send the GET request to the specified URI.

   ```
   final response = await http.get(uri);
   ```

3. **Handle the Response:** The response object contains the server's response to your request.

```
if (response.statusCode == 200) { // Status code 200 indicates success
final data = jsonDecode(response.body); // Assuming JSON response //
Process the data... } else { // Handle errors... }
```

Understanding the Response

The `response` object provides valuable information:

- **Status Code:** A numerical code indicating the status of the request. Common codes include:
  - ○ **200 OK:** The request was successful.
  - ○ **404 Not Found:** The requested resource was not found.
  - ○ **500 Internal Server Error:** The server encountered an error.
- **Body:** The actual data returned by the server, often in JSON format.
- **Headers:** Additional metadata about the response.

Adding Query Parameters

Query parameters are added to the end of a URL after a question mark (?). They are used to pass additional information to the server, such as filtering criteria or pagination options.

```
final uri = Uri.https('api.example.com', '/search', {'q': 'Flutter', 'page':
'2'});
```

This URL translates to:

https://api.example.com/search?q=Flutter&page=2

The parameters in this case are:

- q: search query = 'Flutter'
- page: page number = '2'

Key Points

- **Asynchronous Nature:** Network requests take time, so they're performed asynchronously. Use `async`/`await` or `.then()` to handle the results.
- **Error Handling:** Always handle errors gracefully (e.g., network timeouts, invalid responses) to prevent your app from crashing.
- **Data Parsing:** You'll typically need to parse the response data (e.g., from JSON) into a format that your app can use.

By mastering GET requests and response handling, you'll be able to fetch data from APIs and populate your Flutter apps with dynamic content.

Parsing JSON Data

When you fetch data from an API using a GET request (or other HTTP methods), the server often sends the response in JSON format. JSON (JavaScript Object Notation) is a lightweight and widely used data interchange format that's easy for humans to read and write, and easy for machines to parse and generate.

JSON: The Universal Language of Data

JSON is like a universal language that different systems can understand. It structures data in a hierarchical way, using key-value pairs, arrays, and nested structures. Think of it like a set of labeled boxes containing different types of data.

`dart:convert` and `jsonDecode()`: Your JSON Translator

Dart's built-in `dart:convert` library provides the `jsonDecode()` function, which acts as your trusty translator for converting JSON strings into Dart data structures. Let's see how it works:

```
import 'dart:convert'; // Example JSON string from a server response String
jsonString = ''' { "name": "Alice", "age": 30, "city": "New York",
"interests": ["Flutter", "Dart", "Coding"] } '''; Map<String, dynamic>
jsonData = jsonDecode(jsonString); print(jsonData['name']); // Output: Alice
print(jsonData['interests'][0]); // Output: Flutter
```

In this example:

1. We import the `dart:convert` library.
2. We define a `jsonString` variable containing a JSON string.
3. `jsonDecode()` parses the `jsonString` into a Map<String, dynamic>, where:
   - Keys are strings (e.g., "name", "age", "city", "interests").
   - Values can be of any type (hence `dynamic`).

We can then access the data using the keys:

- `jsonData['name']` gets the value associated with the "name" key (which is "Alice").
- `jsonData['interests']` gets the value associated with the "interests" key, which is a `List`.
- `jsonData['interests'][0]` accesses the first element in the list ("Flutter").

Handling Nested Structures

JSON can contain nested objects and arrays. You can navigate through these structures using dot notation (`.`) for objects and square brackets (`[ ]`) for arrays.

```
print(jsonData['address']['street']); // Access a nested property
```

Converting JSON to Dart Objects

While working with maps is convenient, you can also create custom Dart classes to represent your JSON data more meaningfully. This allows you to give your data stronger types and define methods for working with it.

```
class User { String name; int age; User(this.name, this.age); factory
User.fromJson(Map<String, dynamic> json) { return User(json['name'],
json['age']); } } // ... User user = User.fromJson(jsonData);
```

With these techniques, you'll be able to seamlessly transform raw JSON data into usable information within your Flutter apps.

Handling Errors and Loading States

When dealing with network requests, things don't always go as planned. Network connectivity issues, server errors, or unexpected response formats can all throw a wrench into the works. To create a reliable and user-friendly app, you need to gracefully handle these errors and provide clear feedback to your users.

Why Error Handling is Crucial

- **Prevent App Crashes:** Unhandled errors during network requests can lead to your app crashing, leaving users frustrated and confused. Proper error handling prevents these crashes and allows your app to recover gracefully.
- **Inform the User:** Users need to know what's happening when a network request fails. Displaying clear error messages or alerts helps them understand the issue and take appropriate action (e.g., retrying the request, checking their internet connection).
- **Maintain User Trust:** By handling errors smoothly and providing helpful feedback, you build trust with your users, demonstrating that your app is reliable and well-designed.

Catching Exceptions with `try-catch`

Dart's `try-catch` blocks provide a structured way to handle exceptions (errors) that might occur during code execution. The `try` block contains the code that could potentially throw an exception, while the `catch` block handles the exception if it occurs.

```
Future<void> fetchData() async { try { final response = await
http.get(Uri.parse('https://api.example.com/data')); if (response.statusCode
== 200) { // Success } else { throw Exception('Request failed with status:
${response.statusCode}'); } } catch (error) { print('Error: $error'); // Show
an error message to the user } }
```

In this example, the `try` block attempts to fetch data from an API. If the request fails (e.g., due to a network error or incorrect URL), an exception is thrown. The `catch` block catches the exception, logs an error message, and could display an error alert to the user.

Showing Loading Indicators: Keeping Users Informed

Network requests can take time, especially on slower connections. To avoid leaving users wondering what's happening, display a loading indicator while the data is being fetched. This could be a simple circular progress indicator, a skeleton screen, or a custom animation.

```
bool isLoading = true; // Track loading state // ... inside your build method
if (isLoading) { return const Center(child: CircularProgressIndicator()); }
else { // Display the fetched data }
```

Introducing Error States: Beyond Success or Failure

In addition to loading and success states, consider using an error state to indicate that something went wrong during the data fetching process. This allows you to display a more specific error message or a retry button, giving users a way to recover from the error.

```
enum DataState { loading, success, error } DataState _dataState =
DataState.loading; // Initial state // ... Update _dataState in your fetchData
function based on the request outcome // ... inside your build method if
(_dataState == DataState.loading) { return const Center(child:
```

```
CircularProgressIndicator()); } else if (_dataState == DataState.error) {
return Center(child: Text('Error loading data. Please try again.')); } else {
// DataState.success // Display the fetched data }
```

By implementing robust error handling and providing clear feedback through loading indicators and error states, you can create a more resilient and user-friendly Flutter app.

Asynchronous Operations with Futures

Network requests take time. You send a request to a server, and it might take milliseconds, seconds, or even minutes to receive a response. While your app is waiting, you wouldn't want it to freeze, would you? This is where asynchronous programming and Dart's `Future` class come to the rescue.

The Asynchronous Nature of Network Requests:

In a **synchronous** operation, your code executes line by line, one step at a time. But with network requests, you can't just wait around for the server's response. You need to allow your app to continue running other tasks in the meantime. That's where **asynchronous** operations shine.

Futures: Promises of the Future

A `Future` in Dart is like a promise. It represents a value that will be available at some point in the future, but you don't know exactly when. It's like ordering a pizza: You place the order (make the request), and the pizzeria promises to deliver it (the future result), but you don't know exactly when it will arrive.

`async` and `await`: Your Time Travel Tools

Dart's `async` and `await` keywords make working with futures feel almost like writing synchronous code.

- **async:** You mark a function as `async` to indicate that it will return a `Future`. This tells Dart that the function might perform asynchronous operations.
- **await:** You use the `await` keyword before a `Future` to pause the execution of your function until the `Future` completes and returns its value.

```
Future<String> fetchData() async { // async function returns a Future
final response = await
http.get(Uri.parse('https://api.example.com/data')); // await the
response if (response.statusCode == 200) { return response.body; } else {
throw Exception('Request failed with status: ${response.statusCode}'); }
} // Using the function fetchData().then((data) { // Do something with
the data }).catchError((error) { // Handle errors });
```

In this code snippet:

- `fetchData()` is an async function because it's making a network request and waiting for the response using `await`.
- Once the response is received, the function continues and either returns the response body or throws an error.
- We call `.then()` on the result of `fetchData()` to handle the data when it becomes available and `.catchError()` to catch potential errors.

Handling Success and Errors: `then` **and** `catchError`

Futures offer two primary ways to handle their eventual outcome:

- `.then()`: This method takes a callback function that is executed when the `Future` completes successfully. The callback receives the result value.
- `.catchError()`: This method takes a callback function that is executed if the `Future` completes with an error. The callback receives the error object.

You can chain these methods to create a sequence of actions to be performed depending on the result of the `Future`.

By mastering asynchronous operations with futures, `async`, and `await`, you can write Flutter code that handles network requests gracefully, keeps your UI responsive, and provides a seamless user experience.

Advanced Networking Techniques

While the basics of making GET requests are essential, real-world apps often require more sophisticated networking capabilities. Let's briefly explore some advanced techniques that you'll encounter as you build more complex Flutter apps:

Authentication: Securing Your Data

Many APIs require authentication to ensure that only authorized users can access or modify data. Common authentication methods include:

- **API Keys:** Unique identifiers that grant access to specific API endpoints.
- **OAuth 2.0:** A widely used authorization framework that allows users to grant apps access to their data on other services without sharing their passwords.
- **JWT (JSON Web Tokens):** Compact, self-contained tokens used to transmit information securely between parties.

You'll typically need to include authentication credentials in your HTTP request headers to access protected API endpoints.

POST, PUT, DELETE Requests: Modifying Data

GET requests are great for retrieving data, but what if you want to send data to the server to create, update, or delete resources? That's where other HTTP methods come in:

- **POST:** Used to create new resources on the server.
- **PUT:** Used to update existing resources.
- **DELETE:** Used to delete resources.

These methods typically involve sending a JSON payload in the request body.

```
final response = await http.post( Uri.parse('https://api.example.com/users'),
body: jsonEncode({'name': 'Bob', 'email': 'bob@example.com'}), );
```

WebSockets: Real-Time Communication

While HTTP requests are great for one-off data exchanges, sometimes you need real-time, bidirectional communication between your app and a server. WebSockets provide a way to establish a persistent connection, allowing both the client (your app) and the server to send data back and forth at any time.

This is ideal for applications like chat apps, real-time dashboards, or collaborative tools that require instant updates. Flutter doesn't have built-in WebSocket support, but you can use packages like `web_socket_channel` to easily add this functionality.

Deeper Dive in Later Chapters

We'll delve into these advanced networking techniques in more detail in later chapters, exploring how to implement authentication, handle different HTTP methods, and work with WebSockets in your Flutter apps.

By understanding these concepts, you'll be equipped to build powerful, secure, and dynamic Flutter apps that can interact with servers and APIs in a variety of ways.

Best Practices for Networking in Flutter

Building robust network interactions is crucial for any app that relies on fetching or sending data. Following these best practices ensures your Flutter app communicates efficiently and reliably with servers and APIs.

1. **Error Handling: Anticipate the Unexpected**
   - **Assume Failure:** Always expect network requests to fail. Whether it's due to a poor connection, server issues, or unexpected responses, your app should be prepared.
   - **Try-Catch Blocks:** Use `try-catch` blocks to wrap your network requests. This allows you to catch exceptions (errors) gracefully and provide appropriate feedback to the user.
   - **Error Messages:** Display clear and concise error messages to the user when a request fails. Avoid technical jargon and guide the user on how to resolve the issue (e.g., "Check your internet connection and try again").
   - **Retry Logic:** Consider implementing retry mechanisms to automatically attempt failed requests again after a short delay.
   - **Offline Mode (Optional):** If your app needs to function without an internet connection, consider implementing offline mode. Cache data locally so that users can still access basic functionality even when offline.
2. **Model Classes: Organize Your Data**
   - **Structured Representation:** Create Dart classes (models) to represent the data you receive from APIs. This helps you organize your data, enforce type safety, and makes your code more readable and maintainable.
   - **Parsing Logic:** Encapsulate the logic for parsing JSON or other response formats into your model classes. This keeps your networking code cleaner and easier to test.
   - **Data Validation:** Add validation logic to your models to ensure that the data you receive is in the expected format and meets your app's requirements.
3. **Advanced Networking Libraries:**

While the `http` package is a great starting point, for larger apps or more complex networking requirements, consider using more feature-rich libraries like:

- **dio:** A powerful HTTP client with features like request cancellation, interceptors, global configuration, and file uploading/downloading.
- **chopper:** A code-generation library that simplifies building typed API clients based on your API's interface.
4. **Testing: Don't Just Assume It Works**
   - **Unit Tests:** Write unit tests for your networking code to verify that it handles requests, responses, and errors correctly.
   - **Integration Tests:** Test how your app integrates with real APIs under different network conditions (e.g., slow connections, timeouts).

- **Mock Servers:** Use mock servers during development to simulate API responses and test your app's behavior in isolation from the real network.

Additional Tips:

- **Rate Limiting:** Be mindful of API rate limits and avoid making excessive requests that could lead to throttling or blocking.
- **Background Tasks:** If your app needs to perform network requests in the background, consider using Flutter's `WorkManager` or other background task management tools.
- **Security:** Always prioritize security when transmitting sensitive data over the network. Use HTTPS for all requests and consider encryption for confidential information.

By following these best practices and incorporating them into your Flutter development workflow, you can build apps that are resilient to network challenges, deliver a smooth user experience, and provide a secure and reliable platform for interacting with the world of data and services available online.

Chapter Summary

In this chapter, you embarked on an exploration of network requests and data fetching in Flutter. We began by highlighting the essential role that network communication plays in modern mobile apps, enabling dynamic content, access to cloud services and APIs, and real-time interactions.

You were introduced to the powerful `http` package, Flutter's go-to tool for making HTTP requests. We covered how to add this package to your project and use its core functions (`get`, `post`, `put`, `delete`) to interact with APIs and servers.

We then focused on GET requests, the most common type of request for retrieving data. You learned how to construct GET requests with URLs and query parameters and how to interpret the server's response, including checking status codes and handling the response body.

Next, we tackled the critical task of parsing JSON data, a common format for data exchange over the internet. You learned how to use Dart's `dart:convert` library to decode JSON strings into Dart objects and maps, enabling you to extract and utilize the information effectively.

Recognizing that network requests don't always go smoothly, we emphasized the importance of error handling and graceful degradation. You discovered how to use `try-catch` blocks to catch exceptions, display user-friendly error messages, and provide loading indicators to keep users informed.

We also delved into the asynchronous nature of network requests, introducing the `Future` class and the `async`/`await` keywords. You learned how to use these tools to write cleaner, more readable code that handles network requests efficiently.

Finally, we provided a glimpse into advanced networking techniques like authentication, POST/PUT/DELETE requests, and WebSockets, offering a roadmap for you to explore more sophisticated networking scenarios as you continue your Flutter journey.

Armed with this knowledge, you're now equipped to connect your Flutter apps to the wider world, fetch dynamic data, and create interactive experiences that keep users engaged.

Managing App State (Provider, BLoC, or Riverpod)

Outline

- The Challenge of State Management
- Introduction to State Management Approaches
- Provider: The Simple and Intuitive Approach
- BLoC: The Structured and Scalable Pattern
- Riverpod: The Flexible and Reactive Solution
- Choosing the Right Approach
- Chapter Summary

The Challenge of State Management

Think of your Flutter app as a living organism. It has a memory, a current condition, and it reacts to events. This "memory" and "condition" are collectively known as the app's **state**. It's the data that determines what's displayed on the screen, how the app behaves, and how it responds to user interactions.

Why State Management Matters:

State is the lifeblood of any dynamic app. It's what allows you to build interactive user interfaces, fetch data from the network, and personalize the app experience. However, as your app grows in complexity, managing state effectively becomes increasingly challenging.

Common State Management Challenges:

1. **Shared State:**
- Many apps have data that needs to be accessed and updated by multiple widgets across different parts of the widget tree.
- For example, a shopping cart's contents might need to be displayed on both the product list screen and the checkout screen.
- Without proper state management, keeping this shared state synchronized and consistent can become a nightmare.
2. **Complex State:**
- As your app evolves, your state can become complex, involving nested objects, lists, and relationships.
- Managing this complexity can quickly lead to code that's hard to read, understand, and debug.
- Changes in one part of the state might unexpectedly affect other parts, leading to subtle bugs.
3. **Asynchronous State:**
- Many state changes are triggered by asynchronous operations like network requests.
- Coordinating these asynchronous updates with the rest of your app's state can be tricky.
- Without proper mechanisms, you might end up with race conditions, inconsistencies, or outdated data being displayed.
4. **State Persistence:**
- In some cases, you might want to preserve parts of your app's state even when the user closes the app or switches to a different screen.
- This could be user preferences, login status, or data that was expensive to fetch from a network.
- Implementing state persistence requires careful consideration of storage options (e.g., local storage, databases) and synchronization strategies.

Enter State Management Solutions:

Flutter offers various approaches and libraries to tackle these state management challenges. These solutions provide structured ways to:

- Store and access state from anywhere in your app
- Propagate state changes to relevant widgets
- Handle asynchronous operations gracefully
- Persist state across app sessions

In this chapter, we'll explore some of the most popular state management solutions in Flutter, empowering you to choose the right tools and techniques for your specific project.

Key Takeaway: State management is a fundamental aspect of building robust and scalable Flutter apps. By understanding the challenges and choosing the right approach, you can create apps that handle data effectively and provide a seamless user experience.

Introduction to State Management Approaches

In the world of Flutter, managing state effectively is both an art and a science. Thankfully, you're not alone in this endeavor! Flutter's ecosystem offers a diverse set of state management approaches, each with its own strengths and philosophies.

The Three Musketeers: Provider, BLoC, and Riverpod

In this chapter, we'll focus on three popular and widely used state management solutions:

1. **Provider:**
- **Philosophy:** Keep it simple and intuitive.
- **Mechanism:** Leverages InheritedWidget under the hood for efficient state distribution.
- **Strengths:** Easy to learn, low boilerplate, well-integrated with Flutter's widget tree.
- **Best for:** Small to medium-sized apps or teams who prioritize simplicity and ease of use.
2. **BLoC (Business Logic Component):**
- **Philosophy:** Separate business logic from UI concerns.
- **Mechanism:** Uses streams (reactive programming) to manage state and events.
- **Strengths:** Highly testable, scalable, predictable state changes, well-suited for complex apps.
- **Best for:** Large-scale apps, teams who prioritize separation of concerns, and projects that benefit from a reactive architecture.
3. **Riverpod:**
- **Philosophy:** Flexibility and compile-time safety.
- **Mechanism:** Builds upon Provider, but with a more flexible API and enhanced features.
- **Strengths:** Compile-time safety catches errors early, improved dependency injection, easy testing, and great for complex state scenarios.
- **Best for:** Teams looking for a modern, flexible, and type-safe state management solution.

Other Notable Contenders:

- `setState()`: The most basic approach, ideal for simple state changes within a single widget.
- `ValueNotifier`: A simple way to create reactive state objects.
- `InheritedWidget`: The foundation for many state management solutions, providing a way to share data down the widget tree.
- **Redux:** A predictable state container inspired by the Elm architecture.
- **MobX:** Transparent reactive state management with minimal boilerplate.

Choosing the Right Approach: No Silver Bullet

The best state management solution for your Flutter app depends on various factors:

- **App Complexity:** Simple apps might do well with `setState()` or Provider, while larger apps might benefit from BLoC or Riverpod's structure and flexibility.
- **Team Experience:** Choose a solution that your team is comfortable with and that aligns with your project's conventions.
- **Performance Needs:** If performance is critical, consider BLoC or Riverpod, as they can offer optimizations for complex state interactions.
- **Personal Preference:** Ultimately, the "best" solution is the one that you find the most intuitive and that best suits your project's requirements.

In the following sections, we'll take a closer look at each of the three main approaches (Provider, BLoC, and Riverpod), exploring their strengths, use cases, and implementation details. By the end of this chapter, you'll have a solid understanding of state management in Flutter and be equipped to choose the right tool for your app.

Provider: The Simple and Intuitive Approach

Provider is one of the most popular state management solutions in the Flutter ecosystem. It simplifies the process of managing and sharing state within your app, making your code more organized and easier to maintain.

How Provider Works: Dependency Injection Made Easy

Provider is built upon the concept of dependency injection. In essence, this means that instead of widgets directly creating or managing their state, they receive the state from an external source – a provider.

This approach offers several benefits:

- **Simplified Access:** Widgets can easily access the state they need through a provider, without having to worry about how the state is created or maintained.
- **Automatic Updates:** When the state changes in the provider, any widgets that depend on that state are automatically rebuilt, ensuring that your UI always reflects the latest data.
- **Dependency Management:** Providers can depend on other providers, creating a clear hierarchy of data flow and making it easier to reason about how state is shared and updated in your app.

Using Provider: A Step-by-Step Guide

1. **Add the `provider` Package:** Include the `provider` package as a dependency in your `pubspec.yaml` file:

   ```
   dependencies: provider: ^6.0.0 # Or the latest version
   ```

2. **Create Providers:** Use different types of providers depending on the nature of your state:
- **ChangeNotifierProvider:** For state that can be updated using the `notifyListeners()` method. This is the most common type of provider.

   ```
   ChangeNotifierProvider( create: (context) => MyChangeNotifier(), child:
   MyApp(), // Wrap your app with the provider );
   ```

- **FutureProvider:** For state that is loaded asynchronously using a `Future` (e.g., network requests).

   ```
   FutureProvider( create: (context) => fetchData(), // Asynchronous data
   fetching function initialData: [], // Optional initial data while loading
   child: MyApp(), );
   ```

- **StreamProvider:** For state that is updated continuously using a Stream (e.g., real-time data).

```
StreamProvider( create: (context) => dataStream(), // Stream of data
initialData: 0, // Optional initial data child: MyApp(), );
```

3. **Consume State:** Access the state from providers within your widgets using:
- **context.watch<T>():** Rebuilds the widget whenever the provided state changes.
- **context.read<T>():** Accesses the state without causing the widget to rebuild.

```
final myData = context.watch<MyChangeNotifier>(); // Access the state
```

4. **Update State:** In your ChangeNotifier class, use the notifyListeners() method to trigger UI updates whenever the state changes.

```
class MyChangeNotifier with ChangeNotifier { int _count = 0; int get
count => _count; void incrementCounter() { _count++; notifyListeners();
// Notify listeners (widgets) of the change } }
```

By using Provider, you can create a clean and efficient state management system for your Flutter apps, reducing boilerplate and making your code more testable and maintainable.

BLoC: The Structured and Scalable Pattern

BLoC (Business Logic Component) is a popular and powerful architectural pattern for managing state in Flutter applications. It promotes a clear separation of concerns between the UI (presentation layer) and the business logic, resulting in code that is more organized, testable, and scalable.

The BLoC Philosophy: Separation of Concerns

At its core, BLoC revolves around the idea that your app's UI should be dumb. It shouldn't worry about where data comes from, how it's processed, or what actions to take in response to events. Instead, the UI should simply display the current state of the app and emit events when the user interacts with it.

The business logic, on the other hand, resides in a separate BLoC component. The BLoC receives events from the UI, processes them, and emits new states back to the UI. This separation makes your code easier to understand, maintain, and test.

The BLoC Mechanism: Streams and Events

BLoC relies heavily on Dart's streams (reactive programming) to manage communication between the UI and the business logic.

- **Events:** The UI sends events to the BLoC whenever the user interacts with it (e.g., tapping a button, entering text).
- **States:** The BLoC processes these events and emits new states.
- **Streams:** The UI subscribes to these state streams and rebuilds itself whenever a new state is emitted.

Advantages of BLoC:

- **Testability:** BLoC components are easy to unit test because they don't depend on UI-specific details.
- **Reusability:** BLoCs can be reused across different screens and even different apps.

- **Maintainability:** The clear separation of concerns makes your code more organized and easier to modify.
- **Predictable State Changes:** The unidirectional flow of data (events in, states out) makes it easier to reason about how your app's state changes.
- **Scalability:** The BLoC pattern scales well to large and complex applications.

Implementing a BLoC: A Simplified Example

Let's create a simple counter app using the BLoC pattern:

1. Define Events:

```
abstract class CounterEvent {} class IncrementEvent extends CounterEvent {}
class DecrementEvent extends CounterEvent {}
```

2. Define States:

```
class CounterState { final int count; CounterState(this.count); }
```

3. Create the BLoC:

```
class CounterBloc { int _count = 0; final _counterStateController =
StreamController<CounterState>(); Stream<CounterState> get state =>
_counterStateController.stream; CounterBloc() {
_counterStateController.sink.add(CounterState(_count)); // Initial state }
void increment() { _count++;
_counterStateController.sink.add(CounterState(_count)); } void decrement() {
_count--; _counterStateController.sink.add(CounterState(_count)); } void
dispose() { _counterStateController.close(); } }
```

4. Build the UI:

```
StreamBuilder<CounterState>( stream: counterBloc.state, // Subscribe to the
state stream builder: (context, snapshot) { return Center( child: Column(
mainAxisAlignment: MainAxisAlignment.center, children: [ Text(
'${snapshot.data?.count ?? 0}', style:
Theme.of(context).textTheme.headlineMedium, ), ElevatedButton(onPressed:
counterBloc.increment, child: const Text('Increment')),
ElevatedButton(onPressed: counterBloc.decrement, child: const
Text('Decrement')), ], ), ); }, );
```

In this example, the UI uses `StreamBuilder` to listen for state updates from the `CounterBloc`. Whenever the bloc emits a new state, the `StreamBuilder`'s `builder` function is called, which rebuilds the UI with the updated count.

By following this pattern, you can create well-structured Flutter apps that are easy to maintain and scale, even as your project grows in complexity.

Riverpod: The Flexible and Reactive Solution

Riverpod is a state-management library that builds upon the simplicity of Provider while addressing some of its limitations. It introduces powerful features like compile-time safety, improved testability, and enhanced flexibility, making it a compelling choice for managing state in complex Flutter applications.

Riverpod's Advantages:

- **Compile-Time Safety:** Riverpod leverages Dart's null safety features to catch potential errors during development. This reduces the likelihood of runtime crashes and helps you write more reliable code.
- **Improved Testability:** Riverpod's architecture makes it easy to mock and test your providers in isolation, ensuring that your state management logic works as expected.
- **Flexibility:** Unlike Provider, which requires providers to be created at the top of the widget tree, Riverpod providers can be created and accessed from anywhere in your app, giving you greater flexibility in how you organize your code.
- **Reactive Programming:** Riverpod embraces reactive programming principles, allowing you to easily manage streams of data and react to state changes in a clean and efficient manner.

Using Riverpod: A Step-by-Step Guide

1. **Add the Dependencies:** Include the necessary Riverpod packages as dependencies in your `pubspec.yaml` file:

```
dependencies: flutter_riverpod: ^2.0.0 # Or the latest version
```

2. **Create Providers:** Use different provider types to manage various kinds of state:
- **StateProvider:** For simple state that you want to read and update.

```
final counterProvider = StateProvider((ref) => 0);
```

- **FutureProvider:** For asynchronous operations that return a `Future`.

```
final weatherProvider = FutureProvider((ref) async { final response =
await http.get(Uri.parse('https://api.example.com/weather')); // ...
parse and return weather data });
```

- **StreamProvider:** For asynchronous operations that return a `Stream` of data.

```
final newsFeedProvider = StreamProvider((ref) async* { // ... yield news
articles from a stream });
```

3. **Consume State:** Access the state from providers within your widgets:
- **Consumer Widget:** A widget that allows you to rebuild specific parts of the UI when the provided state changes.

```
Consumer( builder: (context, ref, child) { final count =
ref.watch(counterProvider); // Read the counter state return Text('Count:
$count'); }, );
```

- **`ref.watch(provider)`:** This method allows you to watch a provider and rebuild the widget whenever the state changes.

```
@override Widget build(BuildContext context, WidgetRef ref) { final count
= ref.watch(counterProvider); // Watch the counter state return
Text('Count: $count'); }
```

4. **Update State:** Modify the state within providers using:
- `ref.read(provider).state = new_value:` For StateProvider.
- `ref.invalidate(provider):` To refetch data for FutureProvider and StreamProvider.

```
// Inside a widget ElevatedButton( onPressed: () {
ref.read(counterProvider.notifier).state++; // Increment the counter },
child: const Text('Increment'), );
```

Riverpod offers a flexible and efficient way to manage complex state scenarios in your Flutter applications. By embracing its features and adopting its recommended practices, you can write cleaner, more maintainable, and testable code.

Choosing the Right Approach

Selecting the ideal state management solution for your Flutter project is like choosing the right tool for a job. There's no single "best" approach, as the optimal choice depends on several factors.

Key Factors to Consider:

1. **App Complexity:**
- **Small Apps:** For simple apps with minimal state, `setState()` might be all you need. It's the most basic approach and doesn't require additional dependencies.
- **Medium-Sized Apps:** As your app grows, consider using `Provider`. It's relatively easy to learn, provides good performance, and integrates seamlessly with Flutter's widget tree.
- **Large and Complex Apps:** For apps with intricate state interactions or when performance optimization is crucial, BLoC or Riverpod might be better suited. Their structured approach and reactivity can help manage complex state flows more effectively.
2. **Team Familiarity:**
- The learning curve for different state management solutions varies. If your team is already familiar with a particular approach (e.g., BLoC from other reactive frameworks), it might be more efficient to stick with it.
- However, if your team is open to learning new technologies, consider exploring the benefits of Riverpod, which offers several advantages over Provider.
3. **Performance Requirements:**
- While all state management approaches in Flutter generally offer good performance, BLoC and Riverpod can be more performant in scenarios with frequent state updates or complex state dependencies. Their architecture helps minimize unnecessary widget rebuilds, leading to smoother animations and better responsiveness.

Recommendations for Different Scenarios:

App Complexity	Team Familiarity	Performance Needs	Recommended Approach
Simple	Any	Not critical	`setState()`, Provider

Medium	Familiar with Provider, open to learning Riverpod	Moderate	Provider, Riverpod
Complex	Experienced with reactive programming	High	BLoC, Riverpod

The Best Approach: It Depends

Remember, there's no one-size-fits-all answer when it comes to state management in Flutter. The "best" approach is the one that best aligns with your project's specific needs, your team's experience, and your overall development philosophy.

Here are some additional factors to consider:

- **Testability:** How important is it to be able to easily unit test your state management logic?
- **Scalability:** Will your app's state likely grow and become more complex over time?
- **Maintainability:** How important is it to have clean, well-organized code that's easy to understand and maintain?
- **Learning Curve:** How much time and effort are you willing to invest in learning a new state management approach?

By carefully weighing these factors and experimenting with different solutions, you can choose the state management approach that will empower you to build robust, scalable, and maintainable Flutter applications.

Chapter Summary

In this chapter, you took a deep dive into the realm of state management in Flutter, a crucial aspect of building dynamic and interactive applications. You learned about the fundamental concept of app state and the challenges that arise when dealing with shared state, complex state, asynchronous state, and state persistence.

We introduced you to three powerful state management approaches: Provider, BLoC, and Riverpod. Each of these solutions offers unique advantages and caters to different levels of app complexity and developer preferences.

You learned how Provider simplifies state management with its intuitive approach based on dependency injection, allowing widgets to access and update state seamlessly.

We then explored the BLoC pattern, which promotes a clear separation of business logic from UI components using streams and events. This structured approach enhances code testability, reusability, and maintainability, making it well-suited for large and complex applications.

Finally, you discovered Riverpod, a newer and more flexible state management solution that builds upon Provider's strengths while offering improved compile-time safety and testability.

By the end of this chapter, you gained a comprehensive understanding of state management in Flutter. You learned how to choose the right approach based on your app's size, complexity, performance needs, and team familiarity. Armed with this knowledge, you're now equipped to tackle the challenge of state management in your own Flutter projects and create robust, responsive, and maintainable applications.

Building Interactive Lists and Grids

Outline

- The Importance of Lists and Grids in Mobile UIs
- `ListView`: Your Scrollable List
- `GridView`: Your 2D Display
- Creating Custom List Items
- Handling User Interactions in Lists
- Efficiently Building Large Lists
- Infinite Scrolling and Pagination
- Chapter Summary

The Importance of Lists and Grids in Mobile UIs

Imagine trying to find a specific contact in a long, unorganized list of names. It would be a frustrating and time-consuming task. Lists and grids are the unsung heroes of mobile app design, bringing order and structure to large amounts of data. They play a crucial role in presenting information in a way that is easy for users to browse, understand, and interact with.

The Power of Structured Display

Lists and grids are designed to handle collections of data, such as contacts, products, images, or messages. By arranging these items in a clear and predictable manner, they help users quickly locate the information they need.

- **Visual Clarity:** Lists and grids present items in a structured format, making it easy to scan and compare different elements.
- **Efficient Browsing:** Scrollable lists and grids allow users to navigate through large amounts of data without feeling overwhelmed.
- **Intuitive Interaction:** Users can tap or click on individual items to view details, select options, or perform actions.

Examples of Lists and Grids in the Wild

Lists and grids are ubiquitous in mobile apps. Here are just a few examples:

- **Contacts List:** A list of contacts, usually sorted alphabetically or by recency, making it easy to find a specific person.
- **Product Catalog:** An e-commerce app might display products in a grid layout, allowing users to compare items visually and quickly find what they're looking for.
- **Image Gallery:** Photos or images are often presented in a grid or list, enabling users to swipe or scroll through their collection.
- **Social Media Feeds:** Posts, tweets, or updates are typically displayed in a vertical list, with newer items appearing at the top.
- **To-Do List App:** Tasks or to-dos are listed, often with checkboxes to mark completion or additional information displayed in a structured way.

Beyond the Basics: Interactive Lists and Grids

Lists and grids are not just static displays of data; they can also be highly interactive. Flutter allows you to add features like:

- **Tap Actions:** Tapping on a list item can open a new screen with details, trigger an action, or select the item.
- **Long Press Actions:** Long-pressing an item can reveal additional options like editing or deleting.
- **Swipe Actions:** Swiping on an item can reveal hidden actions or perform specific tasks.
- **Drag and Drop:** Users can reorder items in a list by dragging and dropping them.

By creating interactive lists and grids, you can make your app more engaging and user-friendly, allowing users to easily navigate, select, and manipulate data.

`ListView`: Your Scrollable List

The `ListView` widget is your go-to tool for displaying a collection of items in a scrollable list. Whether it's a simple list of contacts, a long list of news articles, or a product catalog, `ListView` provides the flexibility and efficiency you need to present data in an organized and user-friendly manner.

`ListView` Constructors: Choosing the Right One

Flutter offers three main constructors for creating `ListView` widgets, each tailored for different scenarios:

1. **ListView (Default Constructor):**
   - Ideal for small lists with a known and fixed number of items.
   - You directly pass a list of child widgets to the constructor.
   - Simple to use but can be inefficient for large lists as all widgets are built at once.

     ```
     ListView( children: <Widget>[ ListTile( title: Text('Item 1'), ),
     ListTile( title: Text('Item 2'), ), // ... more items ], );
     ```

2. **ListView.builder:**
   - Designed for large or infinite lists where the number of items is not predetermined.
   - Widgets are built lazily (on demand) as the user scrolls, improving performance.
   - Requires two essential properties:
     - `itemBuilder`: A function that builds each list item widget dynamically.
     - `itemCount`: The total number of items in the list.

       ```
       ListView.builder( itemCount: 100, // Total number of items
       itemBuilder: (BuildContext context, int index) { return
       ListTile( title: Text('Item $index'), ); }, );
       ```

3. **ListView.separated:**
   - Similar to `ListView.builder`, but adds separators between list items.
   - Requires an additional `separatorBuilder` property to create the separator widget.

     ```
     ListView.separated( itemCount: 100, itemBuilder: (BuildContext
     context, int index) { /* ... */ }, separatorBuilder: (BuildContext
     context, int index) { return Divider(); // Add a Divider as the
     separator }, );
     ```

`itemBuilder` and `itemCount` in `ListView.builder`

- **itemBuilder:**
  - A function that takes the `BuildContext` and the `index` of the item to be built.

- ○ It returns the widget to be displayed for that item.
- ○ This function is called repeatedly as the user scrolls, so it should be efficient.
- **itemCount:**
  - ○ Specifies the total number of items in the list.

Building Basic Lists

You can include any type of widget within a ListView. Here are some examples:

- **Text List:**

  ```
  ListView( children: [ Text('Item 1'), Text('Item 2'), Text('Item 3'), ],
  );
  ```

- **Image List:**

  ```
  ListView.builder( itemCount: imageUrls.length, itemBuilder: (context,
  index) { return Image.network(imageUrls[index]); }, );
  ```

By mastering the ListView widget and its various constructors, you'll be able to create flexible, efficient, and visually appealing lists that display any type of content you need.

GridView: Your 2D Display

While lists excel at displaying data linearly, the GridView widget shines when you want to showcase items in a visually appealing grid layout. This is perfect for image galleries, product catalogs, dashboards, and other scenarios where a two-dimensional arrangement enhances the user experience.

GridView Constructors: The Right Fit for Your Grid

Flutter offers three main constructors for creating GridView widgets, each catering to different layout preferences:

1. **GridView.count:**
- **Fixed Number of Columns:** You specify the number of columns you want in the grid.
- **Auto-Row Calculation:** Flutter automatically calculates the number of rows based on the number of items and columns.
- **Ideal for:** When you know the exact number of columns you want and don't mind Flutter managing the row count.

  ```
  GridView.count( crossAxisCount: 2, // Two columns children:
  List.generate(8, (index) { return Center(child: Text('Item $index')); },
  );
  ```

2. **GridView.extent:**
- **Max Item Width:** You specify the maximum width each item can have.
- **Auto-Column Calculation:** Flutter dynamically determines the number of columns based on the available space and the maximum item width.
- **Ideal for:** When you want items to have a consistent width but the number of columns to adjust based on screen size.

```
GridView.extent( maxCrossAxisExtent: 150, // Maximum width of each item
children: List.generate(8, (index) { return Center(child: Text('Item
$index')); }), );
```

3. **GridView.builder:**
- **Dynamic Item Generation:** Similar to `ListView.builder`, this constructor builds grid items lazily as the user scrolls, making it efficient for large datasets.
- **gridDelegate:** A property that controls the layout of the grid, such as the number of columns, spacing, and child aspect ratio.
- **itemBuilder:** A function that builds each grid item based on its index.
- **itemCount:** The total number of items in the grid.
- **Ideal for:** When you have a large or potentially infinite number of items to display.

```
GridView.builder( gridDelegate:
SliverGridDelegateWithFixedCrossAxisCount(crossAxisCount: 2), itemCount:
100, itemBuilder: (context, index) { return Center(child: Text('Item
$index')); }, );
```

GridView **Examples:**

- **Image Grid:**

```
GridView.count( crossAxisCount: 3, children: List.generate(images.length,
(index) { return Image.network(images[index]); }), );
```

- **Product Catalog:**

```
GridView.builder( gridDelegate:
SliverGridDelegateWithFixedCrossAxisCount(crossAxisCount: 2), itemCount:
products.length, itemBuilder: (context, index) { return
ProductCard(product: products[index]); }, );
```

- **Dashboard with Tiles:**

```
GridView.extent( maxCrossAxisExtent: 200, children: [
DashboardTile(title: 'Sales', icon: Icons.monetization_on),
DashboardTile(title: 'Orders', icon: Icons.shopping_cart), // ...more
tiles ], );
```

By mastering the `GridView` widget, you'll be able to create dynamic and visually engaging grid layouts that adapt to different screen sizes and data sets, adding a touch of elegance to your Flutter apps.

Creating Custom List Items

While Flutter's built-in `ListTile` widget is convenient for simple list items, you'll often need to create custom widgets to represent more complex data or to achieve specific visual designs.

Designing Your Custom Item Widget

1. **Create a New Widget Class:** Define a new stateless or stateful widget class, depending on whether your list item needs to manage dynamic data.

```
class ProductItem extends StatelessWidget { // ... (Add properties and
constructor here) @override Widget build(BuildContext context) { // ...
(Build your list item's UI here) } }
```

2. **Add Properties:** Declare properties to store the data for each list item (e.g., product name, image URL, price).

```
final String name; final String imageUrl; final double price; const
ProductItem({ Key? key, required this.name, required this.imageUrl,
required this.price, }) : super(key: key);
```

3. **Build the UI:** Use layout widgets like Row and Column to arrange the elements of your list item. Include widgets like Text, Image, Icon, and others to display the item's data.

```
@override Widget build(BuildContext context) { return Card( child: Row(
crossAxisAlignment: CrossAxisAlignment.start, children: [
Image.network(imageUrl, width: 100), Padding( padding: const
EdgeInsets.all(8.0), child: Column( crossAxisAlignment:
CrossAxisAlignment.start, children: [ Text(name, style:
TextStyle(fontWeight: FontWeight.bold)),
Text('\$${price.toStringAsFixed(2)}'), ], ), ), ], ), ); }
```

Customizing Appearance

You can use various styling techniques to enhance the look of your custom list items:

- **Colors:** Apply colors to the background, text, or icons.
- **Fonts:** Use different fonts and font sizes to create a visual hierarchy.
- **Spacing:** Add padding and margins for better readability and aesthetics.
- **Borders and Shadows:** Apply borders, shadows, or rounded corners to make your list items stand out.

Example: A Product Catalog

```
ListView.builder( itemCount: products.length, itemBuilder: (context, index) {
return ProductItem( name: products[index].name, imageUrl:
products[index].imageUrl, price: products[index].price, ); }, );
```

By creating custom list item widgets, you have complete control over the appearance and layout of each item in your list, allowing you to build highly customized and visually engaging UIs for your Flutter apps.

Handling User Interactions in Lists

Lists become truly powerful when they respond to user interactions. Flutter makes it easy to create interactive lists where users can tap, long-press, or perform other gestures to trigger actions within your app.

Adding Interactivity to List Items

The key to making list items interactive is wrapping them with widgets that detect user input:

1. **InkWell:** A simple way to make a widget respond to taps. It provides visual feedback (like a ripple effect) when tapped.
2. **GestureDetector:** A more versatile widget that allows you to detect a wider range of gestures, such as double taps, long presses, and pans.

```
InkWell( onTap: () { // Code to execute when tapped
_showItemDetails(index); // Show details for the tapped item }, child:
ListTile( // ... your list item content ), );
```

Explanation: The ListTile containing the item is wrapped by InkWell. When the user taps on this tile, the onTap function will be called, which triggers the function to show item details, in this case _showItemDetails().

Handling Tap Events

Inside the onTap callback (or other gesture callbacks), you can implement the desired behavior for the interaction:

- **Navigation:** Navigate to a new screen that displays more details about the tapped item.
- **Data Updates:** Modify the underlying data associated with the list item (e.g., toggle a "favorite" status).
- **Display Details:** Show a dialog, bottom sheet, or other UI element that provides more information about the item.
- **Trigger Actions:** Perform any other relevant actions, such as adding an item to a cart, liking a post, or starting a download.

Using onLongPress for Contextual Actions

The onLongPress callback is triggered when the user performs a long press on a list item. It's often used to provide contextual actions like:

- **Deleting an Item:** Show a confirmation dialog and remove the item from the list if confirmed.
- **Editing an Item:** Navigate to an edit screen where the user can modify the item's details.
- **Sharing an Item:** Allow the user to share the item's content with others.

Visually Indicating Selection

To provide visual feedback when an item is selected, you can use techniques like:

- **Highlighting:** Change the background color of the selected item.
- **Checkmarks:** Display a checkmark icon next to the selected item.
- **Animation:** Create a subtle animation to indicate that the item is active or selected.

Here's an example that shows the ListTile with a different background color when selected:

```
ListTile( //Other properties of ListTile widget selected: selectedIndex ==
index, // highlight if selected selectedTileColor: Colors.grey[200], )
```

By combining these techniques and leveraging Flutter's rich gesture system, you can transform your lists and grids into highly interactive components that respond intuitively to user input, making your app more engaging and user-friendly.

Efficiently Building Large Lists

While Flutter's lists and grids are powerful tools for displaying data, you might encounter performance bottlenecks when dealing with large datasets. Rendering hundreds or thousands of items simultaneously can strain resources and lead to sluggish scrolling and UI jank. Thankfully, Flutter provides a solution: virtualization.

Virtualization: Rendering on Demand

Virtualization is a technique where only the items currently visible on the screen are rendered. As the user scrolls, Flutter dynamically creates and destroys widgets for the items entering and leaving the viewport. This significantly reduces the memory footprint and computational overhead, leading to smoother scrolling and faster load times.

`ListView.builder` and `GridView.builder`: The Virtualization Experts

The `.builder` constructors of `ListView` and `GridView` are your go-to tools for implementing virtualization. Instead of building all items upfront, they only create widgets for the items that need to be displayed at any given moment.

```
ListView.builder( itemCount: 10000, // Large number of items itemBuilder:
(context, index) { return ListTile( title: Text('Item $index'), ); }, );
```

In this example, even though `itemCount` is set to 10,000, Flutter will only build a few list items at a time, significantly improving performance.

Optimizing List Item Widgets: Tips for Peak Performance

To further enhance the performance of your lists and grids, consider the following tips when designing your list item widgets:

1. **Use const Constructors:** When possible, mark your list item widgets as `const`. This tells Flutter that the widget's configuration won't change, allowing it to cache and reuse the widget instances, reducing unnecessary rebuilds.
2. **Simplify `build()` Methods:** Avoid performing complex calculations or network requests within the `build()` method of your list item widgets. If you need to fetch data or perform computations, do it outside the `build` method and pass the results as parameters to the widget.
3. **Minimize Widget Nesting:** Deeply nested widget trees can be expensive to build and render. Strive for flatter widget structures to reduce complexity and improve performance.
4. **Cache Images:** For lists or grids containing images, use the `cached_network_image` package or other caching mechanisms to avoid re-downloading images repeatedly.
5. **Consider SliverList and SliverGrid:** For more advanced use cases, explore the `SliverList` and `SliverGrid` widgets, which provide even finer control over rendering and layout behaviors.

Performance Testing: Measure and Optimize

Always test your app's performance, especially on lower-end devices or with large datasets. Use Flutter's performance profiling tools to identify any bottlenecks and optimize your list or grid implementation accordingly.

By understanding the principles of virtualization and applying these optimization tips, you can ensure that your Flutter lists and grids deliver a smooth, responsive, and enjoyable user experience, even with large amounts of data.

Infinite Scrolling and Pagination

When dealing with large datasets, it's often inefficient and unnecessary to load all the data upfront. Infinite scrolling and pagination are two techniques that allow you to fetch and display data incrementally as the user interacts with your app.

Infinite Scrolling: A Seamless Experience

Infinite scrolling creates the illusion of an endless list or grid. As the user scrolls down and approaches the end of the currently loaded items, your app automatically fetches and appends more data to the list, creating a continuous scrolling experience.

Benefits of Infinite Scrolling:

- **Improved Perceived Performance:** The app appears to load faster initially because it only fetches a small chunk of data to start with.
- **Reduced Memory Usage:** Only the currently visible items and a few surrounding items are loaded into memory, conserving resources.
- **Enhanced User Experience:** Users can seamlessly browse through large datasets without explicit pagination controls.

Pagination: Loading in Chunks

Pagination is a similar concept to infinite scrolling, but it divides the data into distinct pages. As the user reaches the end of a page, the app fetches the next page of data. This approach provides more control over data loading and can be more efficient for very large datasets.

Benefits of Pagination:

- **Precise Control:** You have more control over when and how much data is loaded.
- **Reduced Server Load:** Fetching data in smaller chunks can reduce the load on your backend server.
- **Clearer Progress Indication:** Users can see clear page numbers or indicators, giving them a better sense of their position within the dataset.

Implementing Infinite Scrolling or Pagination in Flutter

Flutter provides several ways to implement infinite scrolling and pagination. You can use the `ScrollController` to listen for scroll events and trigger data fetching when the user reaches a certain point.

Here's a simplified example using `ListView.builder` and a `scrollController`:

```
final ScrollController _scrollController = ScrollController();
ListView.builder( controller: _scrollController, itemCount: items.length + 1,
// +1 for loading indicator itemBuilder: (context, index) { if (index ==
items.length) { return Center(child: CircularProgressIndicator()); // Loading
indicator } else { return ListTile( title: Text('Item $index'), ); } }, );
_scrollController.addListener(() { if (_scrollController.position.pixels ==
```

```
_scrollController.position.maxScrollExtent) { // Reached the end, fetch more
data _fetchMoreData(); } });
```

Packages for Easier Implementation:

Consider using the `infinite_scroll_pagination` package, which simplifies the implementation of infinite scrolling and provides features like error handling and placeholder widgets.

Choosing Between Infinite Scrolling and Pagination

The choice between infinite scrolling and pagination depends on your specific use case and the nature of your data:

- **Infinite Scrolling:** Suitable for continuous, endless feeds like social media or news apps.
- **Pagination:** Better for structured data with a finite number of items or when users need to jump to specific pages.

By carefully considering these factors and choosing the appropriate technique, you can enhance the user experience of your Flutter app by making it more responsive, efficient, and enjoyable to use.

Chapter Summary

In this chapter, you dove into the world of lists and grids, essential components for displaying collections of data in Flutter apps. You learned that these UI elements provide a structured and user-friendly way for users to browse, select, and interact with information.

We explored the `ListView` widget, your primary tool for creating scrollable lists. You learned about different constructors for building lists, including `ListView`, `ListView.builder`, and `ListView.separated`, each catering to different scenarios. You discovered how to use the `itemBuilder` and `itemCount` properties to dynamically create list items and control the list's length. We also provided examples of building basic lists with text, images, and other widgets.

Next, we introduced the `GridView` widget, perfect for displaying items in a grid layout. We discussed three constructors: `GridView.count` for fixed-column grids, `GridView.extent` for grids with maximum item widths, and `GridView.builder` for dynamically building grids. You learned how to use properties like `gridDelegate`, `itemBuilder`, and `itemCount` to create flexible and efficient grids.

You learned how to build custom list item widgets, combining different widgets and styling techniques to create visually appealing and informative items. We demonstrated how to arrange elements within list items using layout widgets like `Row` and `Column` and discussed customizing their appearance with colors, fonts, and spacing.

We then delved into making lists interactive, showing you how to add tap and long-press gestures to list items using `InkWell` and `GestureDetector`. You explored how to handle these interactions to trigger actions like navigation, data updates, and item deletion.

Finally, we addressed performance considerations when working with large lists, introducing the concept of virtualization and explaining how `ListView.builder` and `GridView.builder` implement it. We provided practical tips for optimizing list item widgets and ensuring smooth performance, even with large datasets.

Armed with this knowledge of lists and grids, you're now ready to build dynamic and user-friendly interfaces that effectively present and manage collections of data in your Flutter apps.

Section IV:
Building Real-World Apps

Creating a Simple To-Do List App

Outline

- What We'll Build
- Project Setup
- Building the UI
- Managing the To-Do List State
- Adding and Removing Tasks
- Marking Tasks as Complete
- Styling the App
- Next Steps (Optional)
- Chapter Summary

What We'll Build

In this chapter, we'll roll up our sleeves and build a simple yet functional to-do list app in Flutter. This app will allow users to:

- **Add New Tasks:** Type in a task description and add it to their to-do list.
- **View Tasks:** See a list of all their current tasks.
- **Mark Tasks as Complete:** Check off tasks that have been finished.
- **Delete Tasks:** Remove tasks they no longer need.

The UI will be simple:

- A text field at the top for entering new tasks
- A scrollable list displaying each task with a checkbox to mark completion
- A simple, clean design with intuitive interactions

Why Build a To-Do List App?

This project is the perfect starting point for your Flutter app development journey. Here's why:

- **Practical Application:** To-do list apps are incredibly useful and demonstrate core concepts like state management, user input, and list manipulation.
- **Building Confidence:** Successfully creating your first functional app will boost your confidence and motivation to tackle more complex projects.
- **Hands-On Learning:** There's no better way to solidify your Flutter knowledge than by applying it to a real-world scenario. You'll see how the widgets, layouts, and concepts you've learned come together to create a complete app.

Get Ready to Code!

In the following sections, we'll guide you through the entire process of building this to-do list app, from project setup to adding features and styling. By the end of this chapter, you'll have a working app that you can proudly show off as your first Flutter creation!

Project Setup

Before we start building our to-do list app, let's create a new Flutter project. You have two main options for this: using the command line or an integrated development environment (IDE) like Android Studio or Visual Studio Code (VS Code).

Option 1: Command Line

1. **Open Your Terminal:** Launch your terminal (macOS/Linux) or command prompt (Windows).
2. **Navigate to Your Workspace:** Use the `cd` (change directory) command to navigate to the folder where you want to create your project.
3. **Create the Project:** Run the following command, replacing `simple_todo_app` with your desired project name:

```
flutter create simple_todo_app
```

Flutter will create a new folder named `simple_todo_app` with the basic project structure.

Option 2: Android Studio or VS Code

1. **Open the IDE:** Launch Android Studio or VS Code.
2. **Start a New Project:**
   - **Android Studio:** Click "Start a new Flutter project" on the welcome screen.
   - **VS Code:** Open the Command Palette (Ctrl+Shift+P or Cmd+Shift+P) and type "Flutter: New Project."
3. **Follow the Wizard:** The IDE will guide you through a project creation wizard. Choose "Flutter Application" as the project type and provide the project name (`simple_todo_app`).
4. **Choose a Location:** Select a folder where you want to save your project.
5. **Finish:** The IDE will create the project with the default structure.

Project Structure Overview

Let's take a quick look at the essential parts of your Flutter project:

- **lib folder:** This is where you'll write your Dart code. The `main.dart` file is the entry point of your app.
- **pubspec.yaml:** This file is used to declare your project's dependencies (external packages you use) and assets (images, fonts, etc.).
- **android and ios folders:** These folders contain platform-specific code and configuration for building your app for Android and iOS.
- **test folder:** This folder is where you'll write unit and widget tests for your app.

Create the `main.dart` File

If you used the command line to create the project, you'll already have a `main.dart` file. If you used an IDE, it might have created some boilerplate code in `main.dart`. You can safely replace this code with a simple starting point:

```
import 'package:flutter/material.dart'; void main() { runApp(MyApp()); } class
MyApp extends StatelessWidget { @override Widget build(BuildContext context) {
return MaterialApp( title: 'Simple To-Do App', theme: ThemeData(
primarySwatch: Colors.blue, ), home: Scaffold( appBar: AppBar( title: Text('My
To-Do List'), ), body: Center( child: Text('Your tasks will go here'), ), ),
); } }
```

Create an `assets` Folder (Optional)

If you plan to use any images or icons in your app, create an `assets` folder in your project's root directory to store them. Remember to declare your assets in the `pubspec.yaml` file as explained in Chapter 11.

With your project set up, you're ready to start adding the UI elements and functionality for your to-do list app.

Building the UI

Now that our project is set up, let's start building the user interface (UI) of our to-do list app. We'll combine various widgets to create the necessary elements for adding, displaying, and managing tasks.

Core UI Elements:

1. **App Bar:**
   - **Purpose:** Provides a title for the screen and can include actions like a search button or menu icon.
   - **Widget:** AppBar
   - **Code:**

     ```
     appBar: AppBar( title: Text('My To-Do List'), ),
     ```

2. **Text Field:**
   - **Purpose:** Allows the user to input new task descriptions.
   - **Widget:** TextField
   - **Code:**

     ```
     TextField( controller: _textController, // Controller to manage the
     text input decoration: const InputDecoration(labelText: 'Add a new
     task'), onSubmitted: (value) => _addTask(value), // Add task when
     user presses Enter ),
     ```

     (Remember to declare _textController variable of type TextEditingController in your state class.)

3. **List View:**

   - **Purpose:** Displays the list of tasks.
   - **Widget:** ListView.builder (for dynamic lists)
   - **Code:**

     ```
     ListView.builder( itemCount: _todos.length, itemBuilder: (context, index)
     { return ListTile( title: Text(_todos[index].title), leading: Checkbox(
     ```

```
value: _todos[index].completed, onChanged: (value) => _toggleTodo(index,
value!), ), trailing: IconButton( icon: Icon(Icons.delete), onPressed: ()
=> _removeTodo(index), ), ); }, ),
```

(The _todos variable will hold a list of task objects, and the _toggleTodo and _removeTodo methods will be implemented later.)

4. **Checkbox:**
   - **Purpose:** Allows the user to mark a task as complete.
   - **Widget:** Checkbox
   - **Code:** (See usage within ListTile above)
5. **Add Button (Optional):**
   - **Purpose:** Provides an alternative way to add a new task (besides pressing Enter in the text field).
   - **Widget:** ElevatedButton (or other button types)
   - **Code:** (You would typically place this within a Row with the TextField)

```
ElevatedButton( onPressed: () => _addTask(_textController.text),
child: const Text('Add'), ),
```

Arranging UI Elements with Layout Widgets

- **Column:** Use a Column to arrange the App Bar, text field, and list view vertically.
- **Row:** Optionally, use a Row to place the text field and add button next to each other.
- **Other Layout Widgets:** You can further refine your layout using widgets like Padding (to add spacing around widgets), Container (to add background colors or borders), or Expanded (to make widgets fill available space).

Putting It All Together

You can now assemble these elements into a basic UI structure:

```
// Inside the Scaffold's body: body: Column( children: [ // ... TextField and
optional Add Button in a Row Expanded( child: ListView.builder( // ... List
view code ), ), ], ),
```

With this basic structure, you have the foundation for building a simple to-do list app in Flutter! In the next sections, we will handle state, add and remove tasks, and style the app to make it more appealing.

Managing the To-Do List State

Now that we have the basic UI structure for our to-do list app, we need a way to store and manage the list of tasks. This involves understanding state management, a fundamental concept in Flutter for handling data that changes over time.

Storing Task Data: Lists and Custom Objects

There are a few ways you can store the to-do list data:

1. **List of Strings:** The simplest approach is to use a List<String> to store each task as a string.

```
List<String> _todos = [];
```

2. **List of Custom Objects:** For more flexibility, you can create a custom Task class to represent each to-do item, including properties like the task's title, completion status, and any other relevant details.

```
class Task { String title; bool completed; Task({required this.title,
this.completed = false}); } List<Task> _todos = [];
```

State Management: Tracking Changes

In Flutter, state management refers to the process of keeping track of data that changes over time and updating the UI accordingly. In our to-do list app, the state is the list of tasks itself. When the user adds, removes, or marks a task as complete, the state needs to be updated, and the UI needs to be rebuilt to reflect these changes.

setState(): The Simple Solution

For our simple to-do list app, we can use the setState() method to manage the state. Here's how it works:

1. Store your to-do list data (either as a list of strings or a list of Task objects) in a state variable (e.g., _todos).
2. When the user interacts with the app (e.g., adds a task, toggles a checkbox), modify the _todos list accordingly.
3. Call setState() to tell Flutter that the state has changed. This will trigger a rebuild of the relevant parts of the UI, reflecting the updated to-do list.

Beyond setState(): Larger Projects and Scalability

While setState() is sufficient for our simple app, larger projects with more complex state interactions might benefit from more structured state management solutions like Provider, BLoC, or Riverpod. These approaches offer better organization, separation of concerns, and improved performance in larger apps. However, for our beginner-friendly to-do list, setState() will do the job just fine!

Adding and Removing Tasks

Now that we have a way to store and display our to-do list, let's add the functionality to dynamically add and remove tasks.

Adding Tasks

1. **Capture Input:**
   - Use a TextEditingController to get the text the user entered in the TextField.
   - Create a function (e.g., _addTask) that takes the text as input.

     ```
     final TextEditingController _textController =
     TextEditingController(); void _addTask(String taskText) { // ...
     implementation below }
     ```

2. **Create a Task Object (Optional):**
   - If you're using a custom Task class, create a new Task object with the input text and completed set to false.

```
Task newTask = Task(title: taskText, completed: false);
```

3. **Update the State:**
   ○ Add the new task (or the text directly) to your _todos list.
   ○ Call setState() to trigger a UI rebuild.
   ○ Clear the text field.

```
setState(() { _todos.add(newTask); // If using Task class, or
_todos.add(taskText); for a list of strings });
_textController.clear();
```

4. **Trigger the Function:**
   ○ Call the _addTask function when the user presses Enter in the text field or taps an "Add" button.

```
TextField( // ... Other properties onSubmitted: (value) =>
_addTask(value), ), ElevatedButton( onPressed: () =>
_addTask(_textController.text), child: const Text('Add'), ),
```

Removing Tasks

1. **Add Delete Buttons or Gestures:**
   ○ Add an IconButton with a delete icon (e.g., Icons.delete) to each list item.
   ○ Optionally, you can add a "swipe to delete" gesture using the Dismissible widget.

```
// ... within your `ListTile` in the `ListView.builder`: trailing:
IconButton( icon: Icon(Icons.delete), onPressed: () =>
_removeTodo(index), // `index` is the position in the list ),
```

2. **Create a Remove Function:**
   ○ Create a function (e.g., _removeTodo) that takes the index of the task to be removed.

```
void _removeTodo(int index) { // ... implementation below }
```

3. **Update the State:**
   ○ Remove the task at the specified index from your _todos list.
   ○ Call setState() to trigger a UI rebuild.

```
setState(() { _todos.removeAt(index); });
```

Putting it Together

With these functions in your stateful widget's State class, your to-do list app will be able to add and remove tasks dynamically, providing a more interactive user experience.

```
class _MyToDoAppState extends State<MyToDoApp> { final List<Task> _todos = [];
// Use List<String> if not using a Task class final TextEditingController
_textController = TextEditingController(); // ... functions to add and remove
tasks @override Widget build(BuildContext context) { // UI code with
ListView.builder, etc. } }
```

Marking Tasks as Complete

A key feature of any to-do list app is the ability to mark tasks as complete. This gives users a sense of accomplishment and helps them keep track of their progress.

Checkboxes: The Visual Indicator

In Flutter, we use the Checkbox widget to provide a visual toggle for marking tasks as done. The checkbox's state (checked or unchecked) will correspond to the completion status of the task in your app's state.

Updating State and UI:

Here's how you can integrate a checkbox into your to-do list and update both the state and the UI accordingly:

1. **Incorporate the Checkbox:**
   - Within the ListTile of each task in your ListView.builder, add a Checkbox widget.
   - Set the value property of the Checkbox to the completed property of the corresponding Task object in your list.

   ```
   ListTile( // ... leading: Checkbox( value: _todos[index].completed,
   // Link to the task's completion status onChanged: (value) =>
   _toggleTodo(index, value!), ), // ... ),
   ```

2. **Create the Toggle Function:**
   - Create a function (e.g., _toggleTodo) that handles the checkbox's onChanged event.
   - The function should:
     - Take the index of the task and the new value (true/false) as arguments.
     - Update the completed property of the corresponding Task object in your list.
     - Call setState() to trigger a UI rebuild.

   ```
   void _toggleTodo(int index, bool isChecked) { setState(() {
   _todos[index].completed = isChecked; }); }
   ```

3. **Visual Feedback (Optional):**
   - To provide visual feedback, modify the appearance of the ListTile based on the completed status.
   - For example, you could add a strikethrough effect to the text of completed tasks.

   ```
   ListTile( // ... title: Text( _todos[index].title, style: TextStyle(
   decoration: _todos[index].completed ? TextDecoration.lineThrough :
   null, ), ), // ... ),
   ```

Example: Complete Code for Adding, Removing and Marking Complete

```
class _MyToDoAppState extends State<MyToDoApp> { final List<Task> _todos = [];
final TextEditingController _textController = TextEditingController(); void
_addTask(String taskText) { setState(() { _todos.add(Task(title: taskText,
completed: false)); }); _textController.clear(); } void _removeTodo(int index)
{ setState(() { _todos.removeAt(index); }); } void _toggleTodo(int index, bool
```

```
isChecked) { setState(() { _todos[index].completed = isChecked; }); }
@override Widget build(BuildContext context) { return MaterialApp( title:
'Simple To-Do App', // ... (other UI code including the AppBar) body: Column(
children: [ TextField( controller: _textController, decoration: const
InputDecoration( labelText: 'Add a new task', hintText: 'Enter task'), ),
ElevatedButton( onPressed: () => _addTask(_textController.text), child:
Text('Add Task') ), Expanded( child: ListView.builder( itemCount:
_todos.length, itemBuilder: (context, index) { return ListTile( title: Text(
_todos[index].title, style: TextStyle( decoration: _todos[index].completed ?
TextDecoration.lineThrough : null, ), ), leading: Checkbox( value:
_todos[index].completed, onChanged: (value) => _toggleTodo(index, value!), ),
trailing: IconButton( icon: Icon(Icons.delete), onPressed: () =>
_removeTodo(index), ), ); }, ), ), ], )); } } class Task { String title; bool
completed; Task({required this.title, this.completed = false}); }
```

By implementing these features, you've made your to-do list app truly interactive, allowing users to easily manage and track their tasks.

Styling the App

Now that our to-do list app is functional, let's make it more visually appealing! With Flutter's extensive styling options, you can easily customize the look and feel of your app to match your preferences and brand identity.

Basic Styling Enhancements:

1. **Colors:**
   - **Background:** Use the Scaffold widget's backgroundColor property to set a background color for the app. You can use a light, neutral color for a clean look.
   - **App Bar:** Customize the AppBar's backgroundColor and foregroundColor properties.
   - **Text and Icons:** Use the TextStyle class to change the color of text and icons in your widgets (e.g., list tiles, buttons).

     ```
     Scaffold( backgroundColor: Colors.grey[100], // Light grey
     background appBar: AppBar( backgroundColor: Colors.blue, // Blue app
     bar title: Text( 'My To-Do List', style: TextStyle(color:
     Colors.white), // White text ), ), // ... );
     ```

2. **Padding and Margins:**
   - Use Padding widgets to add spacing around individual widgets.
   - Use Container widgets with padding or margin properties to control spacing around groups of widgets.

     ```
     Padding( padding: const EdgeInsets.all(16.0), // Add padding to all
     sides child: TextField( // ... ), ),
     ```

3. **Custom Fonts:**

- If you have custom fonts, import them into your project's `assets` folder and declare them in the `pubspec.yaml` file.
- Use the `TextStyle` class's `fontFamily` property to apply the custom font to your text.

```
// In pubspec.yaml flutter: fonts: - family: Raleway fonts: - asset:
assets/fonts/Raleway-Regular.ttf - asset:
assets/fonts/Raleway-Bold.ttf // In your code Text( 'This is text in
a custom font', style: TextStyle(fontFamily: 'Raleway'), ),
```

4. **Other Styling Options:**
   - **Rounded Corners:** Use the `BorderRadius` class to add rounded corners to your widgets (e.g., the `TextField`, buttons, or the list items).
   - **Shadows:** Use the `BoxShadow` class to add shadows to your widgets.
   - **Decorations:** The `Container` widget's `decoration` property allows you to add various visual effects like gradients, borders, and background images.

Personalizing Your App:

- **Theme:** If you want to apply a consistent style to your entire app, consider creating a custom theme using `ThemeData` and applying it to your `MaterialApp` widget.
- **Material Design 3:** Flutter 3.0 supports Material Design 3, so experiment with its new color schemes, components and dynamic color.
- **Explore Widgets:** Flutter offers a vast collection of widgets with their own styling options. Explore and experiment to discover the possibilities!

Remember, styling is a creative process. Don't be afraid to experiment with different colors, fonts, and visual elements to create a to-do list app that reflects your unique style and makes you happy to use.

Next Steps (Optional)

Congratulations! You've successfully built your first Flutter app—a simple to-do list. But why stop there? Flutter's flexibility and vast array of features allow you to expand upon this foundation and create a truly powerful and personalized to-do list experience. Here are some ideas to get you started:

1. **Add Due Dates:**
   - Enhance task management by allowing users to set due dates for each task.
   - You can use date and time pickers (`showDatePicker`, `showTimePicker`) to let users select the due date and time.
   - Visually indicate overdue tasks (e.g., change their color or add an icon).
   - Consider sorting the tasks by due date to prioritize upcoming deadlines.
2. **Prioritize Tasks:**
   - Enable users to prioritize tasks based on their importance or urgency.
   - Add a priority level (e.g., high, medium, low) to each task.
   - Allow users to sort the list by priority.
   - Visually differentiate tasks with different priorities (e.g., using colors or icons).
3. **Filter or Sort Tasks:**
   - Implement filtering options to show only completed or uncompleted tasks.
   - Add sorting functionality to order tasks by creation date, due date, or priority.
   - Consider using a `DropdownButton` or a custom filter bar to provide these options.
4. **Persist the To-Do List Data:**
   - Currently, your to-do list data is lost when the app closes. To make the data persistent, you can store it locally on the device using:

- **shared_preferences package:** For simple key-value storage.
- **Local database (SQLite):** For more structured data storage.
- **Cloud storage (Firebase):** For syncing data across multiple devices.
5. **Advanced UI Interactions:**
   - **Drag and Drop Reordering:** Allow users to rearrange tasks by dragging and dropping them.
   - **Swipe Actions:** Enable actions like marking a task complete or deleting it by swiping left or right on a list item.
   - **Custom Animations:** Add custom animations to transitions between screens or when adding or removing tasks.

Explore Further!

These are just a few ideas to get you started. The possibilities are endless! As you become more comfortable with Flutter, explore other features like theming, animations, gestures, and advanced state management techniques to create a truly unique and feature-rich to-do list app.

Feel free to be creative and experiment with different functionalities. Your to-do list app is your playground for learning and exploring the vast capabilities of Flutter!

Chapter Summary

In this chapter, you took a significant step forward in your Flutter journey by learning how to build interactive to-do list apps. We started by defining the goals of our project and envisioning the final product. Then, we guided you through the initial project setup, whether using the command line or a code editor like Android Studio or VS Code.

You learned how to construct the core UI elements of a to-do list app, including the app bar, text field for adding tasks, list view to display tasks, checkbox to mark completion, and an optional "Add" button. We also explored how to arrange these elements using layout widgets like Row and Column.

Next, we tackled the essential concept of state management, explaining how it's used to track changes in your app's data and update the UI accordingly. While we opted for the simple setState() method for this project, we highlighted that larger, more complex apps might benefit from more sophisticated state management solutions.

You then learned how to add new tasks to the list by capturing user input from the text field and updating the state. We also demonstrated how to remove tasks using either delete buttons or swipe gestures. Additionally, you learned how to mark tasks as complete using checkboxes and provide visual feedback through styling.

Finally, we provided suggestions for further enhancements, encouraging you to expand the app's functionality by adding features like due dates, task prioritization, filtering, data persistence, and advanced UI interactions.

By completing this chapter, you've gained valuable hands-on experience in building a functional Flutter app, combining concepts like widgets, layouts, state management, and user input. This project serves as a stepping stone towards creating more complex and feature-rich applications in the future.

Building a News Reader App

Outline

- Overview of the News Reader App
- Project Setup and Dependencies
- Data Models
- Fetching News Data
- Designing the UI
- Displaying the News List
- Implementing Navigation
- Handling User Interactions
- Error Handling and Loading States
- Additional Features and Enhancements
- Chapter Summary

Overview of the News Reader App

In this chapter, we'll embark on building a news reader app that brings the latest headlines right to your fingertips. This app will showcase Flutter's capabilities in fetching data from a real-world API, parsing it, and presenting it in a user-friendly interface.

Key Features and Functionality:

Our news reader app will offer the following:

- **Fetching News:** The app will fetch news articles from a reliable news API (we'll use NewsAPI in this example).
- **Displaying Headlines and Summaries:** Users will see a list of news articles, each featuring a headline, a brief summary, and potentially a thumbnail image.
- **Article Details View:** Tapping on an article will take the user to a detailed view where they can read the full article.
- **Loading and Error Handling:** The app will display a loading indicator while fetching news and gracefully handle errors like network issues or invalid responses.
- **Categorization (Optional):** We might add the ability to filter news by category (e.g., technology, sports, business).

App UI overview:

- A simple app bar with the app title.
- A scrollable list of news articles, each presented as a card with an image, headline, and summary.
- A detailed article view that displays the full article content when a card is tapped.

Core Components: The Building Blocks

Under the hood, our news reader app will be composed of several key components:

1. **Data Model:** A NewsArticle class to represent each news item with properties like title, description, image URL, and source.
2. **API Integration:** The use of the http package to send requests to the NewsAPI and receive JSON responses.

3. **JSON Parsing:** The dart:convert library to decode the JSON data into our NewsArticle model.
4. **State Management:** A state management approach (you could use setState, Provider, or other options) to manage the list of fetched news articles and UI states like loading and error.
5. **UI Widgets:** Widgets like Scaffold, AppBar, ListView.builder, Image, and Text to build the user interface.
6. **Navigation:** The Navigator class to handle navigation between the list of articles and the article details screen.
7. **Error Handling:** Mechanisms to gracefully handle errors like network failures or invalid responses from the API.

By building this news reader app, you'll gain practical experience in working with APIs, handling asynchronous operations, managing state, and building interactive UIs—all essential skills for developing real-world Flutter applications.

Project Setup and Dependencies

Before diving into the code, let's create our Flutter project and equip it with the essential tools we'll need to build our news reader app.

1. Creating a New Flutter Project

You can create a new Flutter project using your preferred method:

Option 1: Command Line

1. **Open Your Terminal:** Launch your terminal (macOS/Linux) or command prompt (Windows).
2. **Navigate to Your Workspace:** Use the cd (change directory) command to go to the folder where you want to create the project.
3. **Create the Project:** Execute the following command, replacing news_reader_app with your desired project name:

```
flutter create news_reader_app
```

Flutter will create a new folder named news_reader_app with the basic project structure.

Option 2: Using an IDE

1. **Open Your IDE:** Launch Android Studio or Visual Studio Code.
2. **Start a New Project:**
   ○ **Android Studio:** Click "Start a new Flutter project" on the welcome screen.
   ○ **VS Code:** Open the Command Palette (Ctrl+Shift+P or Cmd+Shift+P) and type "Flutter: New Project."
3. **Follow the Wizard:** Choose "Flutter Application" as the project type, enter your project name (news_reader_app), and select the desired project location.

2. Adding the http Package

Since our app will be fetching data from a news API, we need the http package to make network requests. If you haven't already added it to your project (as in Chapter 12), follow these steps:

1. **Open pubspec.yaml:** Locate the pubspec.yaml file in your project's root directory.
2. **Add the Dependency:** Under the dependencies section, add the following line:
```
http: ^0.13.5 # (Or the latest version available)
```

3. **Save and Get Packages:** Save the file. Flutter will automatically download and install the `http` package.

3. Additional Dependencies (Optional)

Depending on your app's design and functionality, you might want to add other third-party packages. Some useful options for a news reader app include:

- `flutter_spinkit`: For adding beautiful loading indicators.
- `cached_network_image`: For caching network images to improve performance.
- `url_launcher`: For opening web links in the device's browser.
- `intl`: For formatting dates and times.

To add a package, simply add its name and version to the `dependencies` section of your `pubspec.yaml` file and save it. Flutter will handle the rest.

Get Ready to Code!

With your project set up and the `http` package (and any other necessary dependencies) added, you have all the tools you need to start building your news reader app. We're now ready to define the data models for our news articles and begin fetching news data from the API.

Data Models

In Flutter, like many programming languages, we use data models to represent real-world objects in our code. For our news reader app, we'll create a data model called `NewsArticle` to hold the information about each news story we fetch from the API.

Why Data Models?

Data models serve several important purposes:

1. **Structure:** They provide a clear and organized structure for storing information. Each piece of data (e.g., article title, publication date) has a designated place within the model.
2. **Clarity:** They make your code more readable and self-documenting. When you see a `NewsArticle` object, you instantly know it represents a news story and has specific properties associated with it.
3. **Type Safety:** Data models enforce type safety, ensuring that you're working with the correct data types (e.g., strings for titles, dates for publication times).
4. **Reusability:** You can reuse your data models throughout your app, in different widgets and screens, without having to duplicate code.

The `NewsArticle` Class

Let's create a `NewsArticle` class to represent our news items:

```
class NewsArticle { final String title; // Headline of the article final
String? description; // Summary of the article (might be null) final String
url; // URL to the full article final String? urlToImage; // URL of the image
associated with the article (might be null) final DateTime publishedAt; //
Date and time the article was published NewsArticle({ required this.title,
this.description, required this.url, this.urlToImage, required
```

```
this.publishedAt, }); // Factory constructor to create a NewsArticle from a
Map (JSON data) factory NewsArticle.fromJson(Map<String, dynamic> json) {
return NewsArticle( title: json['title'] ?? '', // Provide a default value if
null description: json['description'], url: json['url'] ?? '', urlToImage:
json['urlToImage'], publishedAt: DateTime.parse(json['publishedAt']), ); } }
```

Explanation:

- Each NewsArticle will hold a title, optional description (some articles might not have one), url, optional urlToImage, and a publishedAt timestamp.
- The fromJson factory constructor allows creating a NewsArticle from the JSON response received from the API. It uses the null-aware operator (??) to set default values if a field is missing from the JSON.

How We'll Use the NewsArticle Model

- We'll fetch a list of NewsArticle objects from the NewsAPI.
- We'll display each NewsArticle's title, description (if available), and urlToImage (if available) in a ListTile or a custom widget in a ListView or GridView.
- When the user taps on a NewsArticle, we'll pass its url property to the detail screen to display the full article.

By defining this data model, we establish a clear structure for handling and presenting news articles in our app, making our code more organized and easier to work with.

Fetching News Data

The heart of our news reader app lies in its ability to fetch fresh news articles from an external source. In this section, we'll use the NewsAPI (https://newsapi.org/) as our news provider and demonstrate how to retrieve news data using HTTP requests and parse it into our NewsArticle model.

Understanding NewsAPI

NewsAPI is a RESTful API that provides access to live news headlines from various sources around the world. It offers different endpoints for fetching top headlines, searching for specific news, and more. To use the API, you typically need to obtain a free API key, which you'll include in your requests.

Fetching News: Making the GET Request

We'll use the http package to make a GET request to the NewsAPI endpoint.

1. **Import the http package:**

```
import 'package:http/http.dart' as http;
```

2. **Define the API Endpoint and Key:**

```
final String apiKey = 'YOUR_API_KEY'; // Replace with your actual API key
final String apiEndpoint =
'https://newsapi.org/v2/top-headlines?country=us';
```

- **Important:** Be sure to replace "YOUR_API_KEY" with the key provided to you by NewsAPI!

3. **Fetch Data Function:**

```
Future<List<NewsArticle>> fetchNewsArticles() async { final response =
await http.get(Uri.parse(apiEndpoint + '&apiKey=$apiKey')); if
(response.statusCode == 200) { final Map<String, dynamic> json =
jsonDecode(response.body); final List<dynamic> articlesJson =
json['articles']; return articlesJson.map((articleJson) =>
NewsArticle.fromJson(articleJson)).toList(); } else { throw
Exception('Failed to load news articles'); } }
```

Explanation:

1. An asynchronous function `fetchNewsArticles()` is created that returns a `Future<List<NewsArticle>>`. This implies the function fetches data and may take time, returning a list of `NewsArticle` objects in the future.
2. We construct the full API endpoint by adding the API key to the base endpoint.
3. We make a GET request to the API endpoint using `http.get()` and `await` the response.
4. If the request is successful (status code 200), we parse the JSON response:
   ○ Extract the 'articles' list from the JSON.
   ○ Use `.map` to create a new `NewsArticle` object for each item in the list by calling the `fromJson` constructor on `NewsArticle`.
   ○ Convert the resulting iterable into a list using `.toList()`.
5. If there is an error in fetching data, throw an `Exception`.

Error Handling:

- We include a `try-catch` block around the network request to catch potential exceptions (e.g., network errors).
- If an exception occurs, we throw an `Exception` with a descriptive error message.
- The caller of `fetchNewsArticles()` (usually in your widget) will need to handle this exception (e.g., by displaying an error message to the user).

Incorporating into Your App

You can call `fetchNewsArticles` within your app to fetch and process news articles. It is typically called in your widget's `initState` function (for stateful widgets) or within a `FutureBuilder` widget.

Designing the UI

The user interface (UI) of our news reader app is where the fetched news data comes to life. We'll use a combination of standard Flutter widgets and a custom widget to create a clean, organized, and visually engaging display of news articles.

UI Elements:

1. **App Bar:**
   ○ **Purpose:** Provides a clear title for the app and, optionally, a search bar for filtering articles.
   ○ **Widgets:**
     ■ `AppBar`: Sets up the app bar structure with a title and actions.
     ■ `Text`: Displays the app title.

- IconButton: An icon button for potential actions (e.g., settings, refresh).
- TextField: (Optional) For implementing a search bar.

```
AppBar( title: const Text('News Reader'), // actions:
[IconButton(icon: Icon(Icons.search), onPressed: () {})], //
Optional search button );
```

2. **News List Display:**
   - **Purpose:** Presents the list of news articles in a scrollable format.
   - **Widgets:**
     - ListView.builder: Dynamically creates NewsCard widgets for each article.

```
ListView.builder( itemCount: articles.length, itemBuilder:
(context, index) { return NewsCard(article: articles[index]);
}, );
```

3. **NewsCard (Custom Widget):**
   - **Purpose:** Represents a single news article, displaying its title, image (if available), and a short description.
   - **Widgets:**
     - Card: Provides a visual container for the article content.
     - ListTile: Organizes the title and description in a list-like format.
     - Image.network (or CachedNetworkImage for caching): Displays the article's image.
     - Text: Displays the article's title and description.

```
class NewsCard extends StatelessWidget { final NewsArticle
article; const NewsCard({Key? key, required this.article}) :
super(key: key); @override Widget build(BuildContext context) {
return Card( elevation: 2, // Add a slight shadow child:
ListTile( leading: article.urlToImage != null // Conditional
for image ? Image.network(article.urlToImage!) : null, title:
Text(article.title), subtitle: Text(article.description ?? ''),
// Handle null description ), ); } }
```

Layout Structure:

We'll use a Scaffold as the base of our UI. Inside the Scaffold:

- The appBar property will hold the AppBar widget.
- The body property will contain the ListView.builder to display the list of NewsCard widgets.

```
Scaffold( appBar: AppBar( title: Text('News Reader'), ), body:
ListView.builder( // ... ListView code ), );
```

In later sections, we'll refine the NewsCard widget's design, implement navigation to article details, and add error handling and loading indicators. This structure provides a solid foundation for building a visually appealing and informative news reader app in Flutter.

Displaying the News List

Now that we have our data model (NewsArticle) and a way to fetch news articles from the API, let's showcase these articles in a visually appealing and informative list.

`ListView.builder`: **The Dynamic List Builder**

We'll utilize the `ListView.builder` widget, which efficiently creates list items on demand as the user scrolls. This ensures smooth performance even when dealing with large lists of news articles.

```
ListView.builder( itemCount: articles.length, itemBuilder: (context, index) {
return NewsCard(article: articles[index]); }, );
```

Explanation:

1. `itemCount`: This property tells the `ListView.builder` how many items it needs to display. In our case, it's the number of news articles we've fetched.
2. `itemBuilder`: This function is called for each index in the list. It builds and returns a NewsCard widget for each article, passing the corresponding `article` object as data.

The `NewsCard` **Widget: Crafting a News Item**

We'll create a custom NewsCard widget to represent each news article. This widget will take a NewsArticle object as input and display the relevant information in a visually organized way.

```
class NewsCard extends StatelessWidget { final NewsArticle article; const
NewsCard({Key? key, required this.article}) : super(key: key); @override
Widget build(BuildContext context) { return Card( elevation: 2, margin: const
EdgeInsets.symmetric(vertical: 8, horizontal: 16), child: ListTile( leading:
article.urlToImage != null ? Image.network(article.urlToImage!, fit:
BoxFit.cover, width: 80, height: 80) : const Icon(Icons.newspaper), title:
Text( article.title, style: const TextStyle(fontWeight: FontWeight.bold), ),
subtitle: Text( article.description ?? 'Tap to read more', maxLines: 2,
overflow: TextOverflow.ellipsis, ), ), ); } }
```

Explanation:

1. **Constructor:** The NewsCard constructor receives a NewsArticle object.
2. **build Method:**
   - It builds a Card widget with a slight elevation.
   - The ListTile is used to display the news content:
     - If the article has an image, we display it as a leading widget with a specified size and aspect ratio.
     - If not, we use a newspaper icon as a placeholder.
     - The article's title is displayed as the title of the ListTile, with bold styling.
     - If the article has a description, we display it with a maximum of two lines and an ellipsis (…) if it's too long. If not, we show "Tap to read more".

Adding Styling: Making It Look Good

You can customize the appearance of the news list and individual NewsCard widgets by applying various styling techniques discussed in Chapter 8:

- Use colors to create visual interest and differentiate elements.
- Experiment with different fonts and text styles.
- Add padding and margins to improve readability and spacing.
- Consider using shadows and rounded corners to give the cards a modern look.

By following these steps and customizing the styling to your liking, you can create a news list that not only presents information effectively but also captivates your users with its visual appeal.

Implementing Navigation

Now that we can display our news articles, let's enable users to dive deeper into a specific article by tapping on it. We'll use Flutter's Navigator class to seamlessly transition between the main news list screen and the article details screen.

Setting the Stage for Navigation

To begin, we need to designate the main news list screen (where the ListView.builder is placed) as the starting point of our app's navigation. This is typically done in the home property of your MaterialApp widget. For this example, let's assume it's called NewsListScreen.

Navigating to the Article Details Screen

1. **Wrap with InkWell (or GestureDetector):** Wrap the NewsCard widget inside an InkWell (or GestureDetector) to make it tappable.

   ```
   InkWell( onTap: () { // Navigation logic (explained below) }, child:
   NewsCard(article: articles[index]), );
   ```

2. **Push the Route:** In the onTap callback of the InkWell, use Navigator.pushNamed to push a new route onto the navigation stack. Pass the selected article's URL as an argument.

   ```
   Navigator.pushNamed( context, '/article_details', // Named route for the
   details screen arguments: articles[index], );
   ```

3. **Define the Detail Route:** In your MaterialApp's routes table, define a named route for the article details screen.

   ```
   MaterialApp( // ... other properties routes: { // ... other routes
   '/article_details': (context) => ArticleDetailScreen(), }, );
   ```

Creating the ArticleDetailScreen

1. **Retrieve Article Data:** In the ArticleDetailScreen widget, access the passed NewsArticle object using ModalRoute.of(context)!.settings.arguments.

   ```
   class ArticleDetailScreen extends StatelessWidget { @override Widget
   build(BuildContext context) { final article =
   ModalRoute.of(context)!.settings.arguments as NewsArticle; return
   Scaffold( appBar: AppBar( title: Text(article.title), ), body: Padding(
   ```

```
padding: const EdgeInsets.all(16.0), child: SingleChildScrollView( child:
Text(article.content ?? 'No content available.'), ), ), ); } }
```

(Remember the news API may not return a `content` property in which case we display a default message.)

2. **Display Article Details:** Build the UI of the detail screen using the article's data. You can display the title, image, full content, publication date, etc.
3. **Optional: Web View:** For a more complete experience, consider using a `WebView` widget to display the article's content directly from its URL (this would require an additional package like `webview_flutter`).

Going Back:

The user can navigate back to the news list by tapping the back button provided by the `AppBar` on the details screen. This automatically pops the `ArticleDetailScreen` route off the navigation stack.

By following these steps, you've successfully implemented navigation between your main news list and individual article details, providing a smooth and intuitive user experience.

Handling User Interactions

User interactions bring your app to life. In this section, we'll enable users to tap on news articles to view details, potentially mark articles as read or save them for later, and consider other interactions that enhance the user experience.

1. Navigating to Article Details on Tap

To make each `NewsCard` tappable, we'll wrap it in an `InkWell` widget. When the user taps the card, we'll navigate to the `ArticleDetailScreen`, passing the selected `NewsArticle` object as an argument.

```
InkWell( onTap: () { Navigator.pushNamed( context, '/article_details',
arguments: article, // Pass the NewsArticle object }); }, child:
NewsCard(article: article), );
```

2. Marking Articles as Read or Saved (Optional)

You can enhance user engagement by adding features like "mark as read" or "save for later." This typically involves:

- **State Management:** Introduce variables in your state to track which articles are read or saved.
- **UI Indicators:** Display visual cues (e.g., icons, color changes) to indicate the article's status.
- **Interaction Logic:** Implement functions to update the state when the user interacts with the corresponding controls (e.g., tapping a "bookmark" icon).

```
// In NewsCard widget trailing: IconButton( icon: Icon( _isSaved ?
Icons.bookmark : Icons.bookmark_border, ), onPressed: () { // TODO:
Update saved status and UI }, ),
```

3. Additional Interactions: Tailor to Your Needs

Consider other user interactions that make sense for your news reader app:

- **Sharing:** Add a button to allow users to share articles via social media or other apps.
- **Commenting/Liking:** Enable users to interact with articles by adding comments or likes (if your app has social features).
- **Customization:** Allow users to personalize the news feed (e.g., by choosing preferred categories).
- **Offline Mode:** Implement offline reading by saving articles locally.

Example: Mark as Read Functionality

```
// Add a read property to NewsArticle and a list of read articles in state
class _NewsListScreenState extends State<NewsListScreen> { // ...
List<NewsArticle> _readArticles = []; void _markAsRead(NewsArticle article) {
setState(() { _readArticles.add(article); article.read = true; }); } // ...
itemBuilder: (context, index) { return InkWell( onTap: () { /*...*/ }, child:
NewsCard( article: articles[index], onMarkAsRead: _markAsRead, // Pass the
markAsRead function to NewsCard ), ); }, // ... } // In NewsCard final
VoidCallback? onMarkAsRead; // Inside ListTile onTap: () {
onMarkAsRead?.call(article); // Call onMarkAsRead to mark as read // Navigate
to details screen },
```

User-Centered Design

Always prioritize the user experience. Make interactions intuitive, provide clear feedback, and ensure that gestures and controls are easy to discover and use.

By combining various input methods and designing thoughtful interactions, you can elevate your news reader app from a simple content viewer to an engaging and user-friendly tool that keeps users informed and coming back for more.

Error Handling and Loading States

In the real world, network requests are not always guaranteed to succeed. Things can go wrong—servers might be down, internet connections might be spotty, or the API might return unexpected data. As a responsible developer, it's your job to anticipate these issues and handle them gracefully, ensuring that your app doesn't crash and that users receive clear feedback about what's happening.

Why Error Handling Matters:

1. **App Stability:** Unhandled errors during network requests can lead to your app crashing, which is a frustrating experience for users. Proper error handling prevents crashes and keeps your app running smoothly.
2. **User Communication:** When a network request fails, you need to inform the user about the issue. Displaying clear and informative error messages helps them understand what went wrong and potentially take corrective action.
3. **Loading States:** While a network request is in progress, it's crucial to provide visual feedback to the user to indicate that the app is working. A loading indicator (e.g., a spinner or a progress bar) reassures the user that something is happening and prevents them from thinking the app is frozen.

Implementing Error Handling:

1. **try-catch Blocks:** Use try-catch blocks to wrap your network requests. The try block contains the code that could potentially throw an exception, and the catch block handles the exception if it occurs.

```
try { final response = await http.get(Uri.parse(apiEndpoint)); // ...
parse and process the response } catch (e) { // Handle the error (e.g.,
display an error message) print('Error fetching news: $e'); }
```

2. **Error Messages:** Inside the `catch` block, display a user-friendly error message using a `SnackBar`, `AlertDialog`, or simply updating the UI.

```
ScaffoldMessenger.of(context).showSnackBar( SnackBar(content: Text('Error
fetching news. Please try again later.')), );
```

Displaying a Loading Indicator:

Use the `CircularProgressIndicator` widget to show a loading spinner while the data is being fetched:

```
// In your widget's build method if (isLoading) { // isLoading is a boolean
variable in your state return const Center( child:
CircularProgressIndicator(), ); } else { // Display the fetched data }
```

Implementing Error States:

Consider introducing a separate error state in your app's state management to handle error scenarios more gracefully. This allows you to display a specific error message, a retry button, or alternative content when a network request fails.

```
enum DataState { loading, success, error } class _NewsListScreenState extends
State<NewsListScreen> { DataState _dataState = DataState.loading; // ...
@override Widget build(BuildContext context) { if (_dataState ==
DataState.loading) { return const Center(child: CircularProgressIndicator());
} else if (_dataState == DataState.error) { return const Center(child:
Text('Error loading news. Please try again.')); } else { // DataState.success
return ListView.builder( // ... ); } } }
```

By incorporating error handling, loading indicators, and error states into your news reader app, you can ensure a more robust and user-friendly experience, even when things don't go according to plan.

Additional Features and Enhancements (Optional)

While our basic news reader app is functional, there's always room for improvement. Here are some exciting features and enhancements you can consider adding to make it even more powerful and user-friendly:

1. **Search Functionality:**
   - Allow users to search for specific articles based on keywords or phrases.
   - Implement a search bar in the app bar or a dedicated search screen.
   - Filter the displayed articles based on the search query.
   - Utilize libraries like `flutter_search_bar` to simplify search bar implementation.
2. **Category Filters:**
   - Enable users to filter news articles by category (e.g., technology, sports, business).
   - Use a `DropdownButton` or a set of buttons/chips to represent different categories.

- Filter the fetched news data based on the selected category.
3. **Refresh Functionality:**
- Add a "pull to refresh" feature to allow users to manually refresh the news list.
- Use the `RefreshIndicator` widget to wrap your `ListView` and implement the refresh logic.
- Fetch the latest news from the API when the user pulls down the list.
4. **Personalized Recommendations:**
- Analyze user behavior (e.g., reading history, preferred categories) to offer personalized news recommendations.
- Use machine learning algorithms or collaborative filtering techniques to suggest articles that users might be interested in.
- Implement a "For You" section or integrate personalized recommendations within the main news feed.
5. **Offline Mode:**
- Cache news articles locally so that users can read them even without an internet connection.
- Consider using a local database (e.g., SQLite) or a caching library like `hive` to store the articles.
- Provide a way for users to manually refresh the cached data when they're online.
6. **Other Enhancements:**
- **Infinite Scrolling:** Implement infinite scrolling to load more articles as the user reaches the end of the list (discussed in Chapter 14).
- **Share Feature:** Allow users to share interesting articles with their friends through various platforms.
- **Text-to-Speech:** Enable a text-to-speech feature for accessibility or hands-free reading.
- **Push Notifications:** Send notifications to users about breaking news or important updates.

By adding these or other features, you can create a news reader app that stands out from the crowd, provides a personalized and engaging experience, and keeps users informed and connected.

Chapter Summary

In this chapter, you took a significant step towards building a real-world Flutter application: a news reader app. You learned the essential building blocks for creating a dynamic app that fetches and displays news articles from an external API.

We started by outlining the app's features and functionality, focusing on fetching news data, displaying articles, and handling navigation and user interactions. Then, we guided you through the project setup, including creating a new Flutter project and adding the necessary dependencies, like the `http` package.

You learned how to define a data model (`NewsArticle`) to represent news articles in your code and how to use the `http` package to make GET requests to the NewsAPI. We discussed the importance of API keys and error handling in the data fetching process.

We then focused on designing the app's UI, introducing the core widgets like `AppBar`, `ListView.builder`, and a custom `NewsCard` widget to display news articles in a visually appealing manner. You learned how to structure the layout using `Scaffold` and `Column`.

We also covered how to implement navigation between the main news list and individual article detail screens using named routes and passing data as arguments. We discussed how to make the news list interactive by adding tap gestures to the `NewsCard` widgets and explored potential features like "mark as read" and "save for later."

Finally, we emphasized the importance of error handling and loading states, showing you how to use `try-catch` blocks, display loading indicators, and implement error states to ensure a smooth and reliable user experience.

By working through this chapter, you've gained practical experience in integrating external APIs, parsing JSON data, managing state, building dynamic UIs, and implementing navigation in a Flutter app. This project lays the foundation for creating more complex and feature-rich applications in the future.

Developing a Weather App with API Integration

Outline

- The Power of Weather Data
- Project Setup and Dependencies
- Weather Data Model
- Fetching Weather Data
- UI Design for Current Weather
- Displaying Current Weather Data
- UI Design for Forecast
- Displaying the Forecast Data
- Handling Locations and Search
- Error Handling and User Feedback
- Adding Polish: Icons and Animations
- Beyond the Basics: Additional Features
- Chapter Summary

The Power of Weather Data

Weather is a force of nature that impacts us all. From deciding what to wear in the morning to planning weekend getaways, accurate and up-to-date weather information is a cornerstone of our daily lives. This is where weather apps come into play, harnessing the power of data to provide insights that help us make informed decisions.

Weather Data in Action

Weather data is far more than just temperature readings. It encompasses a wide range of information that can influence our activities and decisions:

- **Planning Daily Routines:** Knowing the weather forecast allows you to dress appropriately, pack an umbrella, or apply sunscreen, ensuring you're prepared for whatever the day brings.
- **Travel and Transportation:** Weather conditions can significantly impact travel plans. Checking the forecast helps you avoid delays, pack the right gear, and make informed decisions about transportation options.
- **Outdoor Activities:** Whether it's a picnic, hike, or beach day, weather plays a crucial role in determining the feasibility and enjoyment of outdoor activities. Weather apps can provide hourly forecasts, precipitation chances, and UV index information to help you plan accordingly.
- **Agriculture:** Farmers rely on weather data to make crucial decisions about planting, harvesting, and irrigation. Precise forecasts can help them optimize crop yields and minimize losses.
- **Emergency Preparedness:** Weather alerts and warnings about severe weather conditions (like storms, floods, or heatwaves) help people stay safe and take necessary precautions.

Real-Time and Accurate Information: A Game-Changer

The value of weather data is amplified when it's real-time and accurate. Knowing the current conditions and having a reliable forecast empowers you to make the best possible decisions for your day-to-day life.

Weather Apps: Your Personal Meteorologist

Weather apps have become indispensable tools in the modern world. They put a wealth of information at your fingertips, making it easy to:

- **Check the Current Weather:** See the current temperature, humidity, wind speed, and other relevant details at a glance.
- **Get Hourly Forecasts:** Plan your activities with detailed hourly breakdowns of weather conditions.
- **View Extended Forecasts:** Look ahead to the next few days or even weeks to plan trips or events.
- **Receive Alerts:** Get notified about severe weather events or changes in the forecast.
- **Customize Your Experience:** Tailor the app to your location, preferences, and units of measurement.

By providing this valuable information in a user-friendly format, weather apps have become essential companions for millions of people worldwide, helping them stay informed, safe, and prepared.

Project Setup and Dependencies

Before we start coding our weather app, let's set up a new Flutter project and gather the tools we'll need to fetch weather data and build a beautiful interface.

1. Creating Your Flutter Project

Creating a new Flutter project is a breeze. You can use your favorite IDE or the Flutter CLI:

Option 1: Command Line (Recommended)

1. Open your terminal.
2. Navigate to your desired directory.
3. Run the following command, replacing `weather_app` with your preferred name:

```
flutter create weather_app
```

Option 2: Using an IDE

1. Open Android Studio or VS Code with the Flutter plugin installed.
2. Click on "Start a new Flutter project" or use the command palette (Ctrl+Shift+P or Cmd+Shift+P) to create a new project.
3. Follow the instructions, selecting "Flutter Application" as the project type, entering your project name, and choosing a suitable location for the project.

2. Adding the `http` Package

To fetch weather data from an API, we'll need to make HTTP requests. The `http` package is a staple in Flutter for handling network communication.

1. **Open `pubspec.yaml`:** This file is in your project's root directory and manages your project's dependencies.
2. **Add the Dependency:** Under the `dependencies` section, add the following line:

```
dependencies: http: ^0.13.5 # Replace with the latest version
```

3. **Save and Fetch:** Save the file. Run `flutter pub get` in your terminal to download and install the package.

3. Installing Additional Packages (Optional)

To enhance your weather app's features and UI, consider adding the following packages:

- **`geolocator`:** A package for accessing the device's location services.

```
flutter pub add geolocator
```

- **flutter_spinkit:** A collection of cool and customizable loading indicators.

```
flutter pub add flutter_spinkit
```

- **intl:** A package for formatting dates, numbers, and other data types for different locales.

```
flutter pub add intl
```

- **weather_icons:** A package containing a variety of weather icons to visually represent different weather conditions.

```
flutter pub add weather_icons
```

Project Ready for Weather Magic

With your project setup and the essential dependencies in place, you're now prepared to build your weather app! We'll start by defining the data models to structure the weather data we'll be working with.

Weather Data Model

Before we start fetching weather data from an API, let's create a solid foundation for organizing the information we'll receive. Data models are Dart classes that represent the structure of the data we expect to work with. In this case, we'll define models for current weather conditions and weather forecasts.

Why Data Models?

Data models serve several crucial purposes in our weather app:

1. **Structure and Organization:** They provide a clear and logical way to represent the complex weather data we'll be receiving from the API. This makes it easier to work with the data in our code.
2. **Type Safety:** Data models enforce types for each piece of data (e.g., temperature as a number, description as a string). This helps prevent errors and makes our code more reliable.
3. **Code Readability:** By using descriptive class names and property names, we make our code self-documenting and easier for others (or our future selves) to understand.

The `Weather` Class: Your Current Conditions Snapshot

Our `Weather` class will encapsulate the data related to the current weather conditions at a specific location.

```
class Weather { final String cityName; // Name of the city final double
temperature; // Temperature in Celsius (or your preferred unit) final String
description; // Description of weather conditions (e.g., "clear sky," "light
rain") final String iconCode; // Code for the weather icon (e.g., "01d" for
clear sky) Weather({ required this.cityName, required this.temperature,
required this.description, required this.iconCode, }); factory
Weather.fromJson(Map<String, dynamic> json) { return Weather( cityName:
json['name'], temperature: json['main']['temp'].toDouble(), description:
json['weather'][0]['description'], iconCode: json['weather'][0]['icon'], ); }
}
```

Explanation: The constructor takes the parameters for our weather data and stores them as final variables. The `fromJson` factory constructor allows for the creation of a `Weather` object from a JSON map. This is essential since the weather API we are using would give the weather data as a JSON object.

The `Forecast` Class: Peeking into the Future

Our `Forecast` class will represent a collection of weather forecasts for multiple days or hours.

```
class Forecast { final List<DailyForecast> dailyForecasts; // List of daily
forecasts Forecast({required this.dailyForecasts}); factory
Forecast.fromJson(Map<String, dynamic> json) { final List<dynamic> daily =
json['daily']; return Forecast( dailyForecasts: daily.map((item) =>
DailyForecast.fromJson(item)).toList(), ); } } class DailyForecast { final
DateTime date; final double minTemperature; final double maxTemperature; final
String iconCode; DailyForecast({ required this.date, required
this.minTemperature, required this.maxTemperature, required this.iconCode, });
factory DailyForecast.fromJson(Map<String, dynamic> json) { return
DailyForecast( date: DateTime.fromMillisecondsSinceEpoch(json['dt'] * 1000),
minTemperature: json['temp']['min'].toDouble(), maxTemperature:
json['temp']['max'].toDouble(), iconCode: json['weather'][0]['icon'], ); } }
```

Explanation:

- `Forecast`: This class has a `List<DailyForecast>` called `dailyForecasts`. This list would contain the forecast for multiple days (as returned by our weather API). We have a factory constructor to map JSON to the `Forecast` object.
- `DailyForecast`: This is similar to our `Weather` class but has additional properties like `date`, `minTemperature` and `maxTemperature` to include all the data returned from our weather API.

Structuring the API Data

These data models align with the structure of responses typically returned by weather APIs like OpenWeatherMap. When you fetch weather data, the API will return a JSON object, and you'll use these models to parse that JSON into a format that's easy to work with in your Flutter app.

By creating these data models upfront, you lay a solid foundation for the rest of your weather app development. You'll be able to neatly organize and manipulate weather data, leading to a more maintainable and scalable codebase.

Fetching Weather Data

Now that we have our data models ready, let's dive into fetching real-time weather data from a weather API. For this example, we'll use OpenWeatherMap, a popular and reliable weather data provider.

OpenWeatherMap API: Your Weather Oracle

OpenWeatherMap (https://openweathermap.org/) offers a free tier that provides a wealth of weather data, including current conditions, forecasts, and historical data. To use the API, you'll need to sign up for a free account and obtain an API key.

Sign Up and Get Your API Key: Head over to the OpenWeatherMap website and create an account. Once you're logged in, navigate to the API keys section to generate your free API key. Keep this key secure, as it's essential for accessing the API.

Constructing the API Endpoint URL

OpenWeatherMap's API endpoints follow a specific structure:

https://api.openweathermap.org/data/2.5/weather?q={city name}&appid={API key}&units={units}

or

https://api.openweathermap.org/data/2.5/weather?lat={latitude}&lon={longitude}&appid={API key}&units={units}

- `q={city name}` (or `lat={latitude}&lon={longitude}`)**:** Specifies the location for which you want the weather data. You can either provide the city name or the latitude and longitude coordinates.
- `appid={API key}`**:** Your unique API key obtained from OpenWeatherMap.
- `units={units}` **(Optional):** Specifies the unit system for the returned data. You can use `metric` for Celsius or `imperial` for Fahrenheit. The default is Kelvin.

Fetching Data with `http` Package

We'll use the `http` package to send a GET request to the OpenWeatherMap API endpoint. Here's an example function that fetches both current weather and forecast data:

```
import 'package:http/http.dart' as http; import 'dart:convert';
Future<Map<String, dynamic>> fetchWeatherData(String cityName) async { final
weatherUrl = Uri.parse(
'https://api.openweathermap.org/data/2.5/weather?q=$cityName&appid=$apiKey&uni
ts=metric'); final forecastUrl = Uri.parse(
'https://api.openweathermap.org/data/2.5/onecall?lat=$latitude&lon=$longitude&
exclude=hourly,minutely&appid=$apiKey&units=metric'); final weatherResponse =
await http.get(weatherUrl); final forecastResponse = await
http.get(forecastUrl); if (weatherResponse.statusCode == 200 &&
forecastResponse.statusCode == 200) { return { 'weather':
Weather.fromJson(jsonDecode(weatherResponse.body)), 'forecast':
Forecast.fromJson(jsonDecode(forecastResponse.body)), }; } else { throw
Exception('Failed to load weather data'); } }
```

Replace placeholders for `YOUR_API_KEY`, `latitude`, and `longitude` with actual values. Make sure to include error handling in case requests fail.

Remember to handle errors gracefully and provide appropriate feedback to the user in case the network request fails or the API returns an error. You can use a `try-catch` block to catch exceptions and display an error message or a retry button.

By following these steps, you can now fetch real-time weather data from OpenWeatherMap, parse the JSON response into your data models, and prepare to display it in your app's UI.

UI Design for Current Weather

The current weather section is the centerpiece of our weather app. It provides users with an immediate overview of the weather conditions at their chosen location. Let's design a clean and informative UI to showcase this data.

UI Elements:

1. **City/Location Label:**
   - **Purpose:** Clearly displays the name of the city or location for which the weather data is being shown.
   - **Widget:** Text
   - **Display:** Large font size, prominent placement (e.g., top of the screen, center aligned).
2. **Current Temperature:**
   - **Purpose:** Shows the current temperature in the preferred unit (Celsius, Fahrenheit, etc.).
   - **Widget:** Text
   - **Display:** Large, bold font size, placed prominently (e.g., below the city label).
3. **Weather Condition Description:**
   - **Purpose:** Provides a textual description of the current weather conditions (e.g., "Sunny," "Partly cloudy," "Rain").
   - **Widget:** Text
   - **Display:** Smaller font size than temperature, typically below or beside the temperature.
4. **Weather Icon:**
   - **Purpose:** Visually represents the weather conditions using an icon (e.g., a sun icon for sunny, a cloud icon for cloudy).
   - **Widget:** Image.asset() (for local assets) or Image.network() (for icons from the web or a weather icon package like weather_icons).
   - **Display:** Size appropriate to the layout, placed near the temperature and condition description.

Layout Structure: Arranging the Elements

We'll use a combination of layout widgets to organize these UI elements effectively:

- **Scaffold:** Provides the basic app structure with an app bar and body.
- **AppBar:** Holds the app title and any additional actions.
- **Column:** Arranges the city label, temperature, description, and icon vertically.
- **Row:** (Optional) Can be used to position the temperature and icon side-by-side.
- **Center:** (Optional) Can be used to center the entire content within the Scaffold body.

Displaying Fetched Data: Connecting Data and UI

To display the weather data we fetched from the API, we'll use string interpolation within the Text widgets to dynamically insert values.

```
Column( children: [ Text(weather.cityName, style: TextStyle(fontSize: 24)),
Text('${weather.temperature.toStringAsFixed(1)}°C', style: TextStyle(fontSize:
48, fontWeight: FontWeight.bold)), Text(weather.description),
Image.network('http://openweathermap.org/img/wn/${weather.iconCode}@2x.png'),
], );
```

In this example, weather is an instance of our Weather data model. We use string interpolation to display its properties dynamically.

Additional Considerations:

- **Error Handling:** Display an error message if the data fails to load or is invalid.
- **Loading Indicator:** Show a loading spinner (e.g., CircularProgressIndicator) while the data is being fetched.
- **User Interaction:** Allow the user to refresh the data or search for a different location (we'll cover this in later sections).

By carefully arranging these UI elements and integrating the fetched weather data, you'll create a clear, informative, and visually appealing display of the current weather conditions.

Displaying Current Weather Data

Now that we've fetched our weather data, it's time to showcase it in a user-friendly and visually appealing way. We'll utilize the UI elements we designed earlier and integrate the data from our Weather object.

Building the Current Weather UI

```
Widget buildCurrentWeather(Weather weather) { return Column(
mainAxisAlignment: MainAxisAlignment.center, // Center vertically children: [
Text( weather.cityName, style: const TextStyle(fontSize: 32, fontWeight:
FontWeight.bold), ), const SizedBox(height: 16), // Add spacing Row(
mainAxisAlignment: MainAxisAlignment.center, // Center horizontally children:
[ Image.network(
'https://openweathermap.org/img/wn/${weather.iconCode}@2x.png', height: 80, ),
const SizedBox(width: 16), Text(
'${weather.temperature.toStringAsFixed(0)}°C', style: const
TextStyle(fontSize: 64, fontWeight: FontWeight.bold), ), ], ), const
SizedBox(height: 8), Text( weather.description, style: const
TextStyle(fontSize: 20), ), ], ); }
```

In this code:

1. We create a buildCurrentWeather function that takes a Weather object as input and returns a Column widget.
2. The Column arranges the following children:
   - A Text widget to display the city name with a large, bold font.
   - A SizedBox for vertical spacing.
   - A Row to align the weather icon and temperature horizontally:
     - An Image.network widget loads the weather icon from OpenWeatherMap based on the iconCode property.
     - Another SizedBox for horizontal spacing.
     - A Text widget displays the temperature, rounded to the nearest whole number, with a large, bold font.
   - Another SizedBox for vertical spacing.
   - A final Text widget displays the weather condition description.

Incorporating the `buildCurrentWeather` Widget

You can use the `buildCurrentWeather` function within your main widget's `build` method. Assuming you have a `_weather` variable that holds the fetched weather data, you can use it like this:

```
@override Widget build(BuildContext context) { return Scaffold( appBar:
AppBar(title: Text('Weather App')), body: Center( child: _weather != null ?
buildCurrentWeather(_weather!) : const CircularProgressIndicator(), ), ); }
```

(Remember to replace the placeholder for `_weather` with your actual variable.)

Styling Tips:

- **Colors:** Choose a color palette that's visually appealing and easy to read. Consider using light backgrounds with dark text for optimal contrast. Use colors to differentiate sections or highlight important information.
- **Fonts:** Select a legible font family for the text. Use larger font sizes for the city name and temperature to make them stand out.
- **Padding and Spacing:** Add padding around elements to improve readability and visual balance. Use the `SizedBox` widget to create spacing between elements.
- **Icons:** Use high-quality weather icons that are visually appealing and consistent with the overall design of your app.

By applying these styling techniques and customizing the UI elements to your liking, you can create a beautiful and informative current weather display that provides users with a clear and engaging overview of the weather conditions.

UI Design for Forecast

Our weather app would be incomplete without a glimpse into the upcoming weather conditions. The forecast section provides users with a preview of the weather for the next few days or hours, allowing them to plan their activities accordingly.

UI Elements:

1. **Forecast List:**
   - **Purpose:** Presents a scrollable list of daily or hourly weather forecasts.
   - **Widgets:**
     - `ListView.builder`: To dynamically create forecast item widgets.
     - `Column`: To arrange the elements within each forecast item vertically.
2. **Forecast Item:**
   - **Purpose:** Displays the forecast for a specific day or hour.
   - **Widgets:**
     - `Container` or `Card`: To provide a visual container for each forecast item.
     - `Text`: To display the date/time, high/low temperatures, and weather condition description.
     - `Image.network` (or `CachedNetworkImage`): To display the weather icon associated with the forecast.

Layout Structure:

- **`ListView.builder`:** The main container for the forecast list.

- Column (Inside `ListView.builder`): Used to vertically align the elements within each forecast item.
  - Row: (Optional) To arrange elements like the date/time and temperature horizontally.
  - `Image.network`: To display the weather icon.
  - Text: To display the date/time, temperature, and condition description.

Example Layout (Using `ListView.builder` and `Column`):

```
ListView.builder( itemCount: forecast.dailyForecasts.length, itemBuilder:
(context, index) { final dailyForecast = forecast.dailyForecasts[index];
return Card( child: Column( mainAxisAlignment: MainAxisAlignment.center,
children: [ Text(DateFormat('EEEE, MMMM d').format(dailyForecast.date)),
Image.network(
'https://openweathermap.org/img/wn/${dailyForecast.iconCode}@2x.png', ), Text(
'${dailyForecast.maxTemperature.toStringAsFixed(0)}°C /
${dailyForecast.minTemperature.toStringAsFixed(0)}°C', ), ], ), ); }, );
```

Explanation: The above code will render the weather forecast as a list. Each item will be a Card, and the Card will show the date, weather icon, and the maximum/minimum temperatures. The date is converted from its raw format to a human-readable format using `DateFormat` class.

Additional Considerations:

- **Hourly vs. Daily:** You can choose to display either hourly or daily forecasts, depending on your app's requirements.
- **Customizable Layout:** Experiment with different layouts to find the most visually appealing and informative way to present the forecast data. Consider using a `GridView` for a more compact display.
- **Scrolling:** If you have a large number of forecast items, make sure the list is scrollable using `SingleChildScrollView`.

By following these guidelines and leveraging the flexibility of Flutter's layout widgets, you can create a beautiful and informative forecast section that complements the current weather display and provides users with a complete picture of the weather conditions.

Displaying the Forecast Data

Now that we have the forecast data neatly organized in our `Forecast` model, let's craft a UI to present it to the user. We'll build upon the layout structure outlined earlier and populate it with the weather details for each day.

Building the Forecast UI:

1. **Utilize `ListView.builder`:** Continue using `ListView.builder` to dynamically generate widgets for each `DailyForecast` item in the `forecast.dailyForecasts` list.
2. **Enhance the NewsCard Widget:** We'll adapt our existing `NewsCard` widget to display forecast information instead of news articles. Rename the widget to `ForecastCard` and modify its properties and UI elements to match the forecast data.

   ```
   class ForecastCard extends StatelessWidget { final DailyForecast
   forecast; //Constructor const ForecastCard({Key? key, required
   ```

```
this.forecast}) : super(key: key); @override Widget build(BuildContext
context) { return Card( child: Padding( padding: const
EdgeInsets.all(8.0), child: Column( mainAxisAlignment:
MainAxisAlignment.center, children: [
Text(DateFormat('EEEE').format(forecast.date)), // Day of week
Image.network(
'https://openweathermap.org/img/wn/${forecast.iconCode}@2x.png', width:
50, height: 50, ), Text('${forecast.maxTemperature.toStringAsFixed(0)}°C
/ ${forecast.minTemperature.toStringAsFixed(0)}°C'), ], ), ), ); } }
```

Explanation:

1. **Constructor:** This class is similar to our NewsCard, but takes DailyForecast object instead of NewsArticle.
2. **build method:**
- A Card widget holds the forecast data.
- A Column is used to align children vertically.
- The date is formatted to show only the day of the week (e.g., "Monday").
- The weather icon is fetched based on forecast.iconCode.
- The maximum and minimum temperatures are displayed with degree Celsius symbol (°C).

Incorporating the Forecast UI:

Integrate the ListView.builder and ForecastCard into your main screen's layout (e.g., below the current weather section).

```
Column( children: [ buildCurrentWeather(weather), const SizedBox(height: 20),
const Text( 'Forecast:', style: TextStyle(fontSize: 20, fontWeight:
FontWeight.bold), ), Expanded( // This makes list take the remaining available
space child: ListView.builder( itemCount: forecast.dailyForecasts.length,
itemBuilder: (context, index) { return ForecastCard(forecast:
forecast.dailyForecasts[index]); }, ), ), ], );
```

Explanation: We create a new Column widget that displays our previously created buildCurrentWeather on top, followed by a Text widget saying 'Forecast', and the forecast itself using a ListView for each DailyForecast. We use Expanded here to ensure the list view takes up the remaining space on the screen.

Customizing the Forecast Display:

- **Colors:** Choose a color scheme that complements the overall app design. Use colors to distinguish between different days or highlight specific information (e.g., high/low temperatures).
- **Spacing:** Add padding around elements to improve readability and create a cleaner look.
- **Fonts:** Use clear and legible fonts for date/time, temperatures, and condition descriptions.
- **Icons:** Incorporate weather icons that are visually appealing and consistent with the overall design.

By implementing this forecast UI and customizing it to your liking, you'll enhance your weather app's functionality and provide users with valuable insights into the upcoming weather conditions.

Handling Locations and Search

Weather apps are most useful when they provide information relevant to the user's location. In this section, we'll enable our weather app to:

1. Automatically fetch weather data for the user's current location.
2. Allow users to search for weather in a specific city.

1. Obtaining the User's Current Location

We'll use the geolocator package to access the device's location services:

```
import 'package:geolocator/geolocator.dart'; Future<Position?>
_getCurrentLocation() async { bool serviceEnabled; LocationPermission
permission; serviceEnabled = await Geolocator.isLocationServiceEnabled(); if
(!serviceEnabled) { return Future.error('Location services are disabled.'); }
permission = await Geolocator.checkPermission(); if (permission ==
LocationPermission.denied) { permission = await
Geolocator.requestPermission(); if (permission == LocationPermission.denied) {
return Future.error('Location permissions are denied'); } } if (permission ==
LocationPermission.deniedForever) { return Future.error( 'Location permissions
are permanently denied, we cannot request permissions.'); } return await
Geolocator.getCurrentPosition(); }
```

Explanation:

1. Check if location services are enabled.
2. Check and request location permissions.
3. Handle permission denied or permanently denied cases.
4. Get the current location using Geolocator.getCurrentPosition().

2. Implementing a Search Bar

Use the TextField widget to create a search bar. When the user submits a query, trigger a function to fetch weather data for the searched city.

```
TextField( controller: _searchController, onSubmitted: (value) {
_fetchWeatherDataByCity(value); // Fetch data based on city name },
decoration: InputDecoration( labelText: 'Search for a city', suffixIcon:
IconButton( icon: Icon(Icons.search), onPressed: () =>
_fetchWeatherDataByCity(_searchController.text), ), ), );
```

3. Fetching Weather Data Based on Location

We can now modify the fetchWeatherData function that we defined earlier to get latitude and longitude either by a city name or by using the user's location.

```
Future<Map<String, dynamic>> fetchWeatherData({String? cityName, Position?
position}) async { if (cityName != null) { // construct URL for getting
weather data by city name } if (position != null) { // construct URL for
```

getting weather data by latitude & longitude } // Fetch and return weather and forecast data as before }

In your app's initialization (e.g., in initState), you can call _getCurrentLocation() and use the returned Position object to fetch the weather for the user's current location. If the user searches for a city, call _fetchWeatherDataByCity() with the entered city name.

Note: Remember to handle errors that might occur during location retrieval or the search process.

By implementing location and search features, you give users the flexibility to get weather information for their current location or any city they're interested in, making your weather app even more versatile and user-friendly.

Error Handling and User Feedback

Weather data comes from the internet, and as we know, the internet isn't always sunny. Network connections can drop, servers can have hiccups, and APIs might return unexpected responses. To create a weather app that users trust and enjoy, we must handle these errors gracefully and keep users informed about what's happening.

Why Error Handling is Crucial:

- **User Frustration:** A crashing app or a blank screen with no explanation is a recipe for user frustration. Proper error handling prevents crashes and provides clear feedback to users, helping them understand the situation and take appropriate action.
- **Data Reliability:** Weather data is time-sensitive. If a network request fails, your app should be able to recover and retry the request or provide fallback options (e.g., cached data).
- **App Reputation:** An app that handles errors gracefully is perceived as more polished and professional, leading to higher user satisfaction and better reviews.

Displaying User-Friendly Error Messages

When a network request fails, you should display a clear and concise error message to the user. Avoid technical jargon and focus on providing actionable information. Here are some examples of user-friendly error messages:

- "Unable to fetch weather data. Please check your internet connection and try again."
- "Sorry, we couldn't find that location. Please double-check the spelling or try a different search."
- "Oops! Something went wrong. We're working on fixing it. Please try again later."

You can display these messages using a SnackBar (a brief message at the bottom of the screen), an AlertDialog (a pop-up dialog), or simply by updating the UI to show an error state.

Showing Loading Indicators

While the app is fetching data from the API, it's important to provide visual feedback to the user to indicate that something is happening. A loading indicator, such as a circular progress indicator, spinning animation, or a skeleton loader can help manage user expectations and prevent them from thinking that the app is frozen.

```
// Use a boolean flag in your widget's state to track the loading state bool
isLoading = true; // ... in your build method if (isLoading) { return const
Center(child: CircularProgressIndicator()); } else if (error != null) { //
```

```
display your error message widget here } else { // Display the fetched weather
data }
```

Error Handling and State Management

You can manage the loading and error states using your chosen state management solution (e.g., Provider, BLoC, Riverpod). This allows you to easily trigger UI updates when the state changes.

By diligently handling errors and providing timely feedback, you'll create a weather app that's not only informative but also reliable and enjoyable to use, even when the internet throws a few rainclouds your way.

Adding Polish: Icons and Animations

A well-polished app not only functions well but also delights users with its visual appeal and smooth interactions. Let's enhance our weather app by adding weather icons that accurately represent current conditions and subtle animations that make the UI feel more alive.

Weather Icons: A Visual Language

Weather icons are a universal language for communicating weather conditions. A simple icon of a sun instantly conveys sunny skies, while a cloud with raindrops signifies rain. In Flutter, you have several options for incorporating weather icons into your app:

1. **Using the `weather_icons` Package:**
   This package provides a comprehensive collection of weather icons. Install it by adding the following dependency to your `pubspec.yaml` file:

   ```
   dependencies: weather_icons: ^3.0.0 # Or the latest version
   ```

   Then, import the package and use the `BoxedIcon` widget to display icons:

   ```
   import 'package:weather_icons/weather_icons.dart';
   BoxedIcon(WeatherIcons.day_sunny); // Display a sunny icon
   ```

2. **Using Custom Icons:**
   If you prefer a unique style, you can create your own custom weather icons and include them as image assets in your project.
3. **Using Font Icons:**
   You can use icon fonts like Font Awesome or Weather Icons to display weather icons. This approach offers flexibility and scalability.

Animation: Adding a Touch of Life

Animations can subtly enhance the user experience by making your app feel more responsive and engaging. Consider adding animations for transitions between screens, loading data, or even just to add a playful touch to your weather icons.

- **Implicit Animations:** Flutter provides several widgets with built-in implicit animations, like `AnimatedContainer`, `AnimatedOpacity`, and `AnimatedPositioned`. You can use these to easily create smooth transitions and effects.
- **Explicit Animations:** For more complex animations, you can use the `AnimationController` and `Tween` classes to create custom animations.

Here's an example of using `AnimatedOpacity` to fade in the weather data when it's loaded:

```
AnimatedOpacity( opacity: _isLoading ? 0.0 : 1.0, duration: Duration(seconds:
1), child: buildCurrentWeather(_weather), );
```

Explanation: We add the weather widget (`buildCurrentWeather`) inside an `AnimatedOpacity` widget. We modify our `_isLoading` state variable to false when the data is loaded. This will cause the opacity of our `AnimatedOpacity` widget to go from 0.0 (transparent) to 1.0 (opaque) over 1 second (`Duration(seconds: 1)`), creating a smooth fade-in effect.

A Note on Performance

While animations can add a delightful touch to your app, use them judiciously. Excessive or complex animations can negatively impact performance, especially on lower-end devices. Keep your animations subtle and optimized to ensure a smooth user experience.

By incorporating weather icons and subtle animations, you can transform a basic weather display into an informative and visually captivating experience for your users.

Beyond the Basics: Additional Features

With a solid foundation in place, you can now elevate your weather app by adding exciting features that cater to user needs and preferences. Here are some ideas to spark your creativity:

1. **Hourly Forecast:**
- Provide a more granular view of the weather by displaying hourly forecasts for the next 24 hours or more.
- Use a horizontal scrolling list or a similar UI element to present the hourly data.
- Include temperature, precipitation probability, wind speed, and other relevant information for each hour.
2. **Detailed Weather Information:**
- Go beyond basic temperature and conditions. Display additional details like:
   - Humidity
   - Wind speed and direction
   - Pressure
   - UV index
   - Sunrise and sunset times
   - Air quality
- Use tables, charts, or other visual elements to present the data clearly and concisely.
3. **Push Notifications for Weather Alerts:**
- Keep users informed about severe weather conditions (e.g., storms, extreme temperatures) by sending push notifications.
- Utilize the `flutter_local_notifications` package to implement local notifications.
- Consider integrating with a weather alert API to obtain accurate and timely alerts.
4. **Location-Based Reminders:**
- Allow users to set reminders based on weather conditions.
- For example, a reminder to "Take an umbrella if it rains" or "Wear sunscreen if the UV index is high."
- Use the `geolocator` package to track the user's location and trigger reminders when the conditions match.
5. **Integration with Other Weather APIs:**
- Explore other weather APIs like AccuWeather, WeatherKit, or Weatherbit.
- Offer users the option to choose their preferred weather provider.

- Compare data from different APIs to enhance accuracy and provide a more comprehensive view of the weather.

6. **Customization Options:**
- Let users personalize their weather experience by:
    - Choosing between Celsius and Fahrenheit temperature units.
    - Selecting their preferred language for the app.
    - Customizing the app's theme (light/dark mode, color schemes).
    - Configuring which weather parameters are displayed.

7. **Additional Ideas:**
- **Animated Backgrounds:** Create dynamic backgrounds that change based on the current weather conditions.
- **Radar/Map Views:** Integrate maps or radar views to display precipitation, wind patterns, or other weather-related information visually.
- **Historical Data:** Allow users to view past weather data for comparison and analysis.
- **Wear OS Integration:** Extend your app to Wear OS devices to provide quick access to weather information on the go.

By incorporating these additional features, you can elevate your weather app from a basic tool to a comprehensive weather companion that empowers users to make informed decisions and stay prepared for any weather scenario.

Chapter Summary

In this chapter, you embarked on the journey of building a weather app, a project that combines several key Flutter concepts. You discovered how to harness the power of weather data to create an informative and practical tool for everyday life.

We began by setting up a new Flutter project and introducing the `http` package for making network requests. We then explored the concept of data models and created the `Weather` and `Forecast` classes to structure the weather information we'd be fetching from the OpenWeatherMap API.

You learned how to construct the API endpoint URL, including the location (either the user's current location or a searched city) and your API key. Using the `http` package, you sent a GET request to the API and parsed the JSON response into your data models.

Next, we designed the user interface for both the current weather and forecast sections. We used layout widgets like `Scaffold`, `AppBar`, `Column`, and `Row` to organize the UI elements, and we incorporated widgets like `Text` and `Image.network` to display the fetched data.

We then covered how to obtain the user's current location using the `geolocator` package and implement a search bar to allow users to manually enter a location. You learned how to fetch weather data based on either the current location or the searched city.

Finally, we emphasized the importance of error handling and user feedback in the context of network requests. We discussed how to display loading indicators while data is being fetched and how to present user-friendly error messages in case of issues.

By completing this chapter, you've gained a solid understanding of how to build a weather app in Flutter, from fetching data from a real-world API to creating a visually appealing and informative user interface. This project serves as a stepping stone towards developing more complex, data-driven apps that leverage external services and APIs to provide valuable information and experiences to users.

Designing a Personal Finance Tracker

Outline

- The Value of Personal Finance Tracking
- Project Setup and Data Storage
- Data Models
- UI Design
- Transaction Input and Management
- Categorizing and Tagging Expenses
- Visualizing Spending Trends
- Budgeting Features (Optional)
- Additional Features (Optional)
- Chapter Summary

The Value of Personal Finance Tracking

In today's fast-paced world, it's easy to lose track of our finances. Money seems to slip through our fingers, and we might find ourselves wondering where it all went. That's why personal finance tracking is so crucial – it empowers you to take control of your money, make informed decisions, and pave the way towards achieving your financial goals.

Why Track Your Finances?

1. **Gain Awareness of Your Spending Habits:**
- **Identify Spending Patterns:** Tracking your income and expenses reveals where your money is going. Are you spending too much on dining out? Are there subscription services you no longer use? By analyzing your spending patterns, you can identify areas where you can cut back and save.
- **Make Conscious Choices:** Once you're aware of your spending habits, you can make conscious decisions about how you allocate your money. You can prioritize spending on things that truly matter to you and avoid impulsive purchases.
2. **Budget Effectively:**
- **Set Realistic Goals:** Tracking your income and expenses allows you to create a realistic budget that aligns with your financial goals. Whether it's saving for a down payment on a house, paying off debt, or building an emergency fund, a budget helps you stay on track.
- **Monitor Your Progress:** Regularly reviewing your budget and comparing it to your actual spending helps you identify areas where you might be overspending and adjust your budget accordingly.
- **Achieve Financial Stability:** Budgeting is a powerful tool for achieving financial stability. It helps you avoid overspending, build savings, and prepare for unexpected expenses.
3. **Achieve Your Financial Goals:**
- **Save for the Future:** Whether it's retirement, education, or a dream vacation, tracking your finances helps you save for your long-term goals.
- **Reduce Debt:** By understanding your income and expenses, you can develop a plan to pay off debts faster and save on interest payments.
- **Build Wealth:** Effective financial management can lead to wealth accumulation over time, giving you financial freedom and security.

Mobile Apps: Your Financial Companion

Gone are the days of manually recording expenses in a notebook. Personal finance tracking apps have revolutionized how we manage our money, making it more convenient and accessible than ever before.

- **Real-Time Tracking:** Apps allow you to track your spending on the go, right after you make a purchase. This ensures accurate and up-to-date records.
- **Categorization and Insights:** Many apps automatically categorize your expenses, providing insights into your spending habits and helping you identify areas for improvement.
- **Budgeting Tools:** Apps offer budgeting features, allowing you to set spending limits for different categories and track your progress towards your financial goals.
- **Reminders and Alerts:** Receive reminders to pay bills, track spending limits, and stay on top of your finances.

In this chapter, we'll harness the power of Flutter to build a personal finance tracker app that empowers you to take charge of your financial well-being.

Project Setup and Data Storage

Before we delve into the exciting world of transaction tracking and budgeting, let's set up our Flutter project and choose the most suitable data storage mechanism for our needs.

1. Creating Your Flutter Project

Creating a new Flutter project is a familiar step at this point. You can choose your preferred method, either using the command line:

```
flutter create personal_finance_tracker
```

Or your favorite IDE (Android Studio or VS Code).

2. Choosing Your Data Storage Arsenal

The way you store your financial data plays a significant role in the functionality and user experience of your app. Flutter offers various options, each with its own advantages and trade-offs:

Option 1: `shared_preferences` **(Beginner-Friendly)**

- **What It Is:** A simple key-value storage system that allows you to save basic data types (strings, numbers, booleans) locally on the device.
- **Pros:** Easy to use, suitable for small amounts of data or settings.
- **Cons:** Limited to basic data types, not ideal for complex data relationships or large datasets.

Option 2: `sqflite` **(Intermediate)**

- **What It Is:** A SQLite database wrapper for Flutter. SQLite is a lightweight, file-based database that's perfect for storing structured data within your app.
- **Pros:** More powerful than `shared_preferences`, allows for complex queries and relationships, good for offline data storage.
- **Cons:** Requires some SQL knowledge, might be overkill for very simple apps.

Option 3: Firebase (Advanced)

- **What It Is:** Google's cloud-based platform offers a real-time database (Firestore), cloud storage, authentication, and other powerful services.
- **Pros:** Real-time data synchronization across devices, scalable, easy integration with Flutter.
- **Cons:** Requires setting up a Firebase project, might not be suitable for apps that need to function completely offline.
- **Note:** We will explore Firebase in more detail in Chapter 21.

Making Your Choice:

- **Beginner:** If you're just starting with Flutter or building a simple app, shared_preferences is a great option. It's easy to understand and implement.
- **Intermediate:** If you want more structured data storage and offline capabilities, sqflite is a good choice. It gives you the power of a relational database without adding too much complexity.
- **Advanced:** If you want real-time data synchronization, cloud storage, and other advanced features, Firebase is a powerful option. However, it requires some setup and learning curve.

For this tutorial, we'll focus on shared_preferences for its simplicity and ease of use.

No matter which data storage option you choose, the fundamental concepts of data modeling and handling transactions remain the same.

Data Models

Data models are the backbone of any application that deals with structured information. In our personal finance tracker, data models will help us represent financial transactions and categories in a way that's both organized and easy to work with in our Flutter code.

What Are Data Models?

Think of data models as blueprints for creating objects that hold specific types of information. Each model defines a set of properties (data fields) that represent the characteristics of the object. For instance, a model for a person might have properties like name, age, and address.

Defining the Transaction Class:

Let's start by creating a Transaction class to represent each financial transaction in our app.

```
class Transaction { final double amount; // The amount of the transaction
(positive or negative) final String category; // The category of the
transaction (e.g., "Food", "Rent") final DateTime date; // The date of the
transaction final String description; // A description of the transaction
final bool isExpense; // Whether the transaction is an expense (true) or
income (false) Transaction({ required this.amount, required this.category,
required this.date, required this.description, required this.isExpense, }); //
Method to convert Transaction to a Map for storage in shared_preferences
Map<String, dynamic> toJson() { return { 'amount': amount, 'category':
category, 'date': date.toIso8601String(), 'description': description,
'isExpense': isExpense, }; } // Factory constructor to create Transaction from
a Map (from shared_preferences) factory Transaction.fromJson(Map<String,
dynamic> json) { return Transaction( amount: json['amount'], category:
json['category'], date: DateTime.parse(json['date']), description:
json['description'], isExpense: json['isExpense'], ); } }
```

We will store these Transaction objects as JSON strings in shared_preferences. The toJson()
and fromJson() methods help us to do so.

Defining the `Category` Class:

Next, we'll create a `Category` class to represent expense categories:

```
class Category { final String name; // Name of the category (e.g., "Food",
"Rent") final IconData icon; // Icon associated with the category (e.g.,
Icons.restaurant) Category({ required this.name, required this.icon, }); }
```

Since we're using `shared_preferences` which only supports primitive data types, we'll store the names of categories only. The app can then have a mapping of category names to icons internally.

How We'll Use These Models:

- **Transactions:** We'll create a list of `Transaction` objects to store all the user's financial transactions. The app will use these objects to display transactions in a list or grid, calculate totals for reports, and filter by category or date range.
- **Categories:** We'll create a list of `Category` objects to represent available expense categories. The app will use these to populate dropdown menus when adding or editing transactions.

By defining these data models, we establish a clear structure for representing financial data in our app. This will make our code easier to read, maintain, and extend as we add more features to our personal finance tracker.

UI Design

A well-designed user interface is crucial for a personal finance tracker app. It should present financial information clearly and intuitively, making it easy for users to understand their spending habits and manage their budget effectively. Let's outline the key UI components and how we'll structure them using Flutter's layout widgets.

Main UI Components:

1. **Dashboard:**
   - **Purpose:** Provides an overview of the user's financial health at a glance.
   - **Elements:**
     - **Income Summary:** Displays the total income for a selected period (e.g., month, week).
     - **Expense Summary:** Shows the total expenses for the selected period.
     - **Budget Summary:** (Optional) If the app includes budgeting features, displays the remaining budget or a progress bar indicating budget usage.
2. **Transactions List/Grid:**
   - **Purpose:** Displays a list of recent transactions, typically sorted by date.
   - **Elements:**
     - Each transaction item should show:
       - Amount (with positive/negative sign for income/expense)
       - Category
       - Date
       - Description (optional)
   - **Layout:**
     - `ListView.builder`: For a vertical list of transactions.
     - `GridView.builder`: For a grid layout (especially useful on larger screens).
3. **Transaction Input Form:**
   - **Purpose:** Allows users to add new transactions.

- ○ **Elements:**
  - ■ TextField: For entering the amount.
  - ■ DropdownButton: For selecting the category.
  - ■ DatePicker: For choosing the transaction date.
  - ■ TextField: (Optional) For adding a description.
  - ■ Segmented control or radio buttons: For selecting the type (income or expense).
4. **Categories/Tags View:**
  - ○ **Purpose:** Enables users to manage and filter transactions based on categories or tags.
  - ○ **Elements:**
    - ■ List or grid of categories/tags.
    - ■ Each category/tag can be represented with a name and an icon.
5. **Charts or Graphs:**
  - ○ **Purpose:** Visually represent spending patterns and trends over time.
  - ○ **Elements:**
    - ■ Pie chart: To show spending distribution across categories.
    - ■ Bar chart: To compare spending over different periods.
    - ■ Line chart: To track spending trends over time.

Layout Structure:

- **Scaffold:** The foundation for our app's structure.
- **AppBar:** Contains the app title and potentially navigation icons.
- BottomNavigationBar (Optional): For switching between different sections (e.g., dashboard, transactions, categories).
- **Body (Typically a Column or ListView):**
  - ○ **Dashboard:** A Column with widgets for income, expense, and budget summaries.
  - ○ **Transactions List/Grid:** A ListView.builder or GridView.builder to display transaction items.
  - ○ **Transaction Input Form:** A Form widget with the input fields described above.
  - ○ **Categories/Tags View:** A ListView or GridView for displaying categories/tags.
  - ○ **Charts or Graphs:** Widgets from a charting library like fl_chart or charts_flutter.

Example Layout (Dashboard):

```
Scaffold( appBar: AppBar( title: Text('Personal Finance Tracker'), ), body:
Column( children: [ IncomeSummaryWidget(), // Custom widget for income summary
ExpenseSummaryWidget(), // Custom widget for expense summary
BudgetSummaryWidget(), // Custom widget for budget summary (optional) ], ), );
```

Remember, this is just a starting point. You can customize the layout, add or remove elements, and create unique visual styles to match your app's purpose and aesthetics. The goal is to create a user interface that's both visually appealing and easy to use, empowering users to take control of their finances.

Transaction Input and Management

Empowering users to input and manage their transactions is the heart of a personal finance tracker. In this section, we'll create an intuitive form for adding new transactions and provide the functionality to edit and delete existing ones.

Building the Transaction Input Form

We'll utilize Flutter's `Form` widget to create a structured way for users to enter transaction details. The form will include the following elements:

1. **Amount `TextField`:**
   - **Widget:** `TextFormField` (from the `flutter_form_builder` package)
   - **Purpose:** Allows users to enter the transaction amount as a numerical value.
   - **Key Properties:**
     - `keyboardType: TextInputType.number`: Ensures the numeric keyboard is displayed.
     - `decoration: InputDecoration`: Customize the field's label and appearance.
     - `validator`: Add a validator function to ensure the amount is valid.
   - **Code Example:**

```
TextFormField( decoration: InputDecoration(labelText: 'Amount'),
keyboardType: TextInputType.number, validator: (value) { //
validation logic }, ),
```

2. **Category `DropdownButton`:**
   - **Widget:** `DropdownButtonFormField` (from the `flutter_form_builder` package)
   - **Purpose:** Lets users select a category for the transaction.
   - **Key Properties:**
     - `items`: A list of `DropdownMenuItem` widgets representing the categories.
     - `value`: The currently selected category.
     - `onChanged`: A callback that updates the selected category when the user makes a new choice.
     - `decoration`: Customize the dropdown's appearance.
     - `validator`: Validate that a category is selected.

3. **Date Picker:**
   - **Widget:** `showDatePicker`
   - **Purpose:** Allows users to select the transaction date.
   - **Key Properties:**
     - `context`: The `BuildContext` of the current widget.
     - `initialDate`: The initial date to show in the picker.
     - `firstDate`: The earliest date the user can select.
     - `lastDate`: The latest date the user can select.

```
DateTime selectedDate = DateTime.now(); // Initial state for
date ElevatedButton( onPressed: () async { final DateTime?
picked = await showDatePicker( context: context, initialDate:
selectedDate, firstDate: DateTime(2000), lastDate:
DateTime.now(), ); if (picked != null && picked !=
selectedDate) { setState(() { selectedDate = picked; }); } },
child: Text(DateFormat('yyyy-MM-dd').format(selectedDate)), );
```

4. **Description `TextField` (Optional):**
   - **Widget:** `TextFormField`
   - **Purpose:** Allows users to provide an optional description for the transaction.
   - **Key Properties:**
     - `maxLines`: Set to `null` to allow multiline input.

5. **Transaction Type:**

- ○ **Widget:** SegmentedButton (Cupertino style) or a set of Radio buttons.
- ○ **Purpose:** Allows the user to specify whether the transaction is an expense or income.
- ○ **Key Properties:**
    - ▪ children: Map of transaction type to labels or icons.
    - ▪ onValueChanged: Callback to update the selected type in state.

Adding, Editing, and Deleting Transactions:

- **Adding:** Use the formKey.currentState!.save() method to collect the form data when the user submits it. Create a new Transaction object and add it to your list of transactions.
- **Editing:** Allow users to tap on a transaction in the list to open the form in edit mode. Pre-fill the form with the existing transaction data and update the transaction when the user saves changes.
- **Deleting:** Add a delete button or swipe-to-delete gesture to each transaction item. When the user confirms the deletion, remove the transaction from the list and update the UI.

Updating the UI:

- Use setState() (or your chosen state management solution) to trigger a UI rebuild whenever the list of transactions is modified. This will ensure that the transactions list/grid is updated to reflect the latest changes.

Input Validation and Error Handling:

- Implement input validation within your Form to ensure that the entered data is valid (e.g., the amount is a number, the category is selected).
- Display appropriate error messages to the user if the input is invalid.

Code Example (Partial):

```
final _formKey = GlobalKey<FormState>(); Form( key: _formKey, child: Column(
children: [ // Amount TextField, Category Dropdown, Date Picker, etc.
ElevatedButton( onPressed: () { if (_formKey.currentState!.validate()) {
_formKey.currentState!.save(); // Add/edit the transaction and update the UI.
} }, child: Text('Save Transaction'), ), ], ), );
```

Categorizing and Tagging Expenses

A key aspect of personal finance tracking is understanding *where* your money is going. Categorizing and tagging expenses allows users to analyze their spending patterns, identify areas for potential savings, and make more informed financial decisions.

Implementing Categories:

1. **Category List:**
    - ○ Maintain a list of Category objects (refer to the Data Models section for the structure). You can initialize this list with common categories like:
      ```
      final List<Category> categories = [ Category(name: 'Food', icon:
      Icons.fastfood), Category(name: 'Transportation', icon:
      Icons.directions_car), Category(name: 'Entertainment', icon:
      Icons.movie), // ... other categories ];
      ```
    - ○ Use shared_preferences to store the list persistently.
2. **Category Selection:**

- In the transaction input form, use a `DropdownButtonFormField` (or a similar widget) to display the list of categories.
- Allow users to select a category for each transaction.
- Store the selected category in the `Transaction` object.

3. **Filtering by Category:**
   - Create a filter mechanism on the transactions list/grid screen.
   - Allow users to select a category to filter by.
   - Update the displayed list to show only transactions belonging to the selected category.

   ```
   // Sample filter implementation (pseudocode) filteredTransactions =
   _transactions.where((transaction) => transaction.category ==
   selectedCategory).toList();
   ```

Adding and Managing Custom Categories:

1. **"Add Category" Option:** Provide a button or action in the categories view to allow users to create new categories.
2. **Category Input Form:** Create a form to capture the category name and optionally choose an icon (using packages like `font_awesome_flutter`).
3. **Update Category List:** Add the new `Category` object to the `categories` list and update the `shared_preferences` to persist the changes.

Optional: Tagging Expenses

While categories offer a broad classification of expenses, tags allow for more granular organization.

1. **Tagging UI:** Provide a way for users to add multiple tags to each transaction. This could be a `TextField` with autocomplete suggestions or a list of checkboxes.
2. **Data Storage:**
   - For simple implementations, you can store tags as a comma-separated string within the `Transaction` object and `shared_preferences`.
   - For more complex scenarios, consider using a database to store tags separately and link them to transactions.
3. **Filtering:** Allow users to filter transactions based on one or more tags.

By implementing a categorization and tagging system, you empower users to gain valuable insights into their spending habits, identify trends, and make informed financial decisions. This feature adds significant value to your personal finance tracker app.

Visualizing Spending Trends

Numbers alone can only tell you so much. When it comes to personal finances, visualizing spending trends can be a game-changer. Charts and graphs provide a powerful way to transform raw data into intuitive and actionable insights, helping users grasp their spending habits at a glance.

Why Visualize Spending Trends?

- **Identify Patterns:** Charts reveal patterns that might not be obvious from looking at a list of transactions. You can quickly spot which categories you spend the most on, how your spending fluctuates over time, and where there might be opportunities to save.
- **Track Progress:** Visual representations of your spending can help you track your progress toward financial goals. Are you on track to meet your savings target? Is your spending in line with your budget?

- **Motivation and Engagement:** Seeing a visual representation of your financial progress can be highly motivating and encourage positive spending behaviors.

Types of Charts for Finance Tracking

Flutter offers several packages to easily create interactive and aesthetically pleasing charts. Some popular options include:

- `fl_chart`: A powerful and flexible charting library with a wide range of chart types (bar, line, pie, scatter, etc.). It offers extensive customization options to create charts that match your app's design.
- `charts_flutter`: A charting library based on the popular JavaScript library D3.js. It provides a rich set of pre-built chart types and supports complex data visualizations.
- `syncfusion_flutter_charts`: A comprehensive charting package with a variety of chart types, including financial charts like candlestick charts and technical indicators.

Choosing the Right Chart:

The type of chart you choose depends on the specific data you want to visualize:

- **Pie Charts:** Ideal for showing the proportion of spending in different categories. Each slice represents a category, and the slice size indicates the relative amount spent.
- **Bar Charts:** Great for comparing spending amounts across categories or over time. Each bar represents a category or time period, and the bar's height indicates the corresponding amount.
- **Line Charts:** Perfect for tracking spending trends over time. The line shows how spending has fluctuated over days, weeks, or months.

Implementing Charts: A Glimpse

Integrating charts into your Flutter app is straightforward with the help of charting packages. Here's a simplified example using `fl_chart` to create a pie chart:

```
PieChart( PieChartData( sections: [ PieChartSectionData( title: 'Food', value:
foodSpending, color: Colors.blue, ), // ... more sections for other categories
], ), );
```

In this example, `foodSpending` represents the total amount spent on food. You would typically calculate this value by iterating over your list of `Transaction` objects.

Empowering Users with Data

By incorporating charts and graphs into your personal finance tracker, you empower users to gain valuable insights into their spending habits. This can lead to better financial awareness, improved decision-making, and ultimately, a greater sense of control over their financial well-being.

Budgeting Features (Optional)

Budgeting is a powerful tool for gaining control over your finances. It helps you allocate your income wisely, track your spending, and ensure that you're on track to meet your financial goals. Let's explore how we can integrate budgeting features into our personal finance tracker app.

The Power of Budgeting

- **Financial Awareness:** Budgeting encourages you to think critically about your spending habits and prioritize where your money goes.
- **Goal Setting:** It enables you to set clear financial goals (e.g., saving for a vacation, paying off debt) and create a roadmap for achieving them.
- **Spending Control:** By setting spending limits for different categories, you can avoid overspending and make more conscious choices about your purchases.
- **Reduced Stress:** Knowing where your money is going and having a plan in place can significantly reduce financial stress and anxiety.

Implementing Budgeting in Your App

1. **Budget Data Model:**
   - Create a Budget class to represent budget information:

```
class Budget { final String category; // Category the budget applies
to final double amount; // Maximum spending limit for the category
final String period; // Budgeting period (e.g., "monthly", "weekly")
Budget({ required this.category, required this.amount, required
this.period, }); }
```

- Store a list of Budget objects in your data store (shared_preferences or a database).
2. **Setting Budgets:**
   - Create a UI for users to set budgets for different categories.
   - You can use TextFormField for the amount, DropdownButton for the category (populated with your existing categories), and radio buttons or a similar widget for the period (monthly/weekly).
   - Store the created Budget objects in your data store.
3. **Tracking Spending:**
   - As users add transactions, calculate the total spending for each category within the budget period.
   - Compare the spending to the corresponding budget amount.
4. **Displaying Visual Indicators:**
   - Use progress bars, charts, or other visual elements to show users how much they've spent in each category relative to their budget.
   - Consider color-coding the indicators (e.g., green for under budget, yellow for nearing the limit, red for over budget) to provide quick visual cues.
   - Display the remaining budget amount or percentage.

Example: Progress Bar for a Category

```
LinearProgressIndicator( value: categorySpending / budget.amount, // Calculate
the progress ratio backgroundColor: Colors.grey[200], valueColor:
AlwaysStoppedAnimation<Color>( categorySpending > budget.amount ? Colors.red :
Colors.green, ), // Change color based on progress );
```

Additional Budgeting Features:

- **Alerts and Notifications:** Notify users when they are close to reaching or exceeding their budget limits.
- **Budget History:** Allow users to view past budgets and track their spending over time.
- **Budget Goals:** Enable users to set savings goals and track their progress.

By incorporating budgeting features into your personal finance tracker, you empower users to gain better control over their spending, achieve their financial goals, and ultimately, improve their financial well-being.

Additional Features (Optional)

Now that you have a solid foundation for your personal finance tracker app, let's explore some additional features that can elevate it to the next level and make it even more valuable for users. These enhancements can be tailored to your specific needs and interests, allowing you to create a personalized financial management tool.

1. **Bill Reminders and Recurring Transactions:**
   - **Bill Reminders:** Help users stay on top of their bills by implementing reminders for due dates. Allow users to set reminders for individual bills, specify their frequency, and receive notifications before the due date.
   - **Recurring Transactions:** Automate the tracking of recurring expenses or income (e.g., rent, subscriptions, salary) by allowing users to create repeating transactions.
2. **Account Linking:**
   - **Bank Account Integration:** Enable users to connect their bank accounts to automatically import transactions. This eliminates manual data entry and ensures accurate, up-to-date records.
   - **Transaction Categorization:** Implement smart categorization to automatically assign categories to imported transactions based on transaction descriptions or patterns.
3. **Goal Setting and Tracking:**
   - **Savings Goals:** Allow users to set financial goals (e.g., saving for a down payment, paying off a loan) and track their progress over time.
   - **Visual Progress Tracking:** Use progress bars, charts, or other visual elements to display progress towards goals, motivating users to stay on track.
   - **Reminders and Milestones:** Send reminders or celebrate milestones (e.g., reaching a specific savings amount) to keep users motivated and engaged.
4. **Investment Tracking:**
   - **Portfolio Management:** Allow users to track their investments (e.g., stocks, mutual funds, cryptocurrencies).
   - **Real-Time Updates:** Fetch current market data to display the value of their investments in real-time.
   - **Performance Tracking:** Provide charts and graphs to visualize investment performance over time.
5. **Data Export and Backup:**
   - **CSV Export:** Enable users to export their transaction data in CSV format for further analysis or backup.
   - **Cloud Backup:** Offer options for cloud-based backup and synchronization to ensure that users never lose their valuable financial data.
6. **Multi-Currency Support:**
   - **Currency Conversion:** Allow users to track transactions in multiple currencies.
   - **Exchange Rate Integration:** Fetch current exchange rates from a reliable source to convert between currencies accurately.
7. **Security Features:**
   - **Biometric Authentication:** Add an extra layer of security by implementing fingerprint or facial recognition authentication to protect sensitive financial data.
   - **Data Encryption:** Encrypt stored data on the device to safeguard user information.

Your App, Your Way

Remember, these are just suggestions! You have the creative freedom to tailor your personal finance tracker to your specific needs and preferences. Explore these features, combine them, or come up with your own innovative ideas.

Flutter provides you with the tools and flexibility to create a powerful and personalized finance management tool. The only limit is your imagination!

Chapter Summary

In this chapter, you embarked on the journey of building a personal finance tracker app, a practical tool for managing and understanding your finances. We explored the significance of personal finance tracking in promoting financial awareness, effective budgeting, and the achievement of financial goals.

We guided you through the initial steps of setting up a new Flutter project and discussed various data storage options, including `shared_preferences`, `sqflite`, and Firebase. We then delved into creating data models (`Transaction` and `Category`) to represent the core financial data in your app.

You learned how to design the main UI components of a finance tracker, including the dashboard, transaction list/grid, input form, categories view, and charts/graphs. We discussed how to use layout widgets like `Scaffold`, `AppBar`, `Column`, and `Row` to structure these components.

Next, we focused on implementing transaction input and management features. You learned how to create a form for adding new transactions using `TextField`, `DropdownButton`, and `DatePicker`, and how to validate user input. We also discussed how to add, edit, and delete transactions from the data store and update the UI accordingly.

We then explored how to implement categorization and tagging for expenses, allowing users to better organize their transactions and gain insights into their spending patterns.

To visualize spending trends, we introduced the concept of data visualization using charts and graphs. You learned how to leverage libraries like `fl_chart` to create informative visualizations that help users understand their financial behavior.

We also discussed optional budgeting features, showing how to implement budget setting, tracking, and visual indicators to help users stay on top of their spending goals.

Finally, we explored additional features that you can consider adding to enhance your personal finance tracker, such as bill reminders, recurring transactions, account linking, goal setting, investment tracking, data export, multi-currency support, and security features.

By completing this chapter, you've gained a solid understanding of how to build a basic personal finance tracker in Flutter. With the knowledge and tools you've acquired, you can now customize and expand this app to create a personalized financial management tool tailored to your specific needs and preferences.

Section V:
Advanced Flutter Topics (Optional)

Testing Your Flutter Apps (Optional)

Outline

- The Importance of Testing
- Types of Flutter Tests
- Setting Up the Test Environment
- Unit Testing
- Widget Testing
- Integration Testing
- Test-Driven Development (TDD) in Flutter
- Mocking Dependencies
- Continuous Integration (CI) and Code Coverage
- Chapter Summary

The Importance of Testing

Imagine building a house without checking if the foundation is solid or the walls are straight. It's a recipe for disaster, right? Similarly, in software development, testing is the foundation upon which you build reliable, maintainable, and high-quality applications.

Why Testing is Your Safety Net

1. **Catch Bugs Early:** Testing helps you uncover errors and unexpected behaviors in your code early in the development process. The earlier you find bugs, the easier and cheaper they are to fix. Imagine trying to fix a critical bug in a complex app that's already been deployed – not fun!
2. **Ensure Code Quality:** Tests act as a safety net for your codebase. They verify that your app functions as expected, even after making changes or adding new features. This helps prevent regressions (where new code breaks existing functionality).
3. **Increase Developer Confidence:** When you have a comprehensive suite of tests, you can confidently refactor your code, experiment with new features, and make changes without fear of breaking something unexpectedly.
4. **Improve Design:** Writing tests often forces you to think more carefully about your code's design and structure, leading to cleaner, more modular code that's easier to understand and maintain.
5. **Documentation:** Well-written tests can serve as living documentation, providing examples of how your code should be used and what outputs to expect.

Manual vs. Automated Testing: The Tortoise and the Hare

- **Manual Testing:** Involves manually interacting with your app to verify its functionality. It's essential for exploratory testing and evaluating the overall user experience. However, it can be time-consuming, repetitive, and prone to human error.

- **Automated Testing:** Involves writing code that automatically exercises your app's features and verifies their behavior. Automated tests can be run quickly and repeatedly, providing faster feedback and catching bugs that might be missed in manual testing.

Why Automated Testing is a Superpower

- **Speed:** Automated tests can be executed in a fraction of the time it takes to perform manual testing. This is especially important for regression testing, where you need to quickly verify that your changes haven't broken anything.
- **Reliability:** Automated tests are consistent and less prone to human error. They ensure that your app's functionality is always tested in the same way, providing reliable results.
- **Efficiency:** Automated tests can be run automatically as part of your development workflow (e.g., using continuous integration), saving you valuable time and effort.
- **Coverage:** Automated tests can help you achieve higher test coverage, meaning that a larger portion of your codebase is being tested. This increases your confidence in the overall quality of your app.

In the following sections, we'll dive into the different types of automated tests you can write for your Flutter apps and how to create a comprehensive testing strategy to ensure your code is rock-solid.

Types of Flutter Tests

Flutter offers a robust testing framework that allows you to write different types of tests to ensure your app functions correctly and meets your quality standards. Let's explore the three main types of tests you'll encounter in Flutter development:

1. Unit Tests: Microscopic Examination

Unit tests are the smallest and most focused type of test. They zoom in on individual units of your code, such as functions, methods, or classes, and verify that they work as expected in isolation.

- **Purpose:** Isolate and test the smallest possible pieces of logic.
- **Scope:** Typically test a single function, method, or class without interacting with external dependencies (e.g., network requests, databases).
- **Benefits:** Fast, easy to write, and provide quick feedback during development. Help pinpoint the exact location of a bug if a test fails.

2. Widget Tests: UI Under Scrutiny

Widget tests take a step up in scope and test the behavior and UI of individual widgets. They ensure that your widgets render correctly, respond to user interactions as expected, and maintain their state properly.

- **Purpose:** Test the visual appearance and interactive behavior of widgets.
- **Scope:** Typically test a single widget or a small group of related widgets.
- **Benefits:** Verify that your UI elements look and function as intended. Help catch layout issues, styling errors, and interaction bugs.

3. Integration Tests: The Big Picture

Integration tests assess how different parts of your app work together. They simulate user interactions and test the flow of data and events across multiple widgets, screens, and even external systems (like APIs or databases).

- **Purpose:** Test the interaction between multiple components and ensure they work correctly as a whole.

- **Scope:** Test scenarios that involve navigating between screens, fetching data, updating state, and interacting with external dependencies.
- **Benefits:** Verify that your app's overall functionality is intact and that different parts integrate seamlessly. Can catch issues that might not be apparent in unit or widget tests.

A Comprehensive Testing Strategy:

Each type of test plays a specific role in your overall testing strategy:

- **Unit Tests:** The foundation of your testing pyramid. You should have many unit tests to ensure the correctness of your core logic.
- **Widget Tests:** Build upon unit tests to verify the UI and interaction behavior of individual widgets.
- **Integration Tests:** Cap off your testing strategy by validating the overall functionality of your app and its interaction with external systems.

By combining these different types of tests, you create a safety net that catches bugs early, ensures code quality, and gives you the confidence to make changes and enhancements to your Flutter apps without breaking existing functionality.

Setting Up the Test Environment

Before we dive into writing actual tests, let's get your Flutter project ready for testing. Flutter provides a well-structured environment for creating and running tests, and we'll walk through the necessary steps to set it up.

Creating the `test` Directory

By default, Flutter projects already include a `test` directory in the root folder. This is where you'll place all your test files. If the directory doesn't exist for some reason, you can simply create it manually.

Adding Test Files

Inside the `test` directory, you can create individual files for each test you write. The convention is to name your test files with a `_test.dart` suffix (e.g., `widget_test.dart`, `counter_test.dart`). You can organize test files into subdirectories if you have a large number of tests.

The `flutter_test` Package: Your Testing Companion

The `flutter_test` package is your main tool for writing and running tests in Flutter. It provides a rich set of functions and classes to:

- **Define Tests:** The `test` function is used to define an individual test case.
- **Make Assertions:** The `expect` function is used to check whether a condition is true or false.
- **Interact with Widgets:** The `WidgetTester` class allows you to simulate user interactions and test widget behavior.
- **Pump Widgets:** The `pumpWidget` and pump methods are used to render and update widgets in the test environment.

Here's a simple example of a test that verifies that 1 + 1 equals 2:

```
import 'package:flutter_test/flutter_test.dart'; void main() { test('Adding 1
+ 1 equals 2', () { expect(1 + 1, 2); }); }
```

Running Tests:

You have multiple options for running your tests:

- **Command Line:** From your project's root directory, run the following command:
  `flutter test`
    This will run all the tests in the `test` directory.
- **IDE:** If you're using Android Studio or VS Code, they typically provide integrated test runners with a GUI interface for running tests and viewing results.
- **Continuous Integration (CI):** In a professional development environment, you'll likely use a continuous integration (CI) system to automatically run your tests whenever you push code changes. Popular CI platforms for Flutter include Codemagic, GitHub Actions, and Bitrise. (We'll cover CI in more detail later in this chapter.)

By following these steps, you'll have your Flutter project fully equipped and ready for testing, ensuring that you can catch and fix any bugs before they reach your users.

Unit Testing

Unit testing is like taking a magnifying glass to your code and scrutinizing each individual piece to ensure it works correctly in isolation. The goal is to test the smallest possible unit of your code (a function, method, or class) without involving any external dependencies.

Why Unit Test?

- **Early Bug Detection:** Unit tests help you catch errors and unexpected behaviors during development, before they snowball into larger issues.
- **Improved Code Quality:** Well-written unit tests force you to think through edge cases and ensure your code handles various inputs and scenarios correctly.
- **Refactoring Confidence:** With a suite of unit tests, you can confidently refactor your code, knowing that if you break something, the tests will alert you.
- **Living Documentation:** Unit tests act as examples of how your code should be used, serving as valuable documentation for other developers (including your future self).

Writing Unit Tests with `flutter_test`

The `flutter_test` package provides a set of tools to write and run unit tests. The basic structure of a unit test looks like this:

```
import 'package:flutter_test/flutter_test.dart'; void main() {
test('description of what you are testing', () { // Test setup (if needed) //
Call the code you want to test // Use expect() to make assertions about the
results }); }
```

Let's look at an example of a unit test for a simple function that calculates the sum of two numbers:

```
int add(int a, int b) => a + b; void main() { test('add() should correctly add
two integers', () { expect(add(2, 3), 5); expect(add(-5, 10), 5);
expect(add(0, 0), 0); }); }
```

In this test, we call the `add()` function with different inputs and use `expect()` to verify that the output matches our expectations.

The `expect` Function: Your Assertion Arsenal

The `expect` function is the heart of unit testing. It takes two arguments:

- **The actual value:** The result you want to test.
- **The expected value (or matcher):** The value (or a matcher) you expect the actual value to be.

Here are some common matchers used with `expect`:

- `equals`: Checks for equality (e.g., `expect(result, equals(5))`).
- `is`: Checks for type or identity (e.g., `expect(result, isA<int>())`).
- `isTrue`, `isFalse`: Checks for boolean values.
- `isNull`, `isNotNull`: Checks for null values.
- `throwsA`: Checks if a function throws a specific exception.

Designing for Testability: Making Your Code Test-Friendly

To write effective unit tests, it's important to design your code with testability in mind:

- **Modularity:** Break down complex logic into smaller, reusable functions or methods.
- **Dependency Injection:** Avoid hardcoding dependencies (e.g., network clients, databases) into your classes. Instead, inject them as parameters, making it easier to substitute them with mock objects during testing.
- **Avoid Side Effects:** Functions that modify global state or have other side effects can be difficult to test in isolation. Strive for pure functions that only depend on their input and produce a predictable output.
- **Clear Interfaces:** Well-defined interfaces (e.g., function signatures) make it easier to test individual components without knowing their implementation details.
- **Thorough Testing:** Write tests for all your functions, methods, and classes, covering edge cases and error conditions.

By embracing unit testing and designing for testability, you can create a more robust and reliable Flutter app that you can confidently maintain and evolve over time.

Widget Testing

Widget tests take a step beyond unit tests by focusing on the behavior and visual appearance of individual widgets in your Flutter app. They allow you to interact with widgets, trigger events like button taps or text input, and verify that the UI responds correctly.

The Power of the `WidgetTester`

The `WidgetTester` class is your trusty assistant in the world of widget testing. It provides a range of methods to:

- **Build Widgets:** You can use `pumpWidget` to create a widget tree and attach it to the test environment.
- **Find Widgets:** `find.byType`, `find.byKey`, or `find.text` help you locate specific widgets in the widget tree.
- **Interact with Widgets:** Simulate user interactions like tapping buttons (`tap`), entering text (`enterText`), or scrolling (`drag`).
- **Verify Changes:** After interacting with a widget, you can use `pump` or `pumpAndSettle` to rebuild the UI and then check if the expected changes occurred using `expect`.

Example: Testing a Button

```
import 'package:flutter/material.dart'; import
'package:flutter_test/flutter_test.dart'; void main() { testWidgets('MyWidget
has a title and message', (WidgetTester tester) async { // Test setup await
tester.pumpWidget(const MaterialApp( home: Scaffold( body: MyWidget(title:
'T', message: 'M'), ), )); // Test assertion expect(find.text('T'),
findsOneWidget); expect(find.text('M'), findsOneWidget); }); }
```

testWidgets: Your Widget Testing Function

The testWidgets function is specifically designed for writing widget tests. It sets up a test environment, provides a WidgetTester instance, and handles cleanup after the test is finished.

pump vs. pumpWidget: Controlling the Widget Lifecycle

- pumpWidget: Use this at the beginning of your test to inflate the widget tree for the first time.
- pump: Use this to trigger a rebuild of the widget tree after interacting with a widget (e.g., after tapping a button).
- pumpAndSettle: Use this when you expect animations to occur after an interaction. It will wait for animations to complete before proceeding.

Golden Testing: Ensuring Pixel-Perfect UI

Golden tests involve comparing a widget's rendered appearance against a previously saved "golden image" (a reference image that represents the expected appearance). This helps you catch unintended UI changes that might occur due to code modifications.

To create a golden image:

1. Run your test with --update-goldens flag to capture a screenshot of the widget.
2. This screenshot is saved as a golden image in the goldens folder.

Subsequent test runs will automatically compare the widget's appearance with the golden image to ensure consistency.

Best Practices for Widget Testing:

- **Focus on Behavior:** Test the behavior and interactions of your widgets rather than testing implementation details.
- **Test Key Scenarios:** Focus on the most important user flows and edge cases.
- **Isolate Widgets:** Use techniques like dependency injection to isolate widgets from external dependencies (e.g., data providers) during testing.
- **Golden Tests:** Consider using golden tests to catch visual regressions in your UI.

By incorporating widget testing into your development workflow, you can ensure that your Flutter app's UI functions as expected, looks pixel-perfect, and delivers a polished user experience.

Integration Testing

While unit tests focus on individual pieces and widget tests verify the behavior of single UI elements, integration tests take a broader view. They assess how different parts of your Flutter app work together, ensuring that the interactions between widgets, screens, and external systems (like APIs or databases) function as expected.

The Scope of Integration Tests

Integration tests cover a wide range of scenarios, including:

- **Navigation:** Verify that navigating between screens works correctly and that data is passed correctly between screens.
- **Data Fetching:** Test the process of fetching data from an API or database and confirm that the data is displayed correctly in the UI.
- **State Management:** Ensure that your state management solution (e.g., Provider, BLoC) is working as expected and that changes to the state are reflected in the UI.
- **User Interactions:** Test how different UI elements interact with each other (e.g., tapping a button should update a text field).
- **Error Handling:** Verify that your app gracefully handles errors like network failures or invalid input.

Example: Testing Navigation and Data Fetching

Let's say you have a news app (like the one we built in Chapter 16). An integration test might simulate a user:

1. Tapping on a news article in the list.
2. Verify that the app navigates to the correct article details screen.
3. Check that the article details are displayed correctly (title, content, image).

Challenges of Integration Testing

Integration tests can be more complex to write and maintain than unit or widget tests due to:

- **External Dependencies:** They often involve interacting with external systems (APIs, databases), which might require setting up test environments or mocking dependencies.
- **Setup and Teardown:** They may need more elaborate setup and teardown logic compared to smaller, isolated tests.
- **Execution Time:** They can take longer to run than unit or widget tests, especially if they involve network requests.

Strategies for Effective Integration Tests

To write effective integration tests, consider the following tips:

- **Focus on Key User Flows:** Prioritize testing the most critical user interactions and scenarios in your app.
- **Isolate Dependencies:** Use mocking or stubbing techniques to simulate external dependencies and avoid relying on real services during testing.
- **Modularize Tests:** Break down complex integration tests into smaller, more manageable units.
- **Prioritize Reliability:** Make sure your tests are consistent and produce reliable results across different environments and devices.

The `integration_test` Package: Your Integration Testing Companion

Flutter provides the `integration_test` package, which offers a framework for writing and running integration tests. This package provides tools to interact with the Flutter driver, automate UI interactions, and assert on the app's state and behavior.

Conclusion

Integration testing is a vital part of your Flutter app's quality assurance process. By thoroughly testing the interactions between different parts of your app, you can ensure that it functions correctly, delivers a smooth user experience, and meets your high standards for reliability and performance.

Test-Driven Development (TDD) in Flutter

Test-Driven Development (TDD) is a software development approach that flips the traditional coding process on its head. Instead of writing code first and then tests, you write a failing test *before* you write any implementation code. This seemingly counterintuitive approach has profound benefits for your Flutter projects.

The TDD Cycle: Red, Green, Refactor

TDD follows a simple yet powerful cycle:

1. **Red:** Write a test that describes a specific behavior or functionality. Since the code to implement that functionality doesn't exist yet, the test will fail.
2. **Green:** Write the minimum amount of code necessary to make the test pass. Don't worry about perfect code at this stage – just get the test to pass.
3. **Refactor:** Now that you have a working implementation, clean up your code, improve its structure, and eliminate any duplication. Since you have the safety net of your tests, you can refactor confidently, knowing that you haven't broken anything.

Repeat this cycle for each piece of functionality you want to add to your app.

Why TDD Works:

- **Improved Code Quality:** By writing tests first, you're forced to think carefully about the desired behavior of your code before you implement it. This leads to a clearer design and more robust code.
- **Reduced Defect Rate:** Tests catch bugs early, preventing them from creeping into production and causing problems for your users.
- **Faster Feedback Loop:** You get immediate feedback on whether your code works as expected, which allows you to catch errors quickly and iterate rapidly.
- **Living Documentation:** Tests act as executable documentation, providing clear examples of how your code should be used.
- **Refactoring Confidence:** With a suite of tests in place, you can confidently refactor and improve your code without fear of breaking existing functionality.

Applying TDD in Flutter:

TDD is easily applicable to Flutter development. You can write unit tests for your Dart code (business logic, data models) and widget tests for your UI components.

Here's a simplified example of TDD in Flutter:

1. **Red:** Write a widget test for a button that doesn't exist yet. The test expects the button to display specific text and trigger a callback when tapped.
2. **Green:** Create a basic `ElevatedButton` widget with the specified text and `onPressed` callback to make the test pass.
3. **Refactor:** Improve the button's styling or add error handling. Your tests will ensure that these changes don't break the core functionality.

By adopting TDD, you embed testing into your development workflow from the start. This leads to better code quality, fewer bugs, and increased confidence in the reliability of your Flutter apps. While TDD might seem like extra work upfront, it can save you significant time and effort in the long run by preventing costly bugs and making your codebase more maintainable.

Mocking Dependencies

Imagine you're testing a weather app. You don't want your tests to rely on the actual weather conditions or the availability of a network connection. Instead, you want to simulate different scenarios and control the responses you receive. This is where mocking comes to the rescue.

What is Mocking?

Mocking involves creating fake (or "mock") versions of external dependencies that your code relies on. These mock objects mimic the behavior of the real dependencies but allow you to control their responses and behavior during testing.

Why Mock Dependencies?

- **Isolation:** Mocking allows you to test your code in isolation from external factors. You can focus on verifying the logic of your components without worrying about the reliability or state of external systems.
- **Control:** You have full control over the mock objects, so you can simulate different scenarios, error conditions, and responses, making your tests more comprehensive.
- **Speed:** Mock objects are typically faster than interacting with real dependencies (e.g., network requests), leading to faster test execution.
- **Determinism:** Tests using mock objects are more deterministic because you control the mock responses, ensuring that your tests always run the same way.

Mocking with `mockito`

The `mockito` package is a popular tool for creating mock objects in Flutter. Here's how to use it:

1. **Add the Dependency:** Include `mockito` as a dev dependency in your `pubspec.yaml` file.

   ```
   dev_dependencies: mockito: ^5.0.0
   ```

2. **Generate Mock Classes:** Use the `build_runner` tool to generate mock classes for your dependencies.

   ```
   flutter pub run build_runner build
   ```

3. **Use Mock Objects:** In your tests, create instances of the generated mock classes and use them as substitutes for your real dependencies.

Mocking Network Requests

```
import 'package:mockito/mockito.dart'; import 'package:http/http.dart' as
http; class MockClient extends Mock implements http.Client {} // ... in your
test final client = MockClient();
when(client.get(Uri.parse('https://api.example.com/data'))).thenAnswer((_)
async => http.Response('{"data": "mocked"}', 200)); final result = await
fetchData(client: client); // Pass the mock client to your data fetching
function expect(result, 'mocked');
```

Explanation:

1. Create a mock client that simulates the behavior of the `http.Client`.
2. Use when to define the behavior of the mock client's `get` method. In this case, we return a mock response with the JSON data `{"data": "mocked"}`.
3. When `fetchData` calls the `get` method, it will receive the mock response instead of making an actual network request.
4. We then assert that the result of `fetchData` is indeed the expected 'mocked' data.

Mocking Other Dependencies

You can apply a similar approach to mock databases, shared preferences, or any other external components your code interacts with. The key is to create mock objects that simulate the behavior of the real dependencies and provide controlled responses for your tests.

By incorporating mocking into your testing strategy, you can isolate your code, write more comprehensive tests, and achieve faster and more reliable results.

Continuous Integration (CI) and Code Coverage

In the fast-paced world of software development, ensuring code quality and quickly identifying issues is paramount. Continuous Integration (CI) and code coverage are two powerful tools that help you achieve this goal.

Continuous Integration (CI): Your Automated Guardian

CI is a development practice where developers integrate code changes into a shared repository frequently (e.g., multiple times a day). Each integration triggers an automated build and testing process, ensuring that new code doesn't break existing functionality.

Why CI Matters for Flutter Development:

- **Early Issue Detection:** CI catches integration issues early, when they're easier and less costly to fix. This prevents small problems from snowballing into major headaches down the line.
- **Improved Code Quality:** By running tests automatically with every code change, CI ensures that your codebase maintains a high level of quality.
- **Faster Feedback Loop:** Developers receive immediate feedback on the impact of their changes, allowing them to identify and address issues promptly.
- **Increased Confidence:** With a reliable CI system in place, you can confidently deploy new features and releases, knowing that your code has been thoroughly tested.

Code Coverage: Measuring Your Test Effectiveness

Code coverage is a metric that tells you how much of your codebase is actually being exercised by your tests. It's usually expressed as a percentage, where higher percentages indicate better test coverage.

While 100% code coverage doesn't guarantee a bug-free app, it's a good indicator of how thorough your tests are. Aiming for high code coverage helps you ensure that your tests are effectively catching potential issues and reducing the risk of unexpected bugs.

Tools and Services for CI/CD in Flutter:

Flutter has excellent support for CI/CD with various tools and services available:

- **Codemagic:** A popular CI/CD platform specifically designed for Flutter. It offers seamless integration with Flutter projects and provides features like automated building, testing, and deployment.
- **GitHub Actions:** A powerful automation platform that allows you to build custom workflows for your Flutter projects. You can set up actions to run your tests, generate reports, and deploy your app to various platforms.
- **Bitrise:** A mobile-focused CI/CD platform with pre-built steps and workflows for Flutter. It simplifies the setup process and offers a wide range of integrations.
- **Jenkins:** A popular open-source automation server that you can use to build custom CI/CD pipelines for Flutter.
- **Other Options:** Many other CI/CD providers (like CircleCI, Travis CI) can be used with Flutter.

Implementing CI/CD in Your Flutter Projects:

1. **Choose a CI/CD Platform:** Select a platform that aligns with your team's preferences and workflow.
2. **Create a Workflow:** Define the steps of your CI/CD pipeline, including checking out the code, running tests, building the app, and deploying it.
3. **Configure Environment Variables:** Set up environment variables to store sensitive information like API keys or deployment credentials securely.
4. **Monitor and Analyze:** Monitor your CI/CD pipeline for failures and analyze code coverage reports to identify areas where you can improve your tests.

By incorporating continuous integration and tracking code coverage, you can ensure that your Flutter app is thoroughly tested and that you catch potential issues early in the development cycle. This leads to a more reliable and maintainable codebase and helps you deliver high-quality apps that your users will love.

Chapter Summary

In this chapter, you were introduced to the essential world of testing your Flutter apps. We emphasized the importance of testing for building reliable, maintainable, and high-quality apps, discussing how it helps catch bugs early, ensures code quality, and boosts developer confidence.

We explored the differences between manual and automated testing, highlighting the advantages of automated testing in terms of speed, reliability, efficiency, and coverage. We then introduced the three main types of tests in Flutter: unit tests, widget tests, and integration tests, each serving a specific purpose in your overall testing strategy.

You learned how to set up your Flutter project for testing by creating a `test` directory and adding test files. We introduced the `flutter_test` package and its core functions, like `test` and `expect`, which form the backbone of your test cases. You also learned how to run your tests from the command line or within an IDE.

We delved into unit testing, demonstrating how to write tests for individual functions, methods, and classes. We highlighted the use of assertions with `expect` and discussed the importance of designing your code with testability in mind.

Widget testing was introduced as a way to test the UI of individual widgets. You learned how to use the `WidgetTester` to interact with widgets, trigger events, and verify UI changes. We covered the `testWidgets` function for writing widget tests and the difference between pump and `pumpWidget` for controlling the widget lifecycle during tests. We also introduced the concept of golden testing, which ensures visual consistency in your UI.

Finally, we explored integration testing, which tests the interaction between multiple components. We discussed the challenges and strategies for writing effective integration tests and mentioned the `integration_test` package as a helpful tool.

To further enhance your testing practices, we briefly introduced Test-Driven Development (TDD) and discussed how it can lead to better code quality and design. We also covered the concept of mocking dependencies to isolate your code during testing and ensure deterministic results.

We concluded by touching upon continuous integration (CI) and code coverage, emphasizing their importance in automating testing, catching issues early, and maintaining a high-quality codebase. We recommended several tools and services for implementing CI and tracking code coverage in your Flutter projects.

By mastering these testing techniques, you'll be well-equipped to build robust, reliable, and maintainable Flutter apps that delight your users with a seamless experience.

Custom Animations and Transitions (Optional)

Outline

- The Magic of Animations and Transitions
- Implicit Animations: Flutter's Built-in Smoothness
- Explicit Animations: Taking Full Control
- Animation Curves and Controllers
- Tweening: Transforming Values Over Time
- Staggered Animations: Adding Complexity
- Hero Animations: Smooth Transitions Between Screens
- Advanced Custom Animations (Optional)
- Chapter Summary

The Magic of Animations and Transitions

Animations and transitions are the secret ingredients that transform a good app into a great one. They breathe life into static interfaces, creating a more engaging, intuitive, and enjoyable user experience. In Flutter, crafting these visual flourishes is surprisingly easy and rewarding.

Why Animations and Transitions Matter

- **User Feedback:** Animations provide instant visual feedback to user actions, making interactions feel more responsive and natural. Imagine a button that smoothly changes color when pressed – it not only confirms the action but also adds a touch of polish to the UI.
- **Visual Cues:** Transitions guide the user's attention during screen changes or interactions. A fade-out effect as a dialog closes helps users maintain context, while a slide-in animation for a new screen signals a shift in focus.
- **Emotional Connection:** Well-crafted animations can evoke positive emotions, creating a sense of delight and making your app feel more polished and professional.
- **Branding:** Animations can be used to reinforce your brand's personality and create a unique visual identity.

Types of Animations: A Visual Vocabulary

Flutter's animation toolkit provides a diverse set of tools to create a wide range of effects:

- **Fading:** Smoothly transitioning a widget's opacity from 0 (invisible) to 1 (fully visible) or vice versa. This can be used to introduce or remove elements from the screen.
- **Sliding:** Moving a widget across the screen along a specific axis (horizontal or vertical). Sliding animations are commonly used for navigation drawers, modal sheets, and dialogs.
- **Scaling:** Increasing or decreasing the size of a widget over time. This can create a sense of focus or emphasis on specific elements.
- **Color/Opacity Changes:** Gradually changing the color or opacity of a widget to create visual feedback or transitions.
- **Rotation:** Rotating a widget around its center point. This can be used for spinning loading indicators or interactive elements.

Real-World Examples: Animations in Action

You'll find animations and transitions used creatively in many popular apps:

- **Social Media:** Animated likes, comments, and reactions that appear with a flourish.
- **Productivity Apps:** Smooth transitions between tasks, calendar views, or project lists.
- **Games:** Character animations, particle effects, and screen transitions that enhance gameplay.
- **E-commerce:** Animated product showcases, shopping cart transitions, and confirmation animations.

Your Turn to Animate

In the following sections, we'll dive into the technical details of creating custom animations in Flutter, from implicit animations (built-in transitions) to explicit animations (customizable effects). You'll learn how to control animation timing, use different animation curves, and create visually captivating experiences that delight your users.

Implicit Animations: Flutter's Built-in Smoothness

Flutter's built-in implicit animations offer a remarkably easy way to add a touch of magic to your app's UI. These special widgets automatically handle the animation process for you, making smooth transitions between different states a breeze.

How Implicit Animations Work:

Implicitly animated widgets, such as `AnimatedContainer`, `AnimatedOpacity`, and `AnimatedAlign`, take care of the complexities of animation under the hood. When a property of the widget changes (e.g., size, color, opacity), the widget automatically interpolates between the old and new values over a specified duration, creating a visually appealing transition.

Common Implicitly Animated Widgets:

- **`AnimatedContainer`:** Animates changes to a container's size, padding, margin, color, etc.
- **`AnimatedOpacity`:** Animates the opacity of a child widget.
- **`AnimatedAlign`:** Animates the alignment of a child widget.
- **`AnimatedPadding`:** Animates changes to a widget's padding.
- **`AnimatedPositioned`:** Animates the position of a child widget within a `Stack`.

Code Example: Fading a Widget In and Out

```
bool showWidget = true; AnimatedOpacity( opacity: showWidget ? 1.0 : 0.0,
duration: Duration(seconds: 1), child: Container( width: 200, height: 200,
color: Colors.blue, ), );
```

Explanation: When showWidget is true, the `AnimatedOpacity` widget sets its opacity to 1.0 (fully visible), When showWidget becomes `false`, the opacity transitions to 0.0, making it disappear gradually over 1 second.

Benefits of Implicit Animations:

- **Simplicity:** You don't need to create animation controllers or tweens manually. The widget handles everything for you.
- **Ease of Use:** Just change the widget's properties, and the animation happens automatically.
- **Performance:** Implicit animations are generally optimized for performance, making them suitable for simple transitions.

Limitations:

- **Limited Customization:** You have less control over the animation's details, such as the easing curve or specific timing.
- **Complexity:** For intricate animations or sequences of animations, explicit animations (which we'll cover later) provide more flexibility.

When to Use Implicit Animations:

Implicit animations are a great choice when you need:

- **Simple Transitions:** Fading, scaling, moving, or changing the color of a widget.
- **Quick and Easy Animations:** You want to add some visual flair without writing complex animation code.
- **Optimized Performance:** You're concerned about performance and want to use Flutter's built-in optimizations.

By leveraging the convenience of implicit animations, you can quickly and easily enhance the visual appeal and interactivity of your Flutter apps, adding a touch of polish that users will appreciate.

Explicit Animations: Taking Full Control

While implicit animations are convenient for basic transitions, they can feel limiting when you want to create more complex, custom animations that don't fit the mold of pre-defined behaviors. That's where explicit animations step in, giving you fine-grained control over every aspect of the animation process.

Core Concepts of Explicit Animations: The Choreography

Explicit animations involve orchestrating the movement and transformation of your widgets using a combination of essential elements:

1. **AnimationController:**
   - The director of the show, this controller manages the animation's timeline and progress. It produces a value that ranges from 0.0 (the beginning of the animation) to 1.0 (the end).
   - You can start, stop, reverse, repeat, or even control the speed of the animation using the AnimationController.
2. **Animation:**
   - The actor that plays the role of the animated value. It listens to the AnimationController and receives the current value representing the animation's progress.
   - You can create Animation objects for different types of values: double (for size, position, opacity), Color (for color transitions), or even custom types.
3. **Tween:**
   - The makeup artist that transforms your animated value. It defines the start and end values for the animation and provides the in-between values as the animation progresses.
   - You can use Tween classes like Tween<double>, ColorTween, or SizeTween to animate specific properties.

Fading a Widget: A Simple Explicit Animation

```
AnimationController controller = AnimationController( duration: const
Duration(seconds: 2), vsync: this, ); Animation<double> animation =
Tween<double>(begin: 0, end: 1).animate(controller); @override void
initState() { super.initState(); controller.forward(); // Start the animation
} @override Widget build(BuildContext context) { return Scaffold( // ... body:
```

```
Center( child: FadeTransition( opacity: animation, // Attach animation to
Opacity child: Container( // ... your widget to animate ), ), ), ); }
```

Explanation:

1. We create an `AnimationController` that runs for 2 seconds and uses the Ticker provider of the current context (`this`).
2. We create an `Animation<double>` using a Tween to specify a start value of 0.0 and an end value of 1.0. We pass our `AnimationController` to the `animate` method of Tween to drive it.
3. In `initState`, we call `controller.forward()` to start the animation.
4. In `build`, we create a `FadeTransition` widget that uses our animation value to change its opacity.

Explicit vs. Implicit: A Matter of Control

- **Explicit Animations:** More flexible and customizable, but require more setup and understanding of animation concepts. Ideal for complex animations or when you need precise control over timing and behavior.
- **Implicit Animations:** Simpler and easier to use, but less flexible. Suitable for basic transitions and animations where you don't need fine-grained control.

By understanding the power of explicit animations, you gain the ability to craft unique and engaging visual experiences in your Flutter apps that go beyond the standard transitions.

Animation Curves and Controllers

While basic animations bring movement to your app, animation curves and controllers let you add finesse and personality to the motion. Think of it like choosing the right music for a scene in a movie – the curve and controller determine the rhythm and feel of the animation.

Animation Curves: Beyond Linear Motion

An animation curve describes how an animation's values change over time. Instead of a simple linear progression, you can introduce easing, acceleration, deceleration, or even bouncing effects to make your animations more visually interesting and natural.

Flutter provides various built-in curves:

- `Curves.linear`: A constant speed throughout the animation.
- `Curves.easeIn`: Starts slowly, then accelerates.
- `Curves.easeOut`: Starts quickly, then decelerates.
- `Curves.easeInOut`: A combination of `easeIn` and `easeOut`.
- `Curves.bounceIn`, `Curves.bounceOut`, `Curves.elasticIn`, `Curves.elasticOut`: More playful curves that simulate bouncing or elastic effects.

Using CurveTween:

You can apply a curve to your animation using `CurveTween`:

```
animation = CurvedAnimation(parent: controller, curve: Curves.easeInOut);
```

This modifies our previous animation to use easeInOut curve.

`AnimationController`: **The Conductor**

The `AnimationController` is the heart of an explicit animation. It's a special type of `Animation` that:

- Generates values from 0.0 to 1.0 over a specified duration.
- Controls the animation's state (e.g., playing, stopped, dismissed).
- Provides methods to start, stop, reverse, or repeat the animation.

Key `AnimationController` Properties:

- **`duration`:** The total time the animation should take to complete.
- **`vsync`:** A TickerProvider that ensures your animation is synchronized with the screen's refresh rate, preventing jank.
- **`reverseDuration`:** The duration of the animation when played in reverse (optional).

Controlling the Animation:

- `controller.forward()`: Starts the animation.
- `controller.reverse()`: Reverses the animation.
- `controller.stop()`: Stops the animation.
- `controller.repeat()`: Repeats the animation indefinitely.

`TickerProviderStateMixin`: **Staying in Sync**

When using `AnimationController`, you'll often need to mix in the `TickerProviderStateMixin` to your `State` class. This provides the necessary "ticker" objects that drive the animation and ensure it stays in sync with the screen's refresh rate.

```
class _MyAnimatedWidgetState extends State<MyAnimatedWidget> with
SingleTickerProviderStateMixin { // ... (Your animation code here) }
```

Example: A Bouncing Ball

```
Animation<double> animation = Tween(begin: 100.0, end: 200.0).animate(
CurvedAnimation(parent: controller, curve: Curves.bounceOut), ); // ... (In
your build method) AnimatedBuilder( animation: controller, // Pass the
animation controller builder: (context, child) { return Container( width: 50,
height: 50, margin: EdgeInsets.only(top: animation.value), // Animated margin
decoration: const BoxDecoration(color: Colors.red, shape: BoxShape.circle), );
}, );
```

In this example, the ball is dropped using `Curves.bounceOut` which gives it the bouncing effect.

By mastering animation curves and controllers, you gain precise control over the timing, speed, and feel of your animations, unlocking a new dimension of creativity and user engagement in your Flutter apps.

Tweening: Transforming Values Over Time

While an `AnimationController` manages the timing and progress of your animation, tweens are responsible for the actual transformation of values. They define how a property (like size, position, or color) changes smoothly from its initial value to its final value over the course of the animation.

What is Tweening?

Imagine you want to animate a square growing from 100 pixels wide to 200 pixels wide. You could abruptly change the width from 100 to 200, but that would look jarring. Tweening allows you to create a smooth transition between these values, with the square gradually increasing in size over time.

In Flutter, a Tween object is a stateless object that simply defines the start and end values of an animation. It's responsible for calculating the intermediate values between the start and end points based on the current progress of the animation (provided by the AnimationController).

Types of Tweens:

Flutter offers various built-in tweens to handle different types of values:

- **Tween<double>:** For animating numeric values (e.g., size, position, opacity).
- **ColorTween:** For animating color transitions.
- **SizeTween:** For animating size changes.
- **RectTween:** For animating changes to rectangles (position and size).
- **IntTween:** For animating integers.

Using Tweens:

To use a tween in your animation, you first create an Animation object by calling the animate() method on your Tween, passing in the AnimationController. Then, you use the Animation object to drive the changes in your widget's properties.

Example: Animating a Container's Width

```
AnimationController _controller = AnimationController( duration: const
Duration(seconds: 2), vsync: this, ); Animation<double> _animation =
Tween(begin: 100.0, end: 200.0).animate(_controller); @override Widget
build(BuildContext context) { return Scaffold( // ... body: Center( child:
AnimatedBuilder( animation: _controller, builder: (context, child) { return
Container( width: _animation.value, // Use animated width height: 100.0,
color: Colors.blue, ); }, ), ), ); }
```

Explanation:

1. Create an AnimationController.
2. Create an Animation<double> using Tween specifying start and end width values.
3. Use AnimatedBuilder, which listens to _controller and passes the current value of the animation to its builder each time the animation updates.
4. In the builder of AnimatedBuilder, we use _animation.value to get the current animated value (between 100 to 200) and set the width of the container.

With tweens, you can create smooth and visually pleasing transitions for a wide variety of widget properties, adding a touch of elegance to your Flutter animations.

Staggered Animations: Adding Complexity

While animating a single element can be eye-catching, imagine the possibilities when multiple widgets come to life in a choreographed sequence. Staggered animations introduce this level of complexity, allowing you to orchestrate animations that unfold in a visually pleasing rhythm.

The Concept:

Staggered animations involve animating multiple widgets with different start and end times, creating a cascading effect. This can be achieved by dividing the overall animation duration into intervals, with each widget assigned a specific interval during which its animation will play.

`Interval`: Your Animation Scheduler

Flutter's `Interval` class is your tool for defining these animation schedules. An `Interval` takes two parameters:

- begin: The starting point of the interval, expressed as a percentage of the overall animation duration (0.0 to 1.0).
- end: The ending point of the interval, also as a percentage of the duration.

You can then use the `Interval` object to create a `CurvedAnimation` that applies the interval to your `AnimationController`.

Example: Fading Widgets in Sequence

Let's create a staggered animation where three containers fade in one after the other with a slight delay between each:

```
AnimationController _controller = AnimationController( duration: const
Duration(seconds: 3), vsync: this, ); // Create animations with different
intervals final Animation<double> firstFade = CurvedAnimation( parent:
_controller, curve: const Interval(0.0, 0.33, curve: Curves.easeIn), // First
33% ); final Animation<double> secondFade = CurvedAnimation( parent:
_controller, curve: const Interval(0.33, 0.66, curve: Curves.easeIn), //
Second 33% ); final Animation<double> thirdFade = CurvedAnimation( parent:
_controller, curve: const Interval(0.66, 1.0, curve: Curves.easeIn), // Final
33% ); // ... In your build method FadeTransition(opacity: firstFade, child:
Container(color: Colors.red, width: 100, height: 100)),
FadeTransition(opacity: secondFade, child: Container(color: Colors.green,
width: 100, height: 100)), FadeTransition(opacity: thirdFade, child:
Container(color: Colors.blue, width: 100, height: 100)), // ...
```

Explanation:

1. We create an `AnimationController` with a 3-second duration.
2. We define three `CurvedAnimation` objects, each associated with a different `Interval`. The first animation starts at 0.0 and ends at 0.33 (the first third of the animation). The second starts at 0.33 and ends at 0.66, and so on.
3. We wrap each container with a `FadeTransition` and assign the corresponding animation to its opacity property.

When you run this code, you'll see the containers fade in one after the other, creating a staggered effect.

Beyond Fading:

You can use staggered animations for more than just fading. You can animate size, position, color, or any other animatable property to create complex and engaging visual sequences. Experiment with different combinations of widgets, intervals, and curves to unleash your creativity!

Hero Animations: Smooth Transitions Between Screens

Hero animations add a touch of magic to your app's navigation by creating visually captivating transitions between screens. They focus on a shared element (the "hero") that seamlessly moves from one screen to another, providing a sense of continuity and guiding the user's attention.

The Power of the `Hero` Widget

Flutter's `Hero` widget is your key to crafting hero animations. It allows you to tag a widget on one screen (the "source") and match it with another widget on a different screen (the "destination"). During navigation, Flutter automatically animates the transition of the hero widget, making it appear to fly between screens.

Creating a Hero Animation

To create a hero animation, you need two `Hero` widgets:

1. **Source Hero:** Wraps the widget on the original screen that you want to animate.
2. **Destination Hero:** Wraps the corresponding widget on the destination screen.
3. **Shared Tag:** Both `Hero` widgets must have the same `tag` (a unique identifier, usually a `String`).

```
// On the first screen (e.g., a list of products) Hero( tag:
'productImage-${product.id}', // Unique tag child:
Image.network(product.imageUrl), ); // On the second screen (product
details) Hero( tag: 'productImage-${product.id}', // Same tag as the
source hero child: Image.network(product.imageUrl), );
```

Animation Types:

Flutter offers various animation types for hero transitions:

- **Fade:** The hero widget fades out from the source screen and fades in on the destination screen.
- **Scale:** The hero widget scales up or down during the transition.
- **Translate:** The hero widget moves across the screen from its source position to its destination position.
- **Custom:** You can create your own custom hero animations using `flightShuttleBuilder` property.

Enhancing User Experience

Hero animations serve several important purposes in user experience (UX) design:

- **Visual Continuity:** They create a visual connection between screens, making the transition feel smoother and less jarring.
- **Attention Guidance:** They direct the user's attention to the most important element as they move between screens.
- **Delightful Experience:** Hero animations add a touch of visual flair and make your app feel more polished and professional.

Beyond Images: Animating Other Elements

While hero animations are often used for images, you can apply them to any widget you want to transition smoothly between screens, such as text, icons, or even custom-shaped widgets.

Tip: For optimal performance, try to keep the hero widget relatively simple and avoid complex layouts within it.

By mastering hero animations, you'll be able to create more engaging and delightful navigation experiences in your Flutter apps.

Advanced Custom Animations (Optional)

While Flutter's built-in animations and simple explicit animations cover a wide range of use cases, your creative vision might demand even more intricate and specialized animations. For those who crave ultimate control and want to explore the full potential of animation in Flutter, here's a glimpse into some advanced techniques:

1. **Physics-Based Animations:**
- **Real-World Physics:** Create animations that simulate real-world physics principles like gravity, springiness, friction, and momentum.
- **Natural Motion:** Physics-based animations can make your UI elements feel more tangible and responsive, as if they were actual objects obeying the laws of physics.
- **Flutter Tools:** Flutter provides classes like `SpringSimulation`, `FrictionSimulation`, and `GravitySimulation` within the `physics` package to help you build these dynamic animations.
2. **Path-Based Animations:**
- **Following a Path:** Animate widgets along predefined paths (curves, lines, or complex shapes) for unique and eye-catching effects.
- **Creative Possibilities:** Path-based animations open up a world of creative possibilities, from swirling logos to bouncing balls that follow a trajectory.
- **Custom Paths:** Design your own paths or use pre-defined ones from libraries.
3. **Staggered Animations with Custom Curves:**
- **Precise Timing:** Take staggered animations to the next level by customizing the easing curves for each individual animation within the sequence.
- **Smooth Transitions:** Achieve complex, choreographed motion where elements seamlessly move in relation to each other.
4. `AnimatedList`:
- **Dynamic List Animations:** Add, remove, or reorder items in a list with smooth animations.
- **Visual Feedback:** Provide clear visual feedback to users about changes happening within a list.

Further Exploration:

To delve deeper into these advanced animation techniques, check out the following resources:

- **Flutter Documentation:** The official Flutter documentation has a dedicated section on animations: https://docs.flutter.dev/development/ui/animations
- **Physics-Based Animations Cookbook:** Learn how to create physics-based animations: https://docs.flutter.dev/cookbook/animation/physics-simulation
- **Flutter Animation Tutorials:** Find numerous tutorials and examples on various platforms like YouTube and Medium.

Remember, the world of Flutter animations is vast and ever-expanding. By continuously learning and experimenting, you can create truly captivating and unique user experiences that set your apps apart.

Chapter Summary

In this chapter, you took a deep dive into the world of animations and transitions in Flutter. You learned how these elements can elevate user experience, provide feedback, guide attention, and add a touch of delight to your apps.

We started by exploring the concept of implicit animations, showcasing how certain widgets like AnimatedContainer and AnimatedOpacity automatically handle smooth transitions for you. You saw how simple changes to widget properties can result in visually pleasing animations.

Next, we ventured into the realm of explicit animations, where you have complete control over the timing, duration, and behavior of your animations. You learned about the core components of explicit animations — AnimationController, Animation, and Tween — and how they work together to create custom animations.

You discovered how animation curves, such as Curves.easeIn and Curves.bounceOut, can modify the "feel" of your animations, making them more natural and engaging. We discussed how to use AnimationController to control the playback of animations and the importance of TickerProviderStateMixin for synchronization.

You delved deeper into tweening, understanding how it allows you to smoothly transform values like size, position, and color over time. We demonstrated how to use various tween types in combination with AnimationController and Animation to create custom animations.

We then introduced staggered animations, a technique for creating visually interesting sequences where multiple widgets animate with different timings and delays. You learned how to use the Interval class to orchestrate these complex animations.

Finally, we explored hero animations, which create seamless transitions between widgets on different screens. You saw how the Hero widget can be used to define shared elements and provide a visual connection during navigation.

Additionally, we touched upon advanced custom animation techniques like physics-based animations, path-based animations, and AnimatedList, providing you with resources for further exploration and experimentation.

With the knowledge and techniques you've gained in this chapter, you're well-equipped to add a touch of magic to your Flutter apps, creating fluid, interactive, and visually captivating user experiences.

Integrating with Firebase for Authentication and Storage (Optional)

Outline

- Firebase: Your App's Swiss Army Knife
- Setting Up Firebase for Flutter
- User Authentication with Firebase
- Cloud Firestore: Your Cloud Database
- Firebase Storage: Secure File Management
- Real-Time Data with Firebase
- Best Practices and Considerations
- Going Beyond the Basics
- Chapter Summary

Firebase: Your App's Swiss Army Knife

Imagine having a versatile toolkit that handles the backend complexities of your Flutter app, leaving you free to focus on crafting an amazing user experience. That's precisely what Firebase offers.

Firebase, a powerful platform developed by Google, is like a Swiss Army knife for app developers. It provides a comprehensive suite of cloud-based services that simplify the development and management of your app's backend.

Key Features of Firebase: A Multi-Tool Powerhouse

Firebase equips you with an arsenal of features to supercharge your app development:

- **Authentication:** Easily add secure user authentication to your app, supporting email/password, social logins (Google, Facebook, etc.), and phone number authentication.
- **Cloud Firestore:** A flexible and scalable NoSQL database that stores your app's data in the cloud, enabling real-time synchronization across devices.
- **Realtime Database:** A cloud-hosted database that lets you store and sync data in real-time between your users.
- **Cloud Storage:** A secure and scalable solution for storing user-generated content like images, videos, and other files.
- **Cloud Functions:** Run your custom backend code in a serverless environment, triggered by events like user actions or database changes.
- **Machine Learning:** Integrate machine learning capabilities into your app, such as image labeling, text recognition, and language translation.
- **Hosting:** Deploy your web apps or static content (e.g., images, HTML) with Firebase Hosting.
- **Analytics:** Gain insights into your app's usage and user behavior with Firebase Analytics.
- **Crashlytics:** Monitor and troubleshoot crashes in real time to improve your app's stability.
- **...and More:** Firebase offers many other services like A/B testing, push notifications, and remote configuration.

Why Firebase? Streamline Your Backend

Here's how Firebase can simplify your Flutter app development:

1. **No Server Management:** You don't need to set up or maintain your own servers. Firebase handles all the backend infrastructure, scaling automatically to meet your app's needs.
2. **Real-Time Data:** With Firebase's real-time database and Cloud Firestore, changes to data are instantly synchronized across connected devices, providing a seamless and collaborative user experience.
3. **Easy Integration:** Firebase provides excellent SDKs (Software Development Kits) for Flutter, making it easy to integrate Firebase services into your app.
4. **Comprehensive Toolset:** Firebase offers a wide range of features, covering everything from authentication and data storage to machine learning and analytics.
5. **Pay-as-You-Go Pricing:** Firebase offers a generous free tier, and you only pay for the resources you use, making it a cost-effective solution for many projects.

Who Should Use Firebase?

Firebase is an excellent choice for a wide range of Flutter projects, including:

- Apps that require user authentication.
- Apps that store and sync data in real-time.
- Apps that need to handle user-generated content (images, videos, etc.).
- Apps that require backend functionality without the overhead of managing servers.

By integrating Firebase into your Flutter app, you can unlock a wealth of powerful backend features, allowing you to focus on building a great user experience.

Setting Up Firebase for Flutter

Integrating Firebase into your Flutter project is a streamlined process thanks to FlutterFire, a set of Flutter plugins that provide a bridge to Firebase's services. Let's walk through the steps to get you up and running:

1. **Create a Firebase Project:**
   - Visit the Firebase console (https://console.firebase.google.com/) and click "Add project."
   - Follow the instructions to give your project a name, enable Google Analytics (optional), and choose a location.
2. **Register Your Flutter App:**
   - After creating the project, click on the Android icon (if you're developing for Android) or the iOS icon (if you're developing for iOS).
   - Enter your app's package name (you can find this in your `android/app/build.gradle` file or your `ios/Runner.xcodeproj/project.pbxproj` file).
   - Download the configuration file (`google-services.json` for Android or `GoogleService-Info.plist` for iOS).
   - Place the downloaded file in the appropriate location:
     - Android: `android/app` directory.
     - iOS: In the `Runner` subfolder of your Xcode project, and add it to all targets.
3. **Install FlutterFire CLI:**
   Open your terminal and run the following command:
   ```
   dart pub global activate flutterfire_cli
   ```
   This installs the FlutterFire command-line interface (CLI), which simplifies the Firebase setup process.
4. **Configure Your Flutter Project:**
   - Navigate to your Flutter project's root directory in the terminal.
   - Run the following command:

   ```
   flutterfire configure
   ```

- This will guide you through a configuration process where you'll select your Firebase project, choose the platforms you want to support (Android and/or iOS), and specify your app's bundle IDs.
- The FlutterFire CLI will automatically add the necessary Firebase dependencies and configuration files to your project.

5. **Add Firebase Packages:**
   - Depending on the Firebase services you'll be using, add the corresponding packages to your `pubspec.yaml` file:
     - `firebase_core`: Core Firebase plugin (required).
     - `firebase_auth`: For authentication.
     - `cloud_firestore`: For using Cloud Firestore.
     - `firebase_storage`: For using Firebase Storage.

6. **Initialize Firebase:**
   - In your `main.dart` file, add the following code to initialize Firebase:

```
import 'package:firebase_core/firebase_core.dart'; import
'firebase_options.dart'; void main() async {
WidgetsFlutterBinding.ensureInitialized(); await
Firebase.initializeApp( options:
DefaultFirebaseOptions.currentPlatform, ); runApp(MyApp()); }
```

Security Rules: Protecting Your Data

- **Understanding Security Rules:** Firebase provides a security rules language that allows you to control who can access and modify your Firebase data. These rules are essential for protecting user data and ensuring the integrity of your app.
- **Default Rules:** By default, Firebase databases and storage have open access, meaning anyone can read and write data. This is not secure for production apps.
- **Customizing Rules:** You should define custom security rules that restrict access to your data based on user authentication status and other relevant criteria. For example, you might only allow authenticated users to create or modify their own data.
- **Testing Rules:** Thoroughly test your security rules using the Firebase Emulator Suite to ensure they are working correctly and protecting your data.

By following these steps and setting up appropriate security rules, you can leverage the power of Firebase to build secure, scalable, and feature-rich Flutter applications.

User Authentication with Firebase

User authentication is the process of verifying the identity of users who try to access your app. It's a crucial security measure that protects sensitive user data and ensures that only authorized individuals can perform certain actions within your app.

Why User Authentication Matters:

- **Data Protection:** Authentication prevents unauthorized access to user data like personal information, financial details, or private messages.
- **Personalized Experiences:** By identifying users, you can tailor the app's content and features to their individual preferences and needs.
- **Account Management:** Authentication enables users to manage their accounts, update settings, and access their history or purchases.

- **Social Features:** In apps with social components, authentication allows users to interact with others, post content, and join communities.

Firebase Authentication: Your Authentication Swiss Army Knife

Firebase Authentication offers a robust and versatile solution for adding user authentication to your Flutter app. It supports various authentication methods:

- **Email/Password:** Users sign in with an email address and password.
- **Google Sign-In:** Users authenticate using their Google accounts.
- **Facebook Login:** Users authenticate using their Facebook accounts.
- **Phone Number:** Users sign in with their phone numbers (via SMS verification).
- **Apple Sign-In:** Users authenticate using their Apple IDs.
- **Anonymous Sign-In:** Users get a temporary, anonymous account.
- **Custom Authentication:** You can integrate your own authentication system with Firebase.

Implementing Email/Password Authentication

Let's walk through the steps of implementing email/password authentication using the `firebase_auth` package:

1. **Add Dependency:** Add the package to your `pubspec.yaml` and run `flutter pub get`.

   ```
   dependencies: firebase_auth: ^4.1.1 # Latest version
   ```

2. **Import Package:**

   ```
   import 'package:firebase_auth/firebase_auth.dart';
   ```

3. **Registration:** Create a function to handle user registration.

   ```
   Future<UserCredential?> registerWithEmailAndPassword(String email, String
   password) async { try { final credential = await
   FirebaseAuth.instance.createUserWithEmailAndPassword( email: email,
   password: password, ); return credential; // Registration successful } on
   FirebaseAuthException catch (e) { if (e.code == 'weak-password') {
   print('The password provided is too weak.'); } else if (e.code ==
   'email-already-in-use') { print('The account already exists for that
   email.'); } return null; // Registration failed } }
   ```

4. **Login:** Create a function to handle user login.

   ```
   Future<UserCredential?> signInWithEmailAndPassword(String email, String
   password) async { try { final credential = await
   FirebaseAuth.instance.signInWithEmailAndPassword( email: email, password:
   password, ); return credential; // Login successful } on
   FirebaseAuthException catch (e) { // Handle login errors (e.g., invalid
   email, wrong password) return null; // Login failed } }
   ```

5. **Password Reset:** Implement password reset functionality.

```
Future<void> sendPasswordResetEmail(String email) async { try { await
FirebaseAuth.instance.sendPasswordResetEmail(email: email); } catch (e) {
// Handle errors } }
```

6. **Email Verification:** Send verification emails after registration (if desired).

```
User? user = FirebaseAuth.instance.currentUser; if (user!= null &&
!user.emailVerified) { await user.sendEmailVerification(); }
```

Handling Authentication State Changes

Use `FirebaseAuth.instance.authStateChanges()` to listen for changes in the user's authentication state. This stream emits events whenever the user logs in, logs out, or their authentication status changes. Update your UI accordingly.

```
FirebaseAuth.instance.authStateChanges().listen((User? user) { if (user ==
null) { // User is not signed in, show login screen } else { // User is signed
in, show home screen } });
```

By integrating Firebase Authentication into your Flutter app, you can easily add a robust and secure layer of user management, providing a seamless and personalized experience for your users.

Cloud Firestore: Your Cloud Database

Firebase offers two database options: the Realtime Database and Cloud Firestore. In this section, we'll focus on Cloud Firestore, a flexible and scalable NoSQL database that's perfect for storing and syncing your app's data in the cloud.

Cloud Firestore: A NoSQL Powerhouse

Firestore is a document-oriented database, meaning it stores data in documents, which are organized into collections. This structure offers flexibility and makes it easy to model complex data relationships.

- **Documents:** Documents are the basic unit of storage in Firestore. They are essentially key-value pairs, where values can be of various types (strings, numbers, booleans, lists, maps, etc.).
- **Collections:** Collections are containers for documents. They help you organize your data hierarchically.
- **Queries:** Firestore offers a powerful query language for retrieving specific documents or filtering documents based on certain conditions.

Adding the `cloud_firestore` Package

To use Cloud Firestore in your Flutter app, you need to add the `cloud_firestore` package as a dependency in your `pubspec.yaml` file and run `flutter pub get`.

```
dependencies: cloud_firestore: ^4.0.0 # Or the latest version
```

Then you can import it in your dart file using:

```
import 'package:cloud_firestore/cloud_firestore.dart';
```

CRUD Operations with Cloud Firestore

Here's how you can perform basic Create, Read, Update, and Delete (CRUD) operations on Firestore data:

- **Add Data:**

```
final collection = FirebaseFirestore.instance.collection('transactions');
await collection.add({ 'amount': 100.0, 'category': 'Food', 'date':
DateTime.now(), });
```

- **Read Data:**

```
final snapshot = await collection.get(); // Get all documents in the
collection for (var doc in snapshot.docs) { print(doc.data()); }
```

- **Update Data:**

```
final docRef = collection.doc('document_id'); await
docRef.update({'amount': 150.0});
```

- **Delete Data:**

```
await docRef.delete();
```

Structuring Your Data Model

How you structure your Firestore data depends heavily on your app's requirements. Here's an example structure for a personal finance tracker:

```
users (collection)
 - user_id (document)
    - name: "John Doe"
    - email: "john.doe@example.com"
    - transactions (subcollection)
       - transaction_id (document)
          - amount: 100.0
          - category: "Food"
          - date: "2023-12-01T10:00:00Z"
```

In this example, we have a `users` collection, where each document represents a user. Each user document contains a `transactions` subcollection, where each document represents a transaction.

Best Practices:

- **Security Rules:** Define strict security rules to ensure that only authorized users can access and modify data.
- **Data Modeling:** Design your data models carefully, considering the relationships between your data and the queries you'll need to perform.
- **Indexes:** Create indexes for fields you'll frequently query to improve performance.
- **Offline Support:** Utilize Firestore's offline capabilities to allow your app to function even when there's no internet connection.

By understanding and applying these concepts, you can harness the power of Cloud Firestore to create a robust and scalable backend for your Flutter app.

Firebase Storage: Secure File Management

In today's mobile apps, users expect to capture, share, and access a wide range of media content, including images, videos, audio files, and documents. Firebase Storage provides a robust and scalable solution for storing and serving this user-generated content directly from the cloud.

What is Firebase Storage?

Firebase Storage is a cloud-based object storage service tightly integrated with the Firebase platform. It offers several key advantages:

- **Secure and Scalable:** Files are stored in a Google Cloud Storage bucket, ensuring high availability, security, and automatic scaling to meet your app's demands.
- **Direct Uploads:** Users can directly upload files from their devices to Firebase Storage, even on unreliable networks, thanks to resumable uploads.
- **Easy Downloads:** You can easily retrieve files from Firebase Storage within your Flutter app, providing a seamless way to display images, videos, and other content.
- **Download URLs:** Firebase Storage generates secure URLs for your files, which you can use to share or embed them in your app or other web pages.
- **Metadata:** You can attach metadata (e.g., file type, creation date) to your files for easier management and organization.

Adding the `firebase_storage` Package

To use Firebase Storage in your Flutter app, add the `firebase_storage` package as a dependency in your `pubspec.yaml` file and run `flutter pub get`.

```
dependencies: firebase_storage: ^10.0.0 # Or the latest version
```

Then import the package using:

```
import 'package:firebase_storage/firebase_storage.dart';
```

Uploading and Downloading Files

Here's a simplified example of how to upload and download an image:

```
// Uploading an image final storageRef =
FirebaseStorage.instance.ref().child('images/profile.jpg'); await
storageRef.putFile(File(imagePath)); // imagePath is the path to the image
file // Downloading an image URL final url = await
storageRef.getDownloadURL(); Image.network(url); // Display the downloaded
image
```

Security Rules: Keeping Your Data Safe

By default, Firebase Storage requires Firebase Authentication to perform any action on files. This means that only authenticated users can upload, download, or delete files. You can customize these security rules in the Firebase console to control access to your files.

For example, you might want to allow public access to certain files (e.g., profile pictures) or restrict access to private files (e.g., financial documents) to specific users.

Additional Tips for Optimal File Management:

- **Image Compression:** Before uploading large images, consider compressing them to reduce file size and improve upload/download speed. You can use packages like `flutter_image_compress` to compress images within your app.
- **Download Progress:** Provide feedback to the user by displaying the progress of file uploads or downloads using a progress bar or similar indicator.
- **Error Handling:** Handle potential errors during file operations gracefully (e.g., file not found, permission denied) to prevent app crashes.
- **File Organization:** Organize your files in a logical hierarchy within Firebase Storage to keep things tidy and easy to manage.

By integrating Firebase Storage into your Flutter app and following these best practices, you can create a secure, scalable, and efficient system for storing and managing user-generated content, enhancing the functionality and appeal of your app.

Real-Time Data with Firebase

One of Firebase's superpowers is its ability to synchronize data in real time across all connected clients. This means that when data changes in your Firestore database, any app instance listening to that data will receive the update instantly, without the need for manual refreshing or polling. This real-time synchronization opens up exciting possibilities for building collaborative apps, live dashboards, chat applications, and more.

How Real-Time Data Works: A Behind-the-Scenes Look

Firebase achieves real-time data synchronization through WebSockets, a technology that establishes a persistent connection between your app and the Firebase servers. When data changes in the database, Firebase sends a notification to all connected clients, triggering them to update their local data and UI.

Listening for Real-Time Updates in Firestore

To listen for real-time updates in Firestore, you'll use streams and snapshots. Here's how it works:

1. **Create a Query:** Define a query to specify which documents or collections you want to listen to.

```
final collection = FirebaseFirestore.instance.collection('chats');
```

2. **Get a Stream of Snapshots:** Use the `snapshots()` method on the query to get a stream of QuerySnapshot objects.

```
final snapshots = collection.snapshots();
```

3. **Listen to the Stream:** Subscribe to the stream using the `listen()` method. This will trigger a callback function whenever there's a change in the database.

```
snapshots.listen((snapshot) { // Handle the updated snapshot here for
(var doc in snapshot.docs) { print(doc.data()}; } });
```

Explanation:

1. We create a query to listen to changes in the chats collection in our Firestore database.
2. We then create a stream of snapshots by calling `.snapshots()` on our collection.

3. Finally, we call `.listen()` on this stream which will listen for changes in the database, and when there are changes, it would print the document data.

Updating the UI: Reacting to Change

Within the stream listener's callback function, you'll receive a `QuerySnapshot` object that represents the latest state of the data. You can then extract the updated data from this snapshot and use `setState()` (or your preferred state management solution) to trigger a rebuild of the relevant parts of your UI. This ensures that the UI always displays the most up-to-date information.

Practical Tips:

- **Security Rules:** Ensure that your Firebase security rules are configured to restrict access to sensitive data and prevent unauthorized changes.
- **Data Modeling:** Design your Firestore data model with real-time updates in mind. Consider the potential impact of frequent updates on your app's performance and user experience.
- **Unsubscribing:** Remember to unsubscribe from streams when they are no longer needed to avoid memory leaks and unnecessary resource consumption.

By harnessing the power of real-time data in Firebase, you can create dynamic and collaborative Flutter apps that respond instantly to changes, keeping your users engaged and informed.

Best Practices and Considerations

Firebase is an incredibly powerful tool, but like any tool, it's important to use it effectively and be aware of its limitations. Here are some best practices and considerations to keep in mind when integrating Firebase into your Flutter apps:

Best Practices:

1. **Data Modeling:**
   - **Plan Your Data Structure:** Carefully design your Firestore data model before you start building your app. Consider the relationships between your data, the types of queries you'll need to perform, and how your data might evolve over time.
   - **Denormalization:** In some cases, it might be beneficial to duplicate data across multiple documents to optimize read performance. However, be mindful of the potential for data inconsistencies.
   - **Subcollections:** Use subcollections to organize related data within documents (e.g., a "posts" subcollection within a "users" document).
   - **Data Types:** Choose the appropriate data types for your fields to ensure efficient storage and querying.
2. **Security Rules:**
   - **Lock It Down:** Never leave your Firebase database or storage with the default open access rules. This leaves your data vulnerable to unauthorized access and modification.
   - **Validate Data:** Implement validation rules to ensure that data written to your database is in the correct format and meets your application's requirements.
   - **Authenticate Users:** Use Firebase Authentication to control who can access or modify your data.
   - **Test Thoroughly:** Use the Firebase Emulator Suite to test your security rules and ensure they are working correctly.
3. **Performance Optimization:**
   - **Query Efficiently:** Avoid expensive queries that scan large portions of your database. Use indexes to speed up queries on specific fields.

- Limit Data: Only fetch the data you need. Avoid retrieving entire collections if you only need a few documents.
- Offline First: Consider implementing offline capabilities using Firestore's offline persistence feature. This allows your app to continue functioning even when there's no network connection.
4. **Cost Management:**
    - **Monitor Usage:** Keep an eye on your Firebase usage to avoid unexpected costs. Set up budget alerts to get notified when you're approaching your limits.
    - **Optimize Reads and Writes:** Minimize the number of reads and writes to your database. Consider batching operations or caching data where appropriate.

Limitations of Firebase:

- **Cost:** While Firebase offers a generous free tier, costs can escalate quickly for large-scale applications with heavy usage. Be mindful of your usage patterns and choose the appropriate Firebase pricing plan for your needs.
- **Internet Dependency:** Firebase requires an internet connection for real-time data synchronization and other cloud-based features. If your app needs to work offline, you'll need to implement additional mechanisms for local data storage and synchronization.
- **Limited Querying:** While Firestore's query language is powerful, it's not as flexible as SQL. Complex queries might require additional data modeling or client-side filtering.

Testing Your Firebase Integration:

- **Firebase Emulator Suite:** Use the Firebase Emulator Suite to test your app's interaction with Firebase services in a local, simulated environment.
- **Unit and Integration Tests:** Write tests to verify that your app correctly interacts with Firebase Authentication, Firestore, and Storage.
- **Real-World Testing:** Test your app on different devices and network conditions to ensure smooth functionality and data integrity.

By understanding the best practices, potential limitations, and testing strategies for Firebase, you can make informed decisions and build robust Flutter apps that leverage the power of the cloud while delivering a seamless user experience.

Going Beyond the Basics

Firebase is a treasure trove of tools and services that can take your Flutter apps to the next level. While we've covered the essentials of authentication and storage, let's explore some additional Firebase features that can supercharge your app's functionality and user experience.

1. **Cloud Functions:** Your Serverless Sidekick
    - **What it is:** Cloud Functions allow you to run backend code in a serverless environment. This means you can execute code in response to events (like user actions or database changes) without having to manage servers.
    - **Use cases:**
        - Process data: Transform or aggregate data before storing it in Firestore.
        - Send notifications: Trigger push notifications to users based on specific events.
        - Integrate with third-party APIs: Perform server-side API calls to external services.
        - Validate data: Enforce complex validation rules for data integrity.
2. **Crashlytics:** Your App's Guardian Angel
    - **What it is:** Crashlytics provides real-time crash reporting, helping you identify and fix stability issues in your app.
    - **Key features:**

- Detailed crash reports with stack traces and device information.
- User identification for tracking which users are experiencing crashes.
- Issue prioritization based on severity and frequency.
- Real-time alerts for new crashes.

3. **Remote Config:** Instant App Customization
   - **What it is:** Remote Config lets you modify your app's behavior and appearance without requiring users to download an update.
   - **Use cases:**
     - Feature flagging: Enable or disable features for specific user segments.
     - A/B testing: Experiment with different UI layouts or features to see which ones perform better.
     - Personalization: Customize the app experience based on user demographics or behavior.
     - **Note:** Use Firebase Remote Config package to add this functionality to your app.

4. **Firebase ML:** Unleash the Power of AI
   - **What it is:** Firebase ML provides pre-trained machine learning models and APIs that you can easily integrate into your Flutter app.
   - **Use cases:**
     - Image Labeling: Automatically identify objects, places, and activities in images.
     - Text Recognition: Extract text from images or documents.
     - Face Detection: Detect faces in images and identify their features.
     - Barcode Scanning: Read barcodes and QR codes.
     - **Note:** Add the `firebase_ml_vision` package in your app to use Firebase ML Vision kit.

Dive Deeper into Firebase

These are just a few of the many tools and services that Firebase offers. We encourage you to explore the official Firebase documentation and resources to discover the full breadth of its capabilities.

- **Firebase Documentation:** https://firebase.google.com/docs
- **FlutterFire (Firebase for Flutter):** https://firebase.flutter.dev/

By delving into these advanced Firebase features, you can create even more powerful, dynamic, and personalized experiences for your users.

Chapter Summary

In this chapter, you were introduced to Firebase, a powerful backend platform that can simplify the development of your Flutter apps. You learned how Firebase offers a range of essential services, from authentication and real-time databases to cloud storage and machine learning capabilities.

We guided you through setting up Firebase for your Flutter project, explaining how to create a Firebase project, link it to your app, and install the necessary FlutterFire plugins. We emphasized the importance of configuring security rules to protect your user data.

You then explored user authentication with Firebase, understanding different authentication methods and learning how to implement email/password authentication using the `firebase_auth` package. We covered essential concepts like user registration, login, password reset, and email verification.

Next, we dived into Cloud Firestore, Firebase's scalable NoSQL database. You learned about the key concepts of documents, collections, and queries, and how to perform CRUD operations (create, read, update, delete) on your data using the `cloud_firestore` package. We also discussed strategies for designing effective data models to optimize for your app's specific use case.

You also got acquainted with Firebase Storage, a convenient way to store and serve user-generated content like images and videos. We covered how to upload and download files using the `firebase_storage` package and how to implement security rules to control access to your files.

We then explored the exciting world of real-time data with Firebase, demonstrating how to listen to real-time updates in Firestore using streams and snapshots. You learned how to update your app's UI automatically when data changes in the database, making your apps more interactive and responsive.

Finally, we provided best practices and considerations for using Firebase effectively, emphasizing the importance of data modeling, security rules, performance optimization, and cost management. We also encouraged you to explore other Firebase features like Cloud Functions, Crashlytics, and Remote Config to further enhance your app's functionality.

By mastering Firebase's features, you can build robust, scalable, and feature-rich Flutter applications without having to worry about complex backend infrastructure. This chapter has equipped you with the knowledge to integrate Firebase into your projects and take advantage of its powerful cloud-based services.

Publishing Your Flutter App to the App Store and Google Play (Optional)

Outline

- The Journey to the App Stores
- Preparing Your App for Release
- Publishing to the Google Play Store
- Publishing to the Apple App Store
- Post-Launch Considerations
- Troubleshooting and Common Issues
- Chapter Summary

The Journey to the App Stores

The moment you launch your app on the Google Play Store or Apple App Store is exhilarating. It's the culmination of your hard work, creativity, and technical skills. But getting there is a journey that involves more than just writing code. It's a process that requires careful planning, preparation, and attention to detail.

Why Publish Your App?

- **Reach a Global Audience:** The app stores provide a massive platform to reach billions of potential users worldwide.
- **Monetization:** You can generate revenue through app sales, in-app purchases, subscriptions, or advertising.
- **Impact and Recognition:** Your app can make a real difference in people's lives, solve problems, entertain, or educate.
- **Personal Achievement:** Publishing an app is a rewarding experience that showcases your skills and creativity.

The Publication Process: More Than Just Code

Publishing your Flutter app to the app stores isn't as simple as just uploading your code. It involves several key steps:

1. **App Preparation:**
   - Rigorous testing on various devices and operating systems to ensure compatibility and a smooth user experience.
   - Optimizing code for performance and reducing app size.
   - Creating eye-catching app icons and screenshots that showcase your app's features.
   - Writing a compelling app description and choosing relevant keywords for better discoverability.
   - (If applicable) Creating a privacy policy if your app collects any user data.
2. **Store Account Setup:**
   - Creating developer accounts on Google Play Console and Apple App Store Connect.
   - Paying registration fees (a one-time fee for Apple, an annual fee for Google).
3. **App Store Listing Creation:**
   - Preparing metadata (title, description, screenshots, icons, etc.) for your app store listing.
   - Complying with each store's specific guidelines and requirements.
4. **App Submission and Review:**

- ○ Uploading your app's compiled binary (APK for Android, IPA for iOS) to the respective store.
- ○ Waiting for the store's review process, which can take a few days.
- ○ Addressing any feedback or issues raised during the review.

Plan Ahead: The Importance of Preparation

Thorough preparation is key to a smooth app publishing experience. Rushing through the process can lead to delays, rejections, or even a poor user experience. Take the time to:

- **Test Extensively:** Test your app on various devices, screen sizes, and operating systems. Get feedback from beta testers to identify and fix any issues.
- **Polish Your App:** Refine your UI, optimize performance, and ensure your app is stable and reliable before submitting it.
- **Review Guidelines:** Carefully read and follow the App Store Review Guidelines and Google Play Developer Policy to avoid rejection.
- **Prepare Marketing Materials:** Create promotional materials like screenshots, videos, and app store descriptions to showcase your app effectively.

Google Play vs. Apple App Store: Different Worlds

While the overall process is similar, there are some key differences between publishing on Google Play and the Apple App Store:

Feature	Google Play Store	Apple App Store
Review Time	Typically faster	Can take longer
Guidelines	More flexible	More strict
Developer Account Fee	One-time fee	Annual fee
Release Process	More automated	More manual steps

Understanding these differences will help you tailor your preparation and submission strategies accordingly.

Preparing Your App for Release

Before you unleash your Flutter app on the world, it's crucial to give it a thorough polish. This involves meticulous testing, optimizing performance, crafting a captivating app store presence, and ensuring legal compliance.

1. Final Testing: Ensuring a Stellar User Experience

- **Test, Test, Test:** Put your app through its paces on various devices, screen sizes, and operating systems. Simulate different user scenarios and try to break your app in every way imaginable. This will help you catch any lingering bugs, crashes, or UI inconsistencies.
- **Beta Testing:** Recruit beta testers to use your app in real-world conditions. Their feedback will be invaluable in identifying issues you might have missed.
- **Accessibility Testing:** Ensure your app is accessible to users with disabilities. Check color contrast, font sizes, and screen reader compatibility.
- **Performance Profiling:** Use Flutter's performance profiling tools to identify and optimize any performance bottlenecks.

2. Code Optimization: Slimming Down and Speeding Up

- **Minify and Obfuscate:** Use tools like `flutter build apk --split-per-abi` to reduce your app's size by removing unnecessary code and resources.
- **Image Optimization:** Compress images without sacrificing too much quality. Use tools like `flutter_image_compress` to optimize images within your Flutter project.
- **Code Splitting:** If your app is large, consider splitting it into smaller chunks that can be loaded on demand, improving initial load times.

3. App Icons and Screenshots: Making a Visual Impact

- **High-Quality App Icons:** Design an eye-catching app icon that represents your app's brand and stands out in the crowded app stores. Consider using tools like Adobe Illustrator or Sketch to create your icons.
- **Compelling Screenshots:** Capture visually appealing screenshots that highlight your app's key features and benefits. Use a device mockup to showcase your app in a realistic setting.

4. App Store Listing: Your App's Marketing Pitch

- **Title and Subtitle:** Choose a clear, concise, and memorable title that accurately reflects your app's purpose. Use the subtitle to briefly describe its core features.
- **Description:** Craft a compelling app description that highlights the benefits and unique features of your app. Use persuasive language and keywords that potential users might search for.
- **Keywords:** Carefully research and select relevant keywords that will help users discover your app in the app store search.

5. Privacy Policy (If Applicable): Protecting User Data

- **Compliance:** If your app collects any user data (even anonymous analytics), you need to create a clear and concise privacy policy that explains what data you collect, how you use it, and how you protect it. Make sure your privacy policy complies with relevant data protection regulations like GDPR or CCPA.
- **Transparency:** Be transparent with your users about your data practices. Let them know what data you collect and how it's used.
- **User Consent:** Obtain explicit user consent before collecting any personal data.

By meticulously preparing your app for release, you'll increase its chances of success on the app stores and create a positive first impression for your users.

Publishing to the Google Play Store

After all your hard work, it's time to unleash your Flutter app on the Google Play Store, making it available to millions of Android users worldwide. Let's break down the steps involved in this exciting process.

1. Creating a Google Play Developer Account

Before you can publish anything, you'll need a Google Play Developer account.

- **Sign Up:** Go to the Google Play Console - https://play.google.com/console/ and sign up for a developer account. There's a one-time registration fee.
- **Complete Your Profile:** Fill in your developer details, including your name, contact information, and payment details.

2. Preparing Your App for Release

Ensure your app is polished and ready for the world:

- **Testing:** Conduct thorough testing on various Android devices and versions to identify and fix any issues. Utilize emulators, physical devices, and beta testers for comprehensive testing.
- **Optimization:** Reduce your app's size by optimizing images, removing unused code, and using code shrinking techniques. This will make your app faster to download and install.
- **App Bundle:** Create an Android App Bundle (.aab), which is Google Play's recommended publishing format. It dynamically delivers optimized APKs for each device configuration, reducing the download size for users.
    - From Android Studio: Build -> Generate Signed Bundle/APK -> Select Android App Bundle then follow the instructions to create a signed bundle.

3. Crafting Your App Listing

Your app listing is your app's storefront on Google Play. Make it shine!

- **Store Listing:**
    - **Title and Short Description:** Craft a catchy title and a brief, informative description that highlights your app's key features and benefits.
    - **Full Description:** Provide a more detailed description of your app's functionality, emphasizing what makes it unique.
    - **Screenshots and Videos:** Upload high-quality screenshots that showcase your app's UI and main features. You can also add a promotional video to give users a better understanding of your app.
    - **Feature Graphic:** A prominent banner image that appears at the top of your store listing.
    - **Icon:** The visual symbol that represents your app on the home screen and in the Play Store.
- **Categorization and Tags:**
    - Choose the most relevant category (e.g., Education, Finance, Health & Fitness) and add appropriate tags to help users discover your app.
- **Privacy Policy:**
    - If your app collects any user data, you must provide a clear and accessible privacy policy that complies with relevant regulations (e.g., GDPR, CCPA).

4. App Releases: Rolling Out Your App

Google Play offers several release options:

- **Production Release:** Makes your app available to all users on Google Play.
- **Staged Rollout:** Gradually release your app to a percentage of users, allowing you to monitor feedback and catch issues before a wider release.
- **Alpha/Beta Testing:** Release your app to a limited group of testers to get valuable feedback before the official launch.

5. Post-Launch Management:

- **Monitor and Respond:** Regularly check your app's statistics, crash reports, and user reviews. Address any issues or concerns promptly.
- **Updates:** Keep your app fresh and engaging by releasing regular updates with new features, bug fixes, and improvements.

Additional Tips:

- **Store Listing Experiments:** Run experiments to test different versions of your app store listing to see which one performs best.
- **Pricing and Distribution:** If you're planning to monetize your app, carefully consider your pricing strategy and distribution options.

- **Pre-launch Report:** Use the pre-launch report to identify potential issues before your app goes live.

Publishing your app to the Google Play Store is an exciting milestone. By following these steps and best practices, you can ensure a smooth launch and set your app up for success in the competitive mobile app market.

Publishing to the Apple App Store

The Apple App Store is the gateway to a vast audience of iPhone and iPad users. While publishing on the App Store requires a bit more effort than Google Play, the potential rewards are significant. Let's explore the steps involved in getting your Flutter app onto this prestigious platform.

1. Enrolling in the Apple Developer Program

To publish apps on the App Store, you need to enroll in the Apple Developer Program.

- **Join:** Visit the Apple Developer website - https://developer.apple.com/programs/enroll/ and enroll as an individual or organization. There is an annual membership fee.
- **Account Setup:** Fill in your information and agree to the Apple Developer Agreement.

2. Creating an App Store Connect Account

Once enrolled, you'll gain access to App Store Connect, your control center for managing apps.

- **App Store Connect:** Go to App Store Connect - https://appstoreconnect.apple.com/ and log in with your Apple ID.
- **Create an App Record:** Start the process by creating a new app record in App Store Connect. Provide basic details like the app name, bundle ID, and primary language.

3. Building Your App Store Listing

Your app listing is your app's "product page" on the App Store. Make it compelling!

- **App Information:** Fill in the app name, subtitle, description, and category. Use persuasive language and highlight your app's key features and benefits.
- **Pricing and Availability:** Set the price for your app (free or paid) and select the countries where it will be available.
- **Screenshots:** Upload high-resolution screenshots that showcase your app's UI and functionality on different iOS devices.
- **App Preview (Optional):** You can create a short video demonstrating your app's features.
- **App Privacy Details:** Detail how your app collects and uses user data.

4. App Store Review Guidelines: The Rules of the Game

Before submitting your app, it's crucial to review Apple's App Store Review Guidelines. These guidelines outline the rules and standards your app must meet to be accepted on the App Store. Some key areas to pay attention to include:

- **Safety:** Your app must be safe and secure, free of malicious code or content.
- **Performance:** Your app should be stable, responsive, and free of crashes.
- **Design:** Your app should have an intuitive and user-friendly interface that adheres to Apple's design principles.
- **Functionality:** Your app should deliver on its promises and function as described.
- **Legal Compliance:** Your app must comply with all legal requirements, including privacy regulations.

5. Building and Uploading with Xcode

- **Build for Release:** In Xcode, configure your project for release and create an archive of your app.
- **Validate and Upload:** Use Xcode's Organizer to validate and upload the app archive to App Store Connect.
- **Submit for Review:** Once uploaded, submit your app for review. The review process typically takes a few days.

6. Beta Testing with TestFlight

- **TestFlight:** Use Apple's TestFlight platform to distribute beta versions of your app to testers for feedback.
- **Feedback and Improvements:** Gather valuable insights from your testers to refine your app before its official release.

7. Releasing Updates and Managing Your App

- **App Store Connect:** Use App Store Connect to manage your app's listing, pricing, availability, and updates.
- **Monitor Performance:** Track your app's downloads, reviews, and crash reports to identify areas for improvement.
- **Engage with Users:** Respond to user reviews and feedback to build a loyal user base.
- **Plan Updates:** Regularly release updates to add new features, fix bugs, and keep your app fresh and engaging.

By following these steps and paying close attention to Apple's guidelines, you can successfully navigate the App Store submission process and share your Flutter masterpiece with the world of iOS users.

Post-Launch Considerations

Congratulations! Your Flutter app has made its debut on the app stores. But the work doesn't stop here. In fact, launching your app is just the beginning of a new phase in your app's lifecycle – one filled with opportunities for growth, improvement, and user engagement.

Essential Tasks After Launch:

1. **Monitor Crash Reports and Analytics:**
- **Crashlytics (Firebase):** Integrate a crash reporting tool like Firebase Crashlytics into your app. This will alert you to any crashes or errors users experience, providing valuable insights into how to improve your app's stability.
- **Analytics (Firebase):** Use a robust analytics platform like Firebase Analytics to track user behavior, engagement, and retention. This data helps you understand how users interact with your app, identify areas for improvement, and measure the impact of updates.
2. **Engage with User Reviews and Feedback:**
- **Read Reviews:** Pay attention to user reviews on the app stores. They can offer valuable feedback about what users like and dislike about your app.
- **Respond to Feedback:** If users leave negative reviews, try to address their concerns promptly and professionally. Show that you value their feedback and are committed to improving your app.
- **Gather Feedback Through Other Channels:** Consider using in-app surveys, feedback forms, or social media to gather additional feedback from your users.
3. **Plan and Implement Updates:**
- **Gather Feedback:** Collect feedback from users and your own internal team to identify areas for improvement and new features to add.

- **Prioritize:** Prioritize features and bug fixes based on their impact on the user experience and your overall app goals.
- **Test Thoroughly:** Before releasing an update, thoroughly test it on various devices and platforms to ensure it doesn't introduce new issues.
- **Release and Promote:** Roll out the update to users and promote it through various channels (app store updates, social media, blog posts) to encourage them to download the latest version.
4. **Promote Your App:**
- **App Store Optimization (ASO):** Optimize your app store listing with relevant keywords, compelling descriptions, and high-quality screenshots to improve its visibility in search results.
- **Social Media:** Promote your app on social media platforms like Twitter, Facebook, and Instagram.
- **Paid Advertising:** Consider running targeted ads on social media or other platforms to reach a broader audience.
- **Content Marketing:** Create blog posts, tutorials, or videos about your app and share them on relevant platforms to generate interest.
- **Reach Out to Reviewers:** Contact app reviewers and bloggers to get your app featured on their websites or publications.

The Importance of Continuous Improvement:

The app stores are dynamic environments, with new apps and updates being released constantly. To stay competitive, it's important to adopt a mindset of continuous improvement. Regularly monitor your app's performance, gather feedback, and release updates to keep users engaged and attract new users.

Remember, launching your app is just the first step. By actively managing, improving, and promoting your app, you can build a loyal user base, create a successful product, and make a lasting impact in the mobile app world.

Troubleshooting and Common Issues

The app publishing process can be smooth sailing, but sometimes you might encounter unexpected storms. In this section, we'll tackle some common challenges that developers face when publishing their Flutter apps to the app stores and offer tips and resources to help you navigate these rough waters.

App Rejection: When Things Don't Go as Planned

One of the most disheartening experiences for developers is having their app rejected by the app store. Here are some common reasons for rejection:

- **Policy Violations:** Carefully review the App Store Review Guidelines (iOS) and Google Play Developer Policy (Android) to ensure your app complies with all the rules and regulations. Common violations include:
  - **Intellectual Property Issues:** Make sure you have the rights to use all content (images, fonts, music) in your app.
  - **Misleading Content:** Avoid making false claims or exaggerating your app's features.
  - **Incomplete Functionality:** Ensure your app is fully functional and doesn't crash or exhibit major bugs.
  - **Privacy Concerns:** Clearly state how you collect and use user data in your privacy policy. Obtain necessary consent for data collection.
- **Technical Issues:** Technical issues like crashes, bugs, or compatibility problems can also lead to rejection. Thoroughly test your app on various devices and OS versions before submitting.
- **Metadata Issues:** Make sure your app's title, description, screenshots, and other metadata are clear, accurate, and comply with the store's guidelines.

Troubleshooting App Rejection:

- **Read the Rejection Notice Carefully:** The rejection email or message from the app store usually provides detailed reasons for rejection. Carefully analyze the feedback and address the specific issues raised.
- **Appeal the Decision:** If you believe your app was rejected unfairly or due to a misunderstanding, you can appeal the decision and provide additional information or clarification.
- **Consult the Community:** Many online forums and communities are dedicated to Flutter and app development. Seek help from other developers who might have encountered similar issues.

Build Errors During Release:

- **Dependencies:** Ensure all your app's dependencies (packages) are up-to-date and compatible with the release version of Flutter.
- **Platform-Specific Configurations:** Double-check your Android and iOS build configurations (e.g., signing settings, permissions) to ensure they are correct for release builds.
- **Build Tools:** Make sure your Android Studio and Xcode installations are up-to-date, and you're using the correct build tools and settings.
- **Proguard (Android):** If you're using Proguard to obfuscate your Android code, ensure it's configured correctly to avoid issues with missing classes or methods.

Signing and Certificate Issues (iOS):

- **Certificates and Provisioning Profiles:** iOS app distribution requires valid certificates and provisioning profiles. Make sure you have the correct ones set up in Xcode and that they are not expired.
- **App Store Connect:** Verify that your app's bundle identifier matches the one you've registered in App Store Connect.
- **Apple Developer Account:** Check that your Apple Developer Program membership is active and that you have the necessary roles and permissions to publish apps.

Resources and Help:

- **Flutter Documentation:** The official Flutter documentation has a dedicated section on releasing apps: https://docs.flutter.dev/deployment/android and https://docs.flutter.dev/deployment/ios
- **Community Forums:** Flutter has a thriving community forum where you can ask questions and get help from experienced developers: https://flutter.dev/community
- **Stack Overflow:** A vast question-and-answer platform where you can find solutions to many common publishing problems.

By proactively addressing these common issues and utilizing the available resources, you can overcome publishing hurdles and ensure a smooth and successful launch for your Flutter app.

Chapter Summary

In this chapter, you embarked on the final steps of your Flutter app development journey: publishing your creation to the app stores. We explored the exciting prospects that await you when your app reaches a global audience and the potential for making a real impact on users' lives.

You learned that preparing your app for release is a multifaceted process. It involves rigorous testing on various devices and platforms, optimizing code for performance, and creating visually appealing assets like app icons and screenshots. Crafting a compelling app store listing with a clear title, informative description, and relevant keywords is essential for discoverability. Additionally, you learned about the importance of having a privacy policy in place to ensure compliance with data protection regulations.

We then delved into the specific steps involved in publishing to the Google Play Store, from creating a developer account to preparing your app bundle and crafting a captivating app listing. We discussed the significance of selecting appropriate categories, content ratings, and target audiences to reach the right users. You also gained insight into alpha and beta testing, releasing updates, and managing your app within the Play Console.

Finally, we provided a comprehensive guide to publishing on the Apple App Store, which includes enrolling in the Apple Developer Program, creating an App Store Connect account, and building a compelling app listing. We stressed the importance of adhering to Apple's strict App Store Review Guidelines to avoid rejection. You also learned about using Xcode to build and upload your app and how to leverage TestFlight for beta testing.

We concluded the chapter by highlighting essential post-launch considerations like monitoring crash reports and analytics, responding to user feedback, and planning future updates to keep your app relevant and engaging. Additionally, we addressed common challenges developers face during the publishing process, providing troubleshooting tips and helpful resources to ensure a smooth and successful launch for your Flutter app.

Appendices

Appendix A: Useful Flutter Resources and Communities

As you continue your Flutter journey, you'll find a wealth of resources and a vibrant community ready to support your learning and development. Here are some essential resources and communities to bookmark and explore:

Official Flutter Resources:

- **Flutter Website:** The official home of Flutter, providing documentation, tutorials, examples, and the latest news.
  - Link: https://flutter.dev
- **Flutter Documentation:** The comprehensive documentation covers everything from getting started to advanced topics.
  - Link: https://docs.flutter.dev/
- **Flutter Cookbook:** A collection of recipes for solving common Flutter problems and implementing specific features.
  - Link: https://docs.flutter.dev/cookbook
- **Dart Website:** Learn more about the Dart language that powers Flutter.
  - Link: https://dart.dev/
- **DartPad:** An online editor for experimenting with Dart code snippets.
  - Link: https://dartpad.dev/

Community Resources:

- **Flutter Community:** The official Flutter community page, where you can find links to forums, events, social media, and other resources.
  - Link: https://flutter.dev/community
- **Flutter Awesome:** A curated list of the best Flutter libraries, tools, tutorials, articles, and more.
  - Link: https://flutterawesome.com/
- **FlutterDev Google Group:** A discussion forum for Flutter developers.
  - Link: https://groups.google.com/g/flutter-dev
- **Flutter on Reddit:** A subreddit dedicated to Flutter discussions and questions.
  - Link: https://www.reddit.com/r/FlutterDev/
- **Flutter on Stack Overflow:** A platform for asking and answering Flutter-related questions.
  - Link: https://stackoverflow.com/questions/tagged/flutter

Learning Platforms:

- **Flutter YouTube Channel:** The official Flutter channel with tutorials, talks, and demos.
  - Link: https://www.youtube.com/flutterdev
- **Udemy, Coursera, and Udacity:** Offer a variety of Flutter courses, from beginner to advanced levels.
- **Codelabs:** Google's interactive coding tutorials, including several Flutter-specific ones.

Staying Updated:

- **Flutter Widget of the Week:** A series of short videos showcasing different Flutter widgets.
  - Link: https://www.youtube.com/playlist?list=PLjxrf2q8roU23XGwz3Km7sQZFTdB996iG

- **Flutter Blog:** Stay informed about the latest Flutter news and updates.
  - Link: https://medium.com/flutter

Additional Resources:

- **Awesome Flutter:** A GitHub repository with a massive collection of Flutter resources.
  - Link: https://github.com/Solido/awesome-flutter
- **Flutter Gallery App:** An official app showcasing the capabilities of Flutter UI.
- **Flutter Community Medium Publications:** Follow publications like Flutter Community and FilledStacks for insightful articles and tutorials.

Getting Involved:

- **Contribute to Open Source:** Flutter is an open-source project. You can contribute to its development, write tutorials or articles, or create new packages to share with the community.
- **Attend Meetups and Conferences:** Connect with fellow Flutter enthusiasts at local meetups or attend Flutter conferences to learn, network, and get inspired.
- **Ask Questions and Share Knowledge:** Participate in online forums, social media groups, and Q&A platforms to help others and get help when you need it.

The Flutter community is incredibly welcoming and supportive. By actively participating, you can accelerate your learning, find solutions to challenges, and connect with like-minded developers from around the world.

Appendix B: Troubleshooting Common Flutter Errors

Flutter is a powerful framework, but like any tool, you'll encounter the occasional hiccup. This appendix provides solutions to some of the most common errors you might encounter as a beginner, empowering you to troubleshoot and overcome challenges with confidence.

1. The Dreaded "Red Screen of Death"

This error screen appears when an unhandled exception occurs during the build, layout, or paint phase of your app. It's a helpful signal that something went wrong.

- **Check the Error Message:** The error message itself usually provides the most valuable clue. Look for the specific exception type (e.g., NoSuchMethodError, TypeError, RangeError) and the associated error message.
- **Inspect the Stack Trace:** The stack trace pinpoints where the error originated in your code. Start by examining the lines mentioned in the stack trace.
- **Common Causes:**
  - **Null References:** Ensure you're not trying to access a property or call a method on an object that is null.
  - **Type Mismatches:** Check if you're passing data of the wrong type to a function or widget.
  - **Incorrect Widget Usage:** Verify that you're using widgets correctly and following their required parameters.
  - **Layout Errors:** Make sure your layouts are properly constrained and don't cause overflow errors (e.g., "RenderFlex overflowed").

2. "No Material Widget Found" Error

This error occurs when you try to use a Material Design widget without having a MaterialApp or Material widget as an ancestor.

- **Solution:** Wrap your widget tree in a MaterialApp widget, which provides the necessary context for Material Design components.

  ```
  MaterialApp( home: Scaffold( // ... your app content ), );
  ```

3. "setState() or markNeedsBuild() called during build" Error

This happens when you try to change the state of a widget during its build method.

- **Solution:** Move the code that modifies the state to a separate function (e.g., a button's onPressed callback) or use a FutureBuilder or StreamBuilder to manage asynchronous state updates.

4. Dependency Issues

Errors related to missing or incompatible dependencies can be resolved by:

- **Running flutter pub get:** This command ensures you have the latest versions of your dependencies installed.
- **Checking Your pubspec.yaml File:** Ensure all dependencies are listed correctly and that their versions are compatible with your Flutter version.

5. Hot Reload Not Working

If Hot Reload stops working, try:

- **Restarting the App:** Sometimes, a simple restart is all you need.
- **Cleaning and Rebuilding:** Run `flutter clean` and then `flutter run` to rebuild your app.
- **Checking for Errors:** Look for any errors in the console or debug logs that might be preventing Hot Reload from working.

6. Emulator/Simulator Issues

- **Check Device Compatibility:** Make sure your emulator or simulator is configured correctly and compatible with your app's requirements.
- **Update Emulator/Simulator:** Keep your emulators and simulators up-to-date.
- **Restart:** If you encounter issues, try restarting the emulator or simulator.

Additional Tips:

- **Read Error Messages Carefully:** Error messages often provide detailed clues about the problem.
- **Consult Flutter Documentation:** Check the official Flutter documentation for troubleshooting guides and solutions to common errors.
- **Search Online:** Many online forums and communities (e.g., Stack Overflow) are dedicated to Flutter development. Search for your error message to see if others have encountered and solved the same problem.
- **Use Debugging Tools:** Flutter offers excellent debugging tools within Android Studio and VS Code. Utilize breakpoints, logging, and the Flutter inspector to diagnose and resolve issues.

Don't be discouraged by errors! Troubleshooting is a natural part of the development process. With practice and the right resources, you'll become adept at identifying and resolving errors, ensuring your Flutter apps are robust and reliable.

Conclusion

Congratulations! You've reached the end of this beginner's guide to Flutter, and you've taken your first steps into the exciting world of mobile app development. We've covered a lot of ground, from understanding the fundamentals of Flutter and Dart to building interactive lists, fetching data from APIs, and even integrating with Firebase and publishing your app to the world.

Reflecting on Your Progress:

Take a moment to reflect on what you've accomplished. You've learned:

- **The Core Building Blocks:** You understand what widgets are, how to create stateless and stateful widgets, design layouts, and style your app's UI.
- **Essential Flutter Concepts:** You've mastered navigation, working with images and assets, making network requests, managing app state, and building interactive lists.
- **Building Real-World Apps:** You've built four functional apps, demonstrating your ability to apply Flutter concepts to real-world scenarios.
- **Advanced Topics (Optional):** You've dipped your toes into the waters of testing, custom animations, Firebase integration, and app publishing.

Keep Learning and Building:

The learning never stops in the world of app development. Flutter is constantly evolving, with new features, updates, and best practices emerging regularly. Continue to explore the resources mentioned in Appendix A, engage with the Flutter community, and experiment with new ideas and projects.

Your Future in Flutter:

Flutter empowers you to bring your app ideas to life, whether you're a budding entrepreneur, a hobbyist developer, or a seasoned pro. With its flexibility, performance, and beautiful UI capabilities, Flutter opens up a world of possibilities for creating mobile apps that delight and engage users.

We encourage you to keep building, keep learning, and most importantly, keep having fun with Flutter! The mobile app development world is your oyster, and with your newfound Flutter skills, you're well-equipped to create amazing experiences.

Thank you for choosing "Flutter Made Easy"! Happy Fluttering!